# The
# Productivity
# Prescription

# About the Author

David Bain is president of his own management consulting firm, David Bain Associates (located in Joliet, Illinois), and publisher of *Productivity Perspectives*, a management newsletter. He has served as general manager, vice president, and consultant to various manufacturing and distribution companies, all of which he has assisted in improving quality, service, and profit by increasing productivity.

Upon receiving his B.S. degree from Southern Illinois University, Bain joined the Buick Motor Division of General Motors and worked in various managerial positions of increasing responsibility in the functional areas of quality, engineering, and manufacturing. At age 31 he had complete responsibility for Buick's Riviera car line assembly plant.

On the basis of "outstanding potential," Bain was selected by GM's top management to attend Michigan State University's two-year Advanced Management Program for experienced managers of proven ability. He received his M.B.A. degree upon completing that program.

Bain left GM in 1972 for the purpose of broadening the scope of his responsibilities beyond engineering and manufacturing so as to include finance and marketing as well. He has served as general manager, vice president, and consultant to diverse manufacturing and distributing businesses whose annual sales have ranged from $3 million to over $1 billion.

Without benefit of major capital investment and by utilizing what resources were available, Bain has assisted in increasing productivity within all the companies with which he has been associated. In all cases, the efforts of David Bain and of those managers and employees who have worked with him have resulted in substantially improved quality, service, and profit.

# The Productivity Prescription

The Manager's Guide to Improving Productivity and Profits

David Bain

**McGraw-Hill Book Company**

New York • St. Louis • San Francisco • Auckland • Bogotá
Hamburg • Johannesburg • London • Madrid • Mexico
Montreal • New Delhi • Panama • Paris • São Paulo
Singapore • Sydney • Tokyo • Toronto

Library of Congress Cataloging in Publication Data

Bain, David
    The productivity prescription. The manager's guide to improving productivity and profits.

    Bibliography: p.
    Includes index.
    1. Industrial productivity.    I Title.
HD56.B34          658.3'14          81-19296
ISBN 0-07-003235-1                  AACR2
ISBN 0-07-003236-X (pbk.)

1234567890   DOCDOC   8932109876

ISBN 0-07-003235-1

ISBN 0-07-003236-X {PBK.}

*The editors for this book were William A. Sabin and Chet Gottfried,
the designer was Jules Perlmutter, and the production
supervisor was Sally Fliess. It was set in Caledonia
by University Graphics, Inc.*

*Printed and bound by R. R. Donnelley & Sons Company.*

This book is dedicated to my wife, Sandy, whose encouragement has sustained me throughout the lengthy process of organizing and then committing my thoughts and experiences to writing; to our sons, Craig, Eric, and Kevin, whose interest in and enthusiasm for the project added to that support; and to all those with whom I have worked, both employees and managers, who have shared my interest in and contributed to improving quality, service, and profit by increasing productivity.

# Contents

viii    Contents

# Introduction

The United States has been in the productivity doldrums for several years, and there is growing concern about the causes of and the solutions to this perplexing problem. No other single issue is of greater common interest to government, business, and labor than the issue of productivity. It is the area in which leaders from all groups alike recognize improvement as the key to meeting their common needs and expectations. Government leaders view improved productivity as critical to balancing budgets, eliminating trade deficits, conserving scarce resources, and improving services provided. Business leaders see it as the means to reduce costs, improve profit margins, and increase market share. Labor leaders see it as the means to control the growth of job-eliminating imports and to improve worker compensation.

While explaining in further detail the reasons why we should be interested in improving productivity, this book is basically a how-to-do-it book. It builds on the concept that a compatibility exists between individual needs and the needs of any organization. Thus, if an approach is structured around these common needs, individuals' satisfaction with their job and organizational results will improve. For various reasons, the leadership of most organizations today goes about fulfilling its responsibilities in a manner that erodes an inherently strong foundation for fulfilling common needs. Yet the organization can fulfill its needs in a manner that both recognizes and supports the fulfillment of employee needs. If we are to improve productivity in the years ahead, we must analyze the impact of the organization on the individual. We must examine the conditions under which the organization is a threat to the individual, the specific organizational patterns of behavior that are the greatest threat, and the means of minimizing such threats. We must discover how to design organizations and systems in a way that individual talents are used to the maximum and human satisfaction and dignity are preserved. We must learn how to make technology serve people not only in the end product but also in the doing.

The ideas within this book are practical, not theoretical. They are intended to bridge the gap between intellectual understanding and emotional involvement. To achieve improvement, we need to understand those factors that contribute to and those that inhibit productivity. Those inhibiting factors are more often internal and controllable than external and noncontrollable. Thus it is within our managerial power to improve productivity.

This book is an action plan aimed at assisting you achieve that worthwhile goal. The ideas presented here have evolved over 20 years, during which I managed diverse organizations, union and nonunion, manufacturing- and service-oriented, continuous operations and job-shop operations, large businesses and small businesses, all in various locations. The ideas have all contributed to the development of a plan which has yet to fail to improve productivity. That success is, of course, due as much to the commitment of the implementing managers as it is to the plan itself. The most important requirement for your achieving similar success is to obtain the same commitment to making the plan work. The first steps toward fulfilling that requirement are to read this book, honestly evaluate, in terms of employee need fulfillment, the work climate for which you are responsible, and then adopt the outlined plan as your own. The price you pay in terms of individual effort will be repaid many times over in the forms of improved productivity and the personal satisfaction gained from having increased your contribution to improving results. Rather than watching what happens, you will influence what happens. And that is what management is all about.

*David Bain*

# Understanding Productivity

# CHAPTER

# 1 Key Aspects

## Productivity—What It Is and What It Is Not

What is productivity? Productivity is the ratio of some output to some input.

$$\text{Productivity} = \frac{\text{output}}{\text{input}}$$

Productivity is not a measure of production or output produced. It is a measure of how well resources are combined and utilized to accomplish specific, desirable results.

$$\text{Productivity} = \frac{\text{output}}{\text{input}} = \frac{\text{results achieved}}{\text{resources consumed}}$$

The concept of productivity recognizes the interplay between various factors in the work place. While the output, or results achieved, may be related to many different inputs, or resources, in the form of various productivity ratios—i.e., output per labor hour, output per unit of material, or output per unit of capital—each of the separate productivity ratios is influenced by a combination of many relevant factors. These influencing factors include the quality and the availability of materials, the scale of operations and the rate of capacity utilization, the availability and throughput capacity of capital equipment, the attitude and skill level of the work force, and the motivation and effectiveness of the management. The manner in which these factors interrelate has an important bearing on the resulting productivity as measured by any, of many possible, ratios.

A basic productivity ratio with which we are familiar is "miles driven per gallon of gasoline." The "input" measure of gasoline is not used as a gauge of

3

the efficiency of the gasoline alone but as an indicator of the efficiency of the car's performance. This takes into consideration many factors, including speed, traffic, traffic lights, and the efficiency of the car's engine, as well as the efficiency of the gasoline itself. The "output" measure of miles driven is a gauge of the effectiveness, or magnitude, of the results accomplished; thus:

$$\text{Productivity} = \frac{\text{total output}}{\text{total input}} = \frac{\text{total results achieved}}{\text{total resources consumed}}$$

$$= \frac{\text{effectiveness}}{\text{efficiency}}$$

Production, performance, costs, and results are components of the productivity effort. They are not singularly equivalent terms. Most people associate the concept of productivity with manufacturing because productivity is most visible, tangible, and measurable within that activity. Economists have supported this traditional definition by defining productivity as output per unit of labor input. This perspective must change so as to include all segments of work. Education, government, service groups, and professional groups must all continue to be interested in and concerned about productivity. Productivity touches us all as consumers, taxpayers, and citizens. When people complain they can no longer afford to meet their weekly food bill, repair their cars, pay their taxes, and clean the polluted environment, they are talking about more than money. They are talking about productivity—the capacity to utilize our existing resources to meet the ever-expanding demands on the individual.

## The Significance of Productivity Growth

Productivity is important in achieving national, business, and personal goals. The primary benefits of greater productivity growth are pretty much common knowledge—more can be produced in the future, using the same or fewer resources, and our standard of living can be raised. The future economic pie can be made bigger by improving productivity, thereby allowing a bigger slice of that pie for each of us. Expanding the future economic pie can help avoid the clashes between contending groups fighting for smaller pieces of a smaller pie.

From a national perspective, productivity improvement is the only source of increased real national wealth. The more productive use of resources reduces waste and conserves scarce or expensive resources. Without productivity improvements to match them, all increases in wages, other costs, and prices contribute to inflation. Steady growth in productivity is the only way our nation can solve such pressing problems as inflation, unemployment, an increasing trade deficit, and an unstable currency.

From a personal perspective, productivity growth is the key to increasing the real standard of living and best utilizing the available resources to improve the quality of life.

In business, productivity improvements can lead to more responsive customer service, increased cash flow, improved return on assets, and greater profits. More profits provide investment capital for the expansion of capacity and the creation of new jobs. Improved productivity contributes to the competitiveness of a business in its markets, both domestic and foreign.

Business profit can be improved by either increasing sales or by reducing costs or by a combination of both. It is not uncommon for management's focus to be on increasing sales volume with a lesser emphasis placed on controlling, if not reducing, costs. This attitude is the result of conditioning brought about by the expanding markets and increasing sales enjoyed by many businesses in the 1960s and extending, for some businesses, through the 1970s. The sale of additional units results in a diminished fixed cost per unit which automatically increases profitability, providing there is no offsetting increase in variable cost per unit. In some businesses, particularly those that are capital or equipment intensive and in which the fixed element of cost is higher, per unit profit can actually increase with higher volume despite significant increases in variable per unit costs.

Managers, like people in general, seem to have a tendency to migrate toward the comfortable. Rather than confront the issue of controlling costs, it is generally more comfortable to ride the wave of increasing demand. Thus increasing productivity, i.e., the reduction of unit costs while at least maintaining or preferably increasing the volume of outputs, has generally not been given proper emphasis. Until we experience either reduced demand for our products or services, or a demand that is growing at a lesser rate than that to which we are accustomed, productivity and cost control tend to take a back seat to efforts to increase sales.

Cost control has a leverage on profit that few managers have stopped to consider. Due to a company's dependence on profit margin, the positive impact of a single dollar of cost reduction on a company's profit has a far greater effect than does an increase in sales of the same magnitude (see Table 1-1).

In its broadest sense, productivity includes all resources and their costs and as such presents the greatest opportunity to improve profit in any for-profit business and to provide more service for every dollar spent in nonprofit organizations.

## The Productivity Trend within the United States

The history of productivity in this country over the past few years does not make for pleasant reading. Following World War II, U.S. labor productivity grew by more than 3 percent per year. In the mid-1960s, productivity started to decline, and the record for the 1970s shows a further erosion of the produc-

**TABLE 1·1.** The Relationship between a Company's Profit Margin and the Amount of Additional Sales Required to Contribute as Much to the Company's Profit as Does a *Single* Dollar of Cost Reduction

| Profit Margin, in % | Additional Sales, in $, vs. Single $ of Cost Reduction |
|---|---|
| 20 | 5.00 |
| 15 | 6.67 |
| 10 | 10.00 |
| 9 | 11.11 |
| 8 | 12.50 |
| 7 | 14.29 |
| 6 | 16.67 |
| 5 | 20.00 |
| 4 | 25.00 |
| 3 | 33.33 |
| 2 | 50.00 |
| 1 | 100.00 |

tivity growth rate. Productivity gains from 1973 to 1977 averaged only 1 percent, while the 1977–1978 growth rate was less than ½ of 1 percent. Table 1-2 illustrates the recent productivity growth rates for various broad sectors of the private business economy.

In 1979, the productivity growth rate for business fell to a minus quantity and continued to decline for six consecutive quarters. Despite more recent, intermittent, nominal, quarterly increases, there continues to be little, if any, growth in U.S. productivity. For all practical purposes, U.S. productivity has shown no growth since 1977. Some of that erosion can be blamed on the ups and downs of the business cycle. It is generally agreed that when the economy heads into a recession, productivity growth begins to decline. During such periods, output usually is reduced more sharply than is employment. Productivity growth can also decline during recessions because of the loss of economies of scale as capacity utilization drops. The 1974–1975 recession was especially sharp and that can explain some of the loss in productivity. Most economists,

**TABLE 1·2.** Percent Growth in U.S. Labor Productivity, 1948–1978*

| Sector | 1949–1955 | 1955–1965 | 1965–1973 | 1973–1977 | 1977–1978 |
|---|---|---|---|---|---|
| Private business economy | 3.4 | 3.1 | 2.3 | 1.0 | 0.4 |
| Nonfarm | 2.7 | 2.6 | 2.0 | 0.9 | 0.6 |
| Manufacturing | 3.3 | 2.9 | 2.4 | 1.5 | 2.5 |
| Nonmanufacturing | 2.4 | 2.4 | 1.7 | 0.6 | 0.3 |

*Data relate to the annual percent change in "output per hour paid" for all persons.
SOURCE: Based on *Economic Report of the President,* Government Printing Office, Washington, D.C., 1979, p. 68.

however, agree that this disturbing news cannot be blamed on the business cycle alone. There exist too many ways to adjust productivity figures to factor out changes in the business cycle. One of the easiest is simply to compare productivity during periods that are approximately the same in the business cycle. No matter how it is evaluated, the results point to one thing—a recent, actual long-term decline in U.S. productivity growth.

Figure 1-1 illustrates that as productivity has fallen, costs have steadily risen. While output has declined, the compensation for that output has soared. When wage increases, salary adjustments, cost-of-living increases, and benefit-package improvements are given without corresponding increases in productivity, business makes up the difference by raising prices. This difference is, by definition, inflation. It hurts each of us because costs are rising faster than productivity and prices are increased to compensate for the difference. These price increases affect the cost-of-living escalators built into many labor contracts. As prices increase, wages go up. As wages go up, prices increase. The result is a closed cycle that increases inflation while decreasing the real output per unit of real input (the productivity ratio). Figure 1-2 graphically illustrates the inflationary cycle. Spiraling inflation is the result of providing rewards and benefits without requiring compensating increases in productivity.

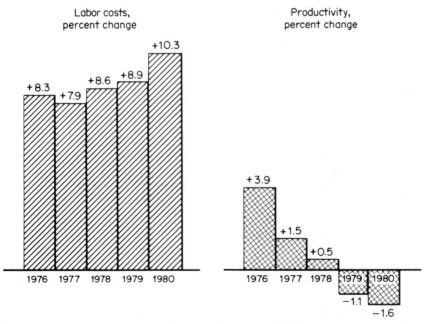

**Figure 1-1.** Labor costs vs. productivity. (Based on data supplied by the U.S. Department of Labor Statistics.)

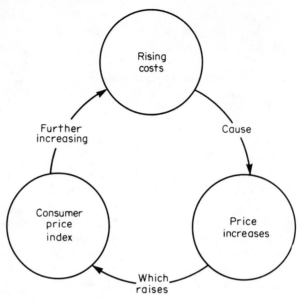

**Figure 1-2.** The inflationary cycle.

Productivity growth presents a worthwhile and continuing challenge worthy of our best efforts.

## Comparing U.S. Productivity with That of Other Nations

At the time of this writing, the United States continues to have the most productive work force in the world. However, in the race for overall productivity growth, the United States has consistently fallen behind the growth rate of most industrialized nations for the last few years. Table 1-3 shows that the gap between U.S. gains and those of other nations is striking, with Japan, Denmark, and Belgium achieving roughly 4 times the productivity gains of the United States.

Unless American firms take proper, decisive, and prompt action aimed at improving the rate of U.S. productivity growth in the 1980s, our long-term leadership will be at an end and our productivity will be below that of other industrialized nations. Figure 1-3 illustrates the projected timetable, per various economic forecasts, of the loss of U.S. productivity supremacy.

Based upon various economic forecasts, and because of different national productivity growth rates, it is projected that the United States will lose its productivity leadership to Germany in 1984. France's productivity is projected to sur-

**TABLE 1-3.** U.S. Manufacturing Productivity Growth as Compared to Other Industrialized Nations

| Country | Average Annual Percent Growth | | Percent Change, 1966–1976 vs. 1960–1966 |
|---|---|---|---|
| | 1960–1966 | 1966–1976 | |
| Japan | 8.8 | 8.9 | +1 |
| Denmark | 5.4 | 8.0 | +48 |
| Belgium | 5.0 | 8.1 | +62 |
| Netherlands | 5.6 | 7.4 | +32 |
| Germany | 6.0 | 5.8 | −3 |
| Italy | 6.7 | 5.3 | −21 |
| Sweden | 6.5 | 5.2 | −20 |
| France | 5.5 | 5.8 | +5 |
| Switzerland | 2.9 | 5.1 | +76 |
| Canada | 4.3 | 3.5 | −19 |
| United Kingdom | 3.7 | 3.1 | −16 |
| United States | 4.0 | 2.2 | −45 |

SOURCE: Based on Timothy Hannan, "The Productivity Perplex," *Business Review of the Federal Reserve Bank of Philadelphia*, March–April 1980, pp. 9–10.

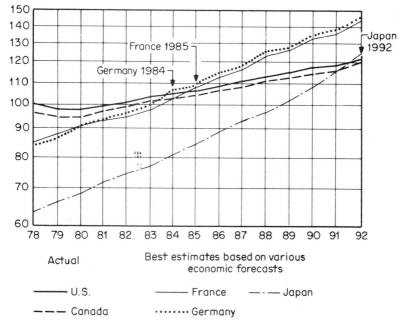

**Figure 1-3.** Actual recent productivity growth and projected trends. Growth rate applied to actual 1978 level of gross domestic product per employee (GNP minus overseas earnings or income). (Reprinted with permission of the American Productivity Center.)

pass the productivity of our work force in 1985, while Japan will do the same by 1992.

National productivity centers are being established at an increasing rate in many countries of the world. In Europe there are twenty national centers; in Asia there are fourteen such centers. One of the most successful national centers is that of Japan. It was established in the 1950s, during a period when Japanese-manufactured products were generally considered to be "second rate" and Japan's per capita income was $200 per year. Today, Japan is recognized world-wide as a quality producer of sophisticated products. Japan's current per capita income is $8000 and its unemployment rate is 2 percent.

When asked the secret of Japan's sustained high growth in productivity, Kohei Goshi, chairman of Japan's Productivity Center, replied:

> The most important reason is the cooperative attitude between management and labor. That includes our lifetime employment system. Once a person is employed, [that person] pretty much stays with the company for a whole working career. He entrusts his entire life to the corporation. He shares his prosperity with the company. We in Japan have learned much from the U.S. about industrial engineering. But we have mixed that technique with more emphasis on the human side. Both the U.S. and Europe need to do that.[1]

Though they no longer sing the company song before each work shift at Toyota and other Japanese auto plants, Japanese auto workers continue to exhibit a sense of pride and mission in their work. Doing a good job is important to them, to their union, to their families, and to their nation. Workers and management share the same objectives. Worker alienation is almost unheard of, and sabotage is unknown. Coke bottles do not rattle in the doors of Japanese-built cars as they sometimes do in those built in the United States.

Each plant has its white-collar and blue-collar Quality Circles in which three to ten employees meet on their own time to discuss quality and find ways to improve the product (see pages 202 to 204 for a discussion on Quality Circles). The rewards given for usable ideas are mostly psychological. Whereas General Motors offers employees up to $10,000 per usable suggestion, a Japanese firm's award of $600 for a patentable idea is considered generous. At Nissan, the maker of Datsun, an original idea is usually awarded with a company button or a ball-point pen.

Trade unionism, though widespread, is passive by U.S. standards. Job classifications are loosely defined, and workers will not hesitate to do any assigned task. The average auto worker in Japan has received wage increases of 212 percent from 1970 to 1978 and, when including benefits, now earns about $9 per hour as compared to the $17 earned by the U.S. counterpart.

---

[1] "How to Stop Sag in Productivity," *U.S. News & World Report*, July 28, 1980, p. 57.

Few of Japan's auto plants can match American facilities in terms of both capacity and design. The Toyota plant near Nagoya is noisy, dark, and cramped. The assembly line produces 60 cars per hour as compared to the pace of 100+ cars per hour of some U.S. auto plants.

The Japanese are not only fussy about the cars they build but also about the cars they buy. All imported cars from the United States, as well as most imports from other countries, must be repainted before they will be accepted by the Japanese consumer. A U.S. auto manufacturer was puzzled by the high level of activity reported within the service department of their dealer located in Tokyo. Sending engineers to Japan to investigate, they found the dealer's service department busily engaged in rebuilding the U.S.-produced and -imported autos prior to their being sold rather than performing repairs after the sale. They reported that, based upon their previous experience, their customers would not accept the American-built cars without extensive rework being performed to raise the quality of those cars to Japanese quality standards.

Due to the increasing number of cars and other Japanese-manufactured products being imported into the United States, relationships between the two nations are at a flash point. To reduce the growing dissatisfaction because of this trade imbalance, the Japanese are manufacturing more of their products in the United States. Japanese television sets are now being produced in the United States, with cars and trucks soon to follow. The results of applying Japanese management techniques to American business have been mixed.

The chairman of the Sony Corporation states his company has applied a combination of 60 percent Japanese management technique and 40 percent American to its television assembly operations, located in the United States, to achieve the best results.[2] It should be noted that Sony spent millions of dollars for new facilities and equipment here. Matsushita Corporation (Quasar) acquired a badly neglected television operation in Franklin Park, Illinois, from Motorola in 1974 and has also spent millions to upgrade the equipment and facility. While experiencing some difficulty in consistently generating a profit, it has successfully avoided attempts to unionize the work force. Participative management is practiced at the Franklin Park facility. The operation is shut down for 15 minutes each Tuesday, and each supervisor encourages the employees to discuss whatever they choose as long as it is related to the job. Management focuses more on consensus than confrontation. Television sets produced at the facility at the time the Japanese took over averaged 150 defects for every 100 completed sets. Today the average number of defects per 100 sets is 4, and *Consumer Reports* consistently ranks Quasar sets the best regarding frequency of repair, though its overall ranking is seventh out of twelve manufacturers.

---

[2]Joseph Winski, "Turning Quasar Around Proves Difficult Task—Even for Japanese," *Chicago Tribune*, September 17, 1980.

While Quasar meets U.S. quality standards, its management concedes they have a long way yet to go to meet Japanese quality standards.

## Exceptions to the Rule of Declining U.S. Productivity

While U.S. productivity has generally declined in recent years, there are some notable exceptions. Howard K. Smith, the noted news commentator for the American Broadcasting Company, pointed this out in his commentary on December 11, 1975:

The Lincoln Electric Company of Cleveland, Ohio, has just paid its 2,300 employees their annual bonuses. The bonuses averaged nearly 12,000 dollars per worker—on top of high weekly wages, not to be sneezed at. Lincoln has a system. It began in the depression in 1934. Mr. Lincoln told his employees business was bad so he couldn't pay. They said, "If we produce more, more cheaply, will you pay us the benefit gained?" He said, "Yes." So a productivity scale was set for each worker. All produced more at cheaper cost. Contracts came in. The increased income was parcelled out in bonuses, reaching nearly 12,000 dollars per worker this year. . . . James F. Lincoln, founder of Lincoln Electric, when asked what it is that causes people to strive for success replied without specific mention of financial incentive as follows, "the answer is recognition of our abilities by our contemporaries and ourselves. The gaining by our skills of the feeling that we have desirable abilities that others covet. The feeling that we are different in some ways that others admire and wish to emulate. The feeling we are outstanding and are so recognized by our fellows."[3]

Texas Instruments (TI) is another exception to the U.S. trend of declining productivity. It first began to formalize an approach to productivity in the late 1940s. Shortly thereafter a work simplification program was established for the purpose of training all employees to apply the principles of productivity improvement. From 1968 through 1978 Texas Instruments' productivity growth averaged 15 percent per year. This was accomplished during the same period that the overall U.S. manufacturing sector improved productivity by an average annual rate of only 1.9 percent. And while that sector increased its prices by an average of 7.2 percent per year, Texas Instruments reduced average prices for its products and services each year.

A. Ray McCord, executive vice president, describes the Texas Instruments' program of productivity improvement as being built around three major strategic systems that act upon productivity to improve it.

[3]Frederick Hornbruch, Jr., *Raising Productivity*, McGraw-Hill, New York, 1977, pp. 279–280, 327–328.

**The growth loop.** Improved productivity reduces cost thereby enabling price cuts which lead to increased market share. This allows more resources to be devoted to technological innovation and enables TI to maintain a leadership position in high growth market segments. This in turn results in billings and earnings growth, permitting investment in new productivity enhancing projects, and the growth cycle repeats.

**The people involvement loop.** Texas Instruments seeks to motivate all employees by providing satisfying and challenging work. As employees perceive that their personal needs are being met, they are motivated to work as individuals and in teams to fulfill the company's needs for improved productivity, and this cycle repeats.

**The success-sharing loop.** Texas Instruments shares its profits with employees. As employees see that achieving increased productivity helps them increase personal net worth, they are motivated to increase productivity still further, and this cycle repeats.

A key element of the Texas Instruments' program of productivity improvement is that because of continuous growth, displaced employees are relocated to other jobs. Often they remain in the same area to work with new equipment in upgraded jobs, such as those of technicians and maintenance specialists. This opportunity to upgrade displaced employees does not exist in many work environments. Instead of losing a job or at best being transferred to a similar job, the displaced TI worker is often moved to a more important and better-paying position; this is a form of positive motivation that can seldom be duplicated in other work situations.

The above are presented not as models but as examples demonstrating that progress in the area of productivity is being achieved by some companies, contrary to the general trend. The methods being used by Lincoln Electric and by Texas Instruments have been developed over a period of several years. Quality control circles, based on worker-management participation, are today commonplace in Japan, but those programs have evolved over a ten-year period. The productivity improvement programs at Lincoln Electric and Texas Instruments have had the total support of top management for an even longer period of time. Sophisticated programs aimed at improving productivity, especially those incorporating incentives, require time, expertise, and considerable resources to implement and administer successfully. The program outlined later in this book is a basic program that requires less skill and fewer resources to implement without compromising the potential gain.

## Factors Affecting Productivity

To realize an improvement in productivity, a manager must affect at least one of the following factors:

**Methods and equipment.** One way to improve productivity is to implement a constructive change in the methods, procedures, and/or equipment with which results are accomplished. Examples include:

- Automating a manual process
- Providing air shields to improve the aerodynamics of over-the-road vehicles
- Reduction in handling (i.e., handle pallet loads of cases rather than individual cases)
- Eliminating wait time (i.e., an employee having to wait for someone or something else before performing the assigned work)

**Utilization of resource capacity.** The precision with which the capacity for accomplishing work is matched with the amount of work to be done provides the second major opportunity for productivity improvement. Examples include:

- Operating a facility and its equipment on a multishift rather than a single-shift basis
- Maintaining on hand only enough inventory as is required to achieve the objective customer-service level
- Using over-the-road vehicles to transport incoming products from vendors rather than returning empty after having made their deliveries
- Installation of shelving or pallet racks to enable full utilization of space, floor to ceiling

**Performance levels.** The ability to elicit and sustain the best efforts of all employees provides the third major opportunity for improving productivity. Examples include:

- Gaining the full benefit of the knowledge and experience of long-term employees
- Establishing a spirit of cooperation and teamwork among all employees
- Motivating employees to accept organizational goals as their own
- Designing and successfully implementing an employee training program

# 2 Limiting Factors

Productivity improvement does not just happen. Dedicated and competent managers make it happen. They do so by setting goals, recognizing obstacles to the achievement of those goals, developing a plan of action to overcome those obstacles, and effectively directing all available resources toward productivity improvement. Several factors act to limit the achievement of productivity-related goals. Some of those limiting factors are internally generated by the organization and its members. Others are generated externally and are thus generally less controllable by the manager. In either case, forces are at work to limit, if not prohibit, productivity growth. By examining and gaining a better understanding of the limiting factors in our own work environments, we are better able to develop an effective plan of action. While limiting factors may vary in nature from one work situation to another, there are some limiting factors that are common, in varying degrees of intensity, to most, if not all. Following is a listing of those common limiting factors.

### Limiting Factor Number One

*Failure of management to set the tone and create a climate conducive to achieving improved productivity.*

Those immortal words of Pogo, "We have seen the enemy and he is us," capture the essence of this limiting factor. Many Americans today feel exploited by business, both as employees and as consumers. Prices continue to rise, and the general feeling is that business profits and rates of return are much greater than they actually are. Profit has become a dirty word. The unscrupulous actions of a few have tended to taint the public attitude toward business in general. The blame for the prevailing negative attitudes toward business and

15

the profit motive rests squarely on the shoulders of business leaders. While hundreds of millions of dollars are spent by businesses each year to advertise the merits of their products, virtually nothing is spent to communicate the importance of profits to the generation of jobs and an improved standard of living for all of us. Rather than regard employees as "partners" with a right to know, they are most often treated in accordance with the "mushroom theory of management"—definitely kept in the dark and sometimes fed horse manure. I am not suggesting that businesses make public any sensitive information but rather that they assume the responsibility for communicating the importance of profits and the common aspects of employee, business, and consumer needs.

Where most business leaders have been reluctant, well-intentioned though ill-advised do-gooders have stepped in not to support the profit motive by explaining its significance but rather to detract from it. As the road to hell is reportedly paved with good intentions, so is the road to losing our nation's cooperative (and competitive) edge.

Managers are responsible for developing and maintaining a work climate favorable to the achievement of organizational goals. Over an extended period of time, the attitudes of any work group are influenced by the person in charge. Not only does the climate of any work situation reflect the individual attitudes and feelings of the group, it also provides a strong indicator of the attitude and feelings of the group's manager. To manage is to lead; to lead is to accept the responsibility for the group's performance. If productivity is not what it should be, who is at fault? Many managers preach productivity to their employees as if it were a matter of obligation. They intimate with their scolding and criticism that poor productivity is the fault of the members of the work group. But they fail to realize that they indict themselves when they complain of lackluster results which are traceable to their own attitudes and behavior.

The formation of attitudes and patterns of behavior that support productivity growth are discussed in detail in a later chapter.

## Limiting Factor Number Two

*This concerns the problem of governmental regulation.*

Increasing regulation of the free-enterprise system has had a negative impact on productivity. Expanding and sometimes injudicious governmental regulations have sapped business resources. Time and money that would best be invested in facilities, equipment, and new technology have instead been consumed in complying with governmental regulations of questionable value. This unfavorable trend equates to forced, legalized, participative management with the government controlling the options available to business.

Realistically, this trend is unlikely to be reversed in the near term, with managerial adjustment to the probability of continued interference being the most practical course of action. To the extent it does not detract from our efforts in more controllable areas, we should, however, continue to oppose unwarranted governmental regulation.

### Limiting Factor Number Three

*Organizational size and maturity have a negative impact upon productivity growth.*

The larger an organization becomes, the greater are the barriers to internal communication, singleness of purpose, and the achievement of results. Regardless of size, as organizations mature, habits, attitudes, and beliefs develop that also present barriers to achieving results. Both organizational size and maturity tend to limit productivity growth.

As organizations mature they develop a crusty rigidity, stubborn complacency, and a reverence for the status quo. When organizations are young, they are flexible, fluid, not yet paralyzed by rigid specialization, and willing to try anything once. As the organization matures, vitality diminishes, creativity fades, flexibility gives way to rigidity, and there is a loss of capacity to meet challenges from unexpected sources. It need not be that way. An organization whose maturing consists simply of acquiring more firmly established ways of doing things is destined for the graveyard—even if it learns to do those things with increasingly greater skill. As rules and procedures proliferate, there is increasing emphasis on the conformity of one's behavior. The person who wins acclaim is not the one who is highly motivated nor the one who gets things done, but rather the one who has an ingrained knowledge of the rules and traditions and a finely tuned sense of how to act in light of those rules and traditions. Whether or not that person actually accomplishes anything becomes of lesser importance. The long process of mastering the rules smothers energy and destroys zest and creativity.

The number of levels in an organization also has an impact on its productivity. It is axiomatic that the more levels, the greater is the cost. While the excess cost shows up in payroll and fringe benefits, the real cost is hidden in the slowness with which the organization can respond to change. Too many levels, including the proliferation of "assistant" and "assistant to" positions, are almost a guarantee that the organization will be affected with arteriosclerosis.

Management efforts tend to become fragmented or duplicated, coordination becomes more difficult, communications are slowed and distorted, and decision making is delayed. "In these times of accelerating change, an organization must be dynamic if it is to maximize opportunities while minimizing costs. In other words, the organization structure needs to be streamlined, not cluttered."[1]

As organizations grow in size, specialization and staff functions increase. Not only does the individual tend to lose the broad perspective, including an under-

[1]Frederick Hornbruch, Jr., *Raising Productivity*, McGraw-Hill, New York, 1977, p. 196.

standing of organizational goals, but conflict tends to develop between operating personnel and staff personnel. The staff personnel, to justify the existence of its position, feels compelled to criticize the actions of operating personnel. As nothing is impossible to the person who doesn't have to do it, limitless opportunities for such criticism exist in most organizations. Staff persons generally have a greater depth and breadth of managerial contacts than does the line manager, especially lower-level line managers. Too frequently, staff persons communicate unfounded criticisms to higher-level managers, who themselves do not understand what is going on "out there." The results can be disastrous. Strong motivation and proper action on the part of the line manager can be turned into apathy and inaction in such a situation. The "how" things are done overshadows the "whether" they are done. A well-designed system of personnel rotation within an organization will reduce, if not eliminate, this problem. Free movement of personnel within an organization reduces barriers to internal communication, diminishes hostility and backbiting, and promotes understanding between individual divisions and departments, plus it results in a freer flow of information and ideas. On one hand, such rotation develops the individual and, on the other, contributes to better understanding between both individuals and functions.

As organizations become larger and more complex, managers and analysts become more and more dependent on "processed" data and depend less and less on first-hand observation and experience. Before reaching them, the raw data detailing what is really going on has been screened, condensed, and sometimes altered. Even when no alteration of the facts has taken place, the system filters out certain kinds of data so that it doesn't reach the people who depend on the system and need it. The information that is either omitted or distorted is usually information that doesn't fit the format of our reporting systems. So the picture of reality that reaches the top of our organizations often bears little resemblance to what is actually taking place. We suffer the consequences when we encounter situations that cannot be understood except in terms of those elements that have been filtered out. That is why every top executive and every analyst should periodically emerge from the ivory tower and take a long, hard look at unprocessed and unfiltered reality. Every sales manager should take a sample case and periodically call on customers; every general should spend some time with the troops in the front lines; and every politician should get out and ring doorbells. Get out of your office from time to time and get in touch with the people in your organization; find out what they are thinking.

## Limiting Factor Number Four

*This pertains to the inability to measure and evaluate the productivity of the work force.*

Our work force has shifted from predominately blue collar to predominately white collar. This shift has taken place before many organizations have been able to determine how to accurately quantify the more physical and tangible real outputs of its blue-collar work force. As the real outputs of white-collar workers are generally less physical and tangible, few organizations have attempted to measure them. Meaningful measurement is the exception rather than the rule in most organizations. Yet measurement is crucial to the achievement of productivity improvement.

Many common measurements, such as output per hour, do not take into consideration changes either in the cost of labor or in the selling price of the product or service produced by that input of labor. Thus the impact on profit is not measured. Dieter Ibielski, of the German Management and Productivity Center, said it all when he stated, "[Management should] put greater emphasis on profit than on productivity, because if a company doesn't have profits, it fails."[2] We are interested in productivity only because it affects the organization's purpose for existence—profitability for a business and improved service for a nonprofit organization. Productivity for the sake of productivity has no significance.

In the absence of measurements, evaluation cannot take place. Once productivity measurements have been installed, they can be monitored and compared to objectives. Unfavorable variances can be promptly recognized and management's attention focused on correcting the related problems.

The subject of measurement and evaluation is covered in detail in a later chapter.

## Limiting Factor Number Five

*Physical resources, the methods by which work is introduced and processed, and technological factors act individually and in combination to limit productivity.*

Physical resources include the facility or work place, its design and layout—the manner in which things are arranged and its size and capacity. For example, in work where tasks are highly interdependent, such as an assembly line or a similar continuous process, a single-floor facility generally offers a higher productivity potential than does a multifloor facility. The design of the facility influences the flow of work and the continuity with which it can be processed. The match between the size of the facility and the volume of work to be processed is also important. An underutilized facility bears the full expense of amortization, maintenance, and operation (full input) while producing limited outputs. As facilities are fixed and the work to be processed often changes both in nature and volume, those facilities tend to be a factor in limiting productivity.

Machines and equipment, as well as raw materials, frequently limit produc-

---

[2]"How to Stop Sag in Productivity," *U.S. News & World Report,* July 28, 1980, p. 58.

tivity. Should machines or equipment be either primitive, worn out, unreliable or misapplied, output will suffer. Rapidly improving technology provides us with machines and equipment with an abundance of features capable of mesmerizing the most callous prospective buyer. It matters not that they aren't designed for the application we plan, or that they will not operate reliably in our work environment, they are so fascinating we cannot resist buying one, or two, or . . . As machinery and equipment are often recommended as a relatively easy way to boost productivity and are sometimes approved, if not purchased, by a person who neither understands them nor the need for them, machinery and equipment can become a factor in limiting productivity.

The quality of raw materials used and the continuity of their supply affect productivity. Many managers have experienced a situation wherein less expensive materials were purchased in an attempt to save money; but because they could not be processed with relative ease, they ended up actually costing money in the form of downtime or restricted output. The continuous supply of needed materials can no longer be taken for granted. Shortages are commonplace; promised delivery dates stretch further into the future; and scarcity that precipitates surcharges are the norm. In some cases, businesses are forced to close, either temporarily or permanently. Money originally scheduled for new equipment and other aids to boost productivity is being diverted to pay the increased cost of materials. Productivity gains can be realized but only with new and creative approaches in our shortage economy. These approaches include better use of materials and improved lead-time planning.

In manufacturing, the design of the product and the ease with which it can be processed have an important bearing on productivity. When a number of varied products are processed through the same facility, the product mix, or proportion in which they are combined, also affects productivity. Improved product design incorporating a sensitivity toward process capability, including human as well as physical resource limitations, coupled with improved scheduling techniques will minimize, if not overcome, these productivity-limiting obstacles.

Technological advances in this country have reached levels where their impact on work processes leaves an unsettling effect. Mechanization, mass production, and automation generally require larger facilities and more modern equipment. These trends require heavy outlays of capital. When technology changes rapidly, a stress is generated on amortization, capital, time, people, and facilities. When these costs rise, money becomes tight and the future cloudy. The result is that management looks at research and development as the area for cutting costs. This places a heavy mortgage on the future. With R&D curtailed, the development of new products, new processes, and new equipment is placed on "hold." Yet for all their expense, such innovative developments are vital to our long-range productivity needs. Since economic squeezes have been with us for some time, cutbacks in R&D programs and expenditures are adversely affecting our current levels of productivity. The effect is both imme-diate and long range. Productivity gains will be hampered for some time as it will take time for innovations to be developed and applied. By providing incen-tives to business, the government can encourage the continuation of R&D pro-grams for the benefit of all.

# 2
# The
# Potential for
# Improvement

# 3 A Positive Prognosis

It has been said that the optimist looks at a partially filled glass of water and sees the glass as half full, while the pessimist sees the glass as half empty; and that the optimist looks at a doughnut and sees the doughnut, while the pessimist focuses on the hole. We have every reason to be optimistic about our prospects for improving productivity. I know it can be done because I have, with the help of many managers in several different but difficult situations, done it. The fact that you are reading this book is a positive indicator that you are interested, and interest is the first step toward accomplishing anything worthwhile.

I am reminded of the story of a person interested in finding the "secret to the universe." This person was consumed by focusing all available resources on discovering that basic truth which would provide understanding of all things including life itself. The days turned into weeks, the weeks into months, and the months into years, as one lead after another failed to materialize. Determined to find the elusive answer and to utilize it for personal gain, the person journeyed to a faraway land. It was said that on a mountain top in this remote land lived a guru and that this guru possessed the coveted secret of the universe. Enduring severe hardships, the person crossed the ocean, walked across stretches of desolate terrain, and, consuming all energy and resources, climbed the treacherous mountain to question the guru. Sure enough, on the mountain peak sat a guru holding with precious care in his arms a stone tablet. Exhausted to the extent it was difficult to speak, the person dug deep down into the reserve of physical energy and pleaded to the guru, "Please, please share with me that knowledge which explains everything and will enable me to reach my human potential, the secret to the universe." As gurus tend to be as compassionate as they are wise, the guru agreed to share the secret. He turned the tablet he was holding around so that it could be seen. With bleary eyes and with difficulty in focusing, the person could see that there was an inscription on the tablet. Drawing upon the little energy remaining, the person crawled closer so the inscription could be read. The inscription appeared to be only five words. Finally, at the point where the inscription could be brought into focus, the five words were seen and impacted the person's brain like a bolt of lightning. Those five words were . . . *"There ain't no free lunch."* That secret applies to us and to our desire to improve productivity. Nothing worthwhile in this world can be accomplished without total commitment and dedicated effort. Improving productivity would be easier were we starting from scratch. We carry the burden of existing conditions that are counter to productivity growth. That is the bad news. The good news is that we are capable of changing those conditions and thereby improving productivity. *You* can do it! Not overnight and not without effort, but you *can* do it.

As the secret to the universe is basic, so must be our plan to improve productivity. A common failing of productivity improvement plans is that they tend to be theoretical, elaborate, and forced onto the scene without the inputs and cooperation of employees. If it is so elaborate it cannot be properly administered, it will not work. Further, there is a tendency to apply productivity improvement programs as power is applied to a light bulb. Where there is nothing, we throw the management switch by attempting to implement changes more rapidly than they can be assimilated. The program fails and we cannot understand why.

I am of the opinion managers tend to underestimate their employees' abilities, including their ability to understand the need for and contribute to meaningful change. The problem is with the method of implementation. While indeed noble, managerial sense of urgency must be tempered with the fact that even bright and dedicated people will experience problems when too much is changed too fast. At the other extreme is management's having no sense of urgency. Such managers talk about the need for improvement but either never get around to implementing the required changes or, if they do, implementing them so slowly that the excitement and interest brought about by a reasonable challenge wanes. Such managers tend to live in constant fear of what could go wrong. They doubt themselves and those with whom they work, and because they dwell on the problems rather than their solutions, they most often see their fears materialize. After all, according to King Solomon, "As a man thinketh in his heart, so is he." If a manager's thoughts focus on positive results, they will be forthcoming. On the other hand, should a manager focus on negative results, then those negative results will surely materialize.

In the last several years, many influences have combined to challenge the validity of the "no free lunch" philosophy. Across-the-board raises and increasing benefit packages are commonplace, and they are provided equally to high and low producers alike. In the process of making more motivated employees equal, at least in terms of compensation, to their less motivated counterparts, labor unions (in conjunction with management which is motivated to avoid a work interruption at any cost) have done themselves and their nation a great disservice. But this dark aspect does have a silver lining. Many of today's employees are concerned because they want their best efforts to be recognized. They hunger for recognition above the level provided by merely doing what is required of everybody on the job. They want the opportunity to excel and be singled out as being very good, if not the best, at what they do.

Regardless of the individual manager's political, economic, and moral philosophy regarding human rights, it is obvious that changes in the work environment have created productivity-inhibiting problems to be solved. These are facts of life every manager must recognize. They are situations which must be effectively dealt with if productivity is to be improved and the organization's goals met. A manager cannot afford to become obsessed with the many demands of subordinates. As managers, we must have a deep concern for what each employee gives in exchange for what he or she gets. The benefits of employment must be to both parties. We refer to this as an *exchange system.*

An exchange system is a method by which employees and employers interact in a way that some of the needs of both are satisfied. This system has been around for centuries. Successful businesses, without fail, use it. An experienced manager is well aware of the responsibility to the organization of making sure employees earn their pay and also knows that it is profitable to management for the employees to use their full potential to realize organizational goals. Further, the experienced manager recognizes that organizational needs will not be met unless employees' needs are also satisfied.

Common sense tells us that if we are to be successful in any endeavor, then we must focus on the related controllable elements rather than on the noncontrollable. The only portion of the entire universe we can, in the short term, influence is our own. You may be a manager operating in a tightly controlled and restricted environment that inhibits employee involvement, or at least what can be communicated to them. You may have a labor contract forced upon you that provides disincentives, rather than rewards, for good performance. You may have schedules forced upon you that are less than realistic and perhaps not compatible with the efficient utilization of resources. It is not a perfect world, nor can you realistically expect a perfect work environment. Some things you can change; others you realistically cannot. By focusing on those factors over which you have the most control, especially the exchange system based on mutual fulfillment of individual and organizational needs, you *can* realize significant improvement in productivity.

# CHAPTER
# 4 Humans vs. Organizations?

"If you dig very deeply into any problem, you will get to people."[1] And so it is with the problem of productivity. Productivity has been defined as the relationship between real inputs and real outputs, or the measure of how well resources are combined and utilized to accomplish an end result desired by the organization. As the highest order of resources, people are responsible for controlling and utilizing all other resources. People design and operate the equipment and the facility; they design and implement methods and procedures; they purchase and use materials; they sell the product or service and produce or provide it. All these things and more are performed, in varying degrees of effectiveness, by people. People are the key factor in improving productivity. If we are to improve productivity, we must understand both the nature of people and of the organizations in which they work.

## The Nature of People

With regard to people, there are four basic assumptions: individual differences, the whole person, motivated behavior, and human dignity.

**Individual differences.** Each person is unique. As no two sets of fingerprints are the same, or as no two snowflakes are exactly alike, so it is with people. We are born with different physical characteristics and with varying capacities. From that point on we are exposed to different people, things, and events that

[1] J. Watson Wilson, "The Growth of a Company: A Psychological Case Study," *Advanced Management Journal*, January 1966, p. 43.

combine to form unique experiences and different personalities. The fact that individuals are different suggests they cannot be effectively managed by a standard technique.

Even if part of a group, an individual remains individual, displaying personal feelings, judgments, actions, and degrees of motivation and satisfaction. A group is powerless until an individual or individuals within the group act to influence the behavior of all its members.

**A whole person.** A person's home life is not separable from work life. Physical condition is not separate from emotional condition. Skill does not exist separately from background and knowledge. Each affects the other.

When we employ a person, we employ the whole person, not just a set of skills or knowledge. Each human being is a single system embodying all the experiences of that person.

**Motivated behavior.** All human behavior is caused by a person's need structure. We can influence behavior by motivating a person to fulfill needs as the person sees them. A person is not motivated by what other people think the person should want, but rather by what that person wants. Management has two ways by which it can motivate any employee. It can either get the employee to see that a desired action will increase need fulfillment, or it can convince the worker to follow a certain course of action to avoid a decreased need fulfillment. "Management's power to motivate is effective only to the extent that, from the employee's point of view, management controls the means by which the employee can satisfy his needs."[2]

**Human dignity.** Because people are of the highest order, they expect to be treated with respect and dignity. Every task, no matter how menial, entitles the person who does it to proper respect and recognition in line with the manner in which it is performed.

## The Nature of Organizations

Organizations are social systems, both formal and informal, and are formed on the basis of mutual interest and need fulfillment.

**Social systems.** Activities within any organization are governed by social laws as well as psychological laws. People's behavior is influenced as much by their group as they are by their individual needs. Just as people have psychological needs, they have social and status needs whose fulfillment is dependent upon the group or organization. Both formal and informal social systems exist side by side within any organization. The formal, or official, system awards status based

[2]Keith Davis, *The Dynamics of Organizational Behavior*, McGraw-Hill, New York, 1957, p. 16.

on assigned level of responsibility. The informal system provides status based on individual needs of the group's members. For example, there sometimes exists both a formal leader, appointed by the organization, and a separate informal leader, appointed by its members.

The organization as a social system incorporates the idea that the environment is one of dynamic change, unlike the static organizational chart. The parts of the system are interdependent and subject to change by the other parts.

**Mutual interest.** Organizations are formed and maintained on the basis of some mutuality of interest among their members. In modern society mutual interest is largely a product of circumstances. Without the required combination of personal skills and resources, we are forced to combine our personal needs. In so doing, we establish a superordinate (or organizational) goal whose achievement enables the fulfillment of personal needs. This has become increasingly true as technology has advanced. While the professions and certain trades are exceptions, business and government embody this concept. In either, no matter how good the managers become, they cannot achieve this goal without the help of others. Nor can their employees operate alone without benefit of the organization and the resources it provides.

## Setting the Tone and Developing a Climate Conducive to Productivity Growth

We are working today with highly educated and enlightened people living in a land of plenty. Our specific job is to motivate those with whom we work to achieve higher levels of productivity. In a sense, one person can never "motivate" another, as motivation is an internal desire and can come only from within the person. However, with an understanding of human motivation, we know what conditions cause people to act. This knowledge enables us, as managers, to create a climate that is favorable to getting them to act. Practically speaking, we can motivate others to perform in a desired manner, but this ability to motivate is dependent upon a general understanding of human motivation for its success.

The most common form of motivation within organizations, especially in business and industry, is what is referred to as either the "law of effect" or the "principle of reinforcement." You reward behavior you want continued and you punish behavior you want eliminated. Applying this concept to an organization, larger pay increases or special recognition would be given to outstanding producers, while employees whose behavior is clearly detrimental to the organization would be given some form of punishment suitable to the offense. In brief, motivation based on the principle of reinforcement is the familiar carrot-and-stick approach.

There are three general types of motivation, or triggering devices, available to managers which enable them to turn employee needs and drives into action. Let's examine the characteristics of each for the purpose of determining how they can best be applied to supporting productivity growth.

## Fear Motivation

Fear motivation is based on negative reinforcement, or punishment. This type of motivation undoubtedly dates back to prehistoric times. It is based on force and the ability to punish or deprive an individual, or group, of something they need. In early times the most effective motivator was the biggest and strongest. If you didn't do what was wanted when the stronger person wanted it done, you might find yourself deprived of life itself. For centuries thereafter workers commonly toiled endless hours for survival wages. In such an environment fear motivation proved to be very effective. Though the individual workers were powerless in such a situation, in time they began to realize that if they were to unite, they could form an equalizing threat. Thus unions came into being. Today, because of the impact of federal and state legislation, unionism, and the relative ease with which employees can change jobs, the effectiveness of fear motivation has been somewhat reduced. The manager—who is aware of the costs of turnover, slowdowns, strikes, and other restrictions of employee output—is sensitive to the problems created in an organization by employee hostility. We are naturally hesitant to use punishment, even when it is obviously called for.

In spite of the problems involved, negative reinforcement or fear motivation has, and will always have, a place in our organizations. It is a fundamental part of the exchange system by which the needs of both employer and employee are satisfied. Unless employees at all levels of the organization are aware that failure to perform adequately will lead to undesirable consequences, the motivational structure of the organization is totally destroyed.

Though necessary and effective when properly implemented, fear motivation tends to be misused in various fashions. A manager concluding that subordinates are uncommitted and unwilling to work may turn to fear motivation. This attitude becomes self-reinforcing as the manager tends to highlight the shortcomings, rather than achievements, of the work group. For some managers, the power to punish offers the only assurance they can find that they are in charge. Other managers punish their subordinates, and sometimes even their fellow managers, in unconscious ways by critical remarks, demeaning treatment, and unreasonable demands. Threats, whether outwardly expressed or implied, become meaningless if never implemented. When punishment is applied in an organization without clear-cut and properly communicated expectations or standards of performance, or without objective measures, or in a nonuniform manner, the question of fairness is raised and generates sympathy for the person being punished and hostility toward the organization.

As it is management's responsibility to communicate and enforce expectations and as it is fact some people, like donkeys, will only respond to a knock on the head, negative reinforcement, or fear motivation, must remain a managerial tool to be applied when warranted. The proper and constructive application of negative reinforcement to the work place is a combination of managerial attitudes and actions which includes accepting the responsibility for the success of subordinates, as well as the maintenance of a work climate conducive to the achievement of organizational objectives. When employees have been properly trained, have been made aware of specific and realistic expectations, and have been advised individually and in a businesslike and nondemeaning manner of their shortcomings as judged by objective measures, including the possible consequences of those shortcomings, we are applying negative reinforcement in a constructive manner. While enlightened management must assume the responsibility for making its employees successful, there should always exist a minimum acceptable level of personal performance below which the achievement of organizational goals is recognized as being compromised. Should an employee fail in one assignment but continue to express a good attitude including a willingness to meet expectations, management would be remiss not to reassign that person, if possible, to another position. In so doing, management communicates its constructive concern for the individual. Realistically, committing ourselves to this course of action will not save all employees, but it will serve to improve the work climate and, in turn, our potential to improve productivity, including minimizing the cost of labor inputs by reducing turnover.

## Incentive Motivation

Incentive motivation is based on positive reinforcement, or reward. We are all familiar with the classic example of incentive motivation depicted by the donkey pulling a cart because there is a stick strapped to his back and, at the end of the stick, a carrot dangles in front of the donkey's nose. There is little doubt that the cart will move forward—provided the stick is short enough, the carrot big enough, the load in the cart light enough, and the donkey hungry enough. When all these elements are present and the timing is perfect, there is no question about the effectiveness of incentive motivation. The weakness lies in the corollary of this system with the human appetite. Every person's wants depend, in large measure, upon what the person already has. As soon as a want is satisfied, it ceases to be a want and no longer motivates behavior. What motivates an employee today will not necessarily continue to do so next month or next year. An organization cannot hope to continue to motivate an employee forever with the same old carrot. Organizations that have sought to motivate their employees solely with incentives and rewards have found themselves defeated by the law of diminishing returns. While there is inherently nothing wrong with offering tangible rewards for outstanding individual or group effort, the offers invariably become progressively less effective when they are expected to carry the primary responsibility for keeping employees productive. More and more tends to be paid for less and less.

Let's look at other weaknesses of incentive motivation as applied within organizations:

1. Commonly, incentive motivation is viewed as a substitute for supervision with disastrous results. Popular opinion is that given a big enough and juicy enough carrot, employees will fall over each other in an effort to raise productivity. For reasons previously stated, such is not the case. The proper administration of incentive programs requires a time-consuming effort by highly skilled managers.
2. Objective appraisal of individual contribution as a part of an incentive program is the exception rather than the rule. With either individual or group incentives, it is difficult to accurately reward in proportion to individual contribution. This becomes apparent to the participants and results in the incentive program becoming a demotivator rather than a motivator.
3. Incentive programs result in real or imaginary differences in work assignments and assigned equipment and may themselves become a greater source of contention. Even when their assumptions are not based on fact, employees tend to rationalize away another's success on the basis of "preferential treatment" by the manager in charge.
4. Over a period of time, incentive compensation comes to be expected just like a regular paycheck. Even when such compensation is of the profit sharing variety, some employees suspect management of manipulating the profits to keep the pay out low.

Many managers have found that incentive motivation, which began with strong acceptance and initially promised to be an effective motivational system, has, in the long run, turned out to be burdensome and less effective. While tangible rewards may not be effective over the long run due to the fact they do not alter the employees' attitude toward their jobs, intangible rewards *can* alter basic attitudes and improve long-term performance.

We have established that both fear motivation and incentive motivation can be temporarily effective, but both are inherently weak because neither one touches the inner "nerve" of accomplishment for its own sake. That brings us to the third, and only lasting, type of motivation.

## Achievement Motivation

Achievement motivation is based on accomplishment for its own sake. The achievement-motivated employees work because of the sense of challenge, accomplishment, and service to others which they feel. The philosophy of achievement motivation is based on a true understanding of human nature. The manager who is committed to this system of motivation rejects the traditional theory that people are basically lazy, shun responsibility, and are indifferent toward organizational goals. By believing in people and their potential for improvement, the manager encourages employees to accept responsibility. Such a manager encourages creativity; achieves organizational goals by helping subordinates reach their personal goals; and manages by objectives and by so doing increases the organizational effectiveness of all those with whom there is any interface. This person is a leader striving toward managerial excellence.

Without question, achievement motivation is the most powerful and lasting force a manager can use. When we change peoples attitudes toward the organization, toward their work, their family, their friends, and most important of all toward themselves, we have altered the basic structure of both the human personality and the organization for the better.

All of us are individually the sum total of the experiences and attitudes, or habits of thought, we have acquired up to this point in our lives. We react, evaluate, judge, and respond according to habits of thought that were formed over many years in environments over which we often had little, if any, control. Though influenced strongly by our past experiences, we continue to change and to react to new opportunities and new challenges. We have the potential to learn new ways of interpreting or perceiving our world. We can add new dimensions as we encounter new experiences and make our judgments and adjust our attitudes accordingly. Here the manager's leadership ability comes into play.

While unable to alter the early environmental influences of coworkers, the manager can influence their current work-place environment and their thoughts about it. If accomplished constructively and with high purpose, the manager can not only change their work-related attitudes and habits for the better but can also improve organizational performance. The manager can help subordinates change some of the basic and critically important attitudes which they, as individuals, hold toward themselves, toward others, toward the organization, and toward their work. The process of achievement motivation is not easy. Altering deeply ingrained attitudes takes time. Frustration can be anticipated as you deal with the never-ending number of ways in which different persons satisfy their needs. There is definitely no free lunch when it comes to applying achievement motivation. Yet because it is the only form of motivation that recognizes each person as a unique individual, it can create opportunities, recognize performance, encourage growth, and sponsor individual expression. Achievement motivation alone can stimulate the type of goal-directed behavior required to build a highly productive organization.

## Maslow's Hierarchy of Human Needs

Psychologist Abraham Maslow asserted that all human behavior is motivated by unsatisfied needs. A need, according to Maslow, is an inner demand—an unfilled condition, a physical or psychic appetite. The individual behaves in ways which are calculated to result in a reduction of this inner appetite. In this context, a variety of needs, or appetites, usually compete for influence over a person's immediate behavior. Maslow contended that the system of human needs operated in the form of a hierarchy, or an ascending scale of priority. Certain and more basic needs tend to outrank others, and some are more fundamental in shaping an individual's behavior. As the more basic needs are satisfied, a person will seek the higher needs. If the basic needs are not met, they claim priority, and efforts to satisfy the higher needs must be postponed. A need priority of five levels was established as follows by Maslow.[3]

1. Basic biological or physical needs
2. Safety and security
3. Belonging and social activity
4. Esteem and status
5. Self-realization and fulfillment

Since each individual is an integrated whole, we are not dealing with single-need persons within the work environment. We are dealing with people who are influenced by a complex web of needs which manifest themselves in many ways. It will help to understand the individual if we review some basic facts about the types of needs.

## Biological Needs

It is highly unlikely that the manager will encounter, in today's work environment, an employee who has a real unsatisfied physical or biological need except for relatively short periods of time. Some of the physical needs are food, water, sleep, and air. If working at all, a person is generally not starving or suffering from thirst, exposure, or a lack of sleep. The physical needs are the most primitive, or basic, in the hierarchy of needs. They must be satisfied if life is to be sustained. They are also the easiest needs to satisfy. Man does not live by bread alone, unless there is no bread. When basic physical needs are satisfied, as they generally are today, other needs tend to occupy the mind and dominate actions.

It should be stressed, however, that because of the basic and vital nature of the physical needs they are important as motivators. To visualize their critical role, consider how much time is spent during the average day just trying to satisfy them. Our need for sleep alone accounts for approximately one-third of the total day. Add to this the time spent preparing and eating our meals, and you have accounted for a sizable chunk of the total time available to us.

You will realize when reflecting upon your physical needs that it is difficult,

[3]Abraham Maslow, "A Theory of Human Motivation," *Psychological Review*, vol. 50, 1943, pp. 370–396.

if not impossible, to separate them from some of our other needs of a social or psychological nature. For example, when you have guests for dinner, you could satisfy their hunger with basic, though nutritious, foods of limited variety. Instead, you might have salad, steak, vegetable, dessert, and a choice of drinks. It becomes obvious that we are motivated by other than our physical needs. The same is true when we emphasize factors other than shelter when purchasing a home and look for more than transportation when buying a car.

## Safety Needs

We are also unlikely to encounter signs of the basic safety needs among our managers or employees except in disguised or subtle forms. In emergency situations, people may have a basic fear for life and safety, but such situations are rare. However, we may find a need for security prevalent among our employees, especially those at the lowest levels of the organization. Security needs may surface in employees' insistence on fair play, on job tenure, job protection, and insurance.

Real security is an internal rather than an external condition. Our feeling of security is more a function of our inner attitudes and values than it is of our external job, salary, position, or length of service. People may have the external factors of job, position, and tenure, yet not have security in the form of personal confidence in their abilities. This should be kept in mind when the temptation arises to give employees everything they ask for. The basic problems do not go away as a single result of external manipulation.

Ultimately, we are all responsible for our own security, and there is only one way to develop it: by increasing and fortifying personal strength, personal ability, and personal talent. As a manager, you fulfill your responsibility by motivating your subordinates to achieve more, to grow, and to develop within your organization.

## Social Needs

One of the strongest motivators in the behavior of any person is the quest for social acceptance—for belonging, for association, for friendship and love. This contributes to people wanting a better home, a bigger car, nice clothes, and more money. These things are modern day symbols of social acceptance. The need a person has for social acceptance is usually an outward manifestation of a deeper need, the need for self-acceptance. If other people accept a person, that acceptance confirms the person has chosen the right value system and is reassured. Their acceptance supports the individual's own self-acceptance. In this light, we can see that even a person's needs for social acceptance are internally motivated.

Most successful managers recognize the power that social needs can generate within their organizations. Accordingly, they strive to provide opportunity, training, and stimulation to their subordinates enabling them to earn more money and meet their social needs. As previously mentioned, money alone is seldom a complete solution. A need when satisfied ceases to be a need. The need either becomes greater or a new need replaces it. That is why "one-note" motivational programs based on only one need and without regard to other needs, as are most incentive programs, seldom work effectively for an extended period of time.

## Ego Needs

Ego needs are essentially needs for self-respect. It is the desire of the individual to feel like a worthwhile person who is making a reasonably significant contribution in life. Its most important facet is that it must be deserved. Many successful businesspeople have taken their children, or other relatives, into their business and elevated them to a high position only to discover that the relative was ungrateful if not disinterested in the opportunity provided. In the process, the child or other relative lost self-respect by the awareness that the high position was neither deserved nor earned. People will go into battle or face other certain danger just to keep, or acquire, self-respect. One employee may be willing to do the dirtiest, most difficult, most dangerous work in the organization to preserve self-esteem because of the need for a job. This employee cannot feel right without a job and will take whatever work is available. Another employee might lose self-esteem by doing such lowly and dirty work, and will go on unemployment when times get tough. Both employees are motivated by self-esteem, but they have different ways of showing it.

To understand and motivate subordinates, you need to know the specific ways they satisfy their psychological needs. If you know their needs and their typical ways of satisfying them, you can anticipate how they will respond to whatever you say or do. Fortunately, there is a definite consistency in the way each individual will go about satisfying needs. Habits are relatively stable as you will know if you've ever tried to break one.

You can be sure that all people want self-respect even though their actions may not indicate it. You can be equally sure that everything you do to help your subordinates, superiors, and peers grow in self-respect will win you their support. In your ability to praise and build up others, you have a force more powerful than you have ever imagined. Every time you help another person grow in self-respect, you add a new dimension of strength and confidence to your own personality. If your managerial practices destroy self-respect, they are progressively destroying the foundation for motivation.

## Self-Fulfillment Needs

Self-fulfillment means to reach one's potential or to become all you are capable of becoming. This is a lofty need whose fulfillment is characterized by a continuous search, on the part of the individual, for self-development. This need is less apparent than the others because most people are too busy satisfying either their social or esteem needs. The struggle that most individuals experience in satisfying their other, more basic, needs generally dilutes and diverts their energies away from self-fulfillment. Therefore, few people have the opportunity to pursue satisfaction of this last important need. That is why self-fulfillment is most often seen in either highest-level managers or exceptional junior executives.

An individual functions as an integrated whole. Presentation of individual needs in a compartmentalized fashion has value in promoting understanding, but nevertheless is artificial. Each behavior is in constant interaction with every other aspect of that person. All individual needs do, however, relate to one central need that we will call *self-preservation* or *self-enhancement*. This theoretical framework assumes a very broad definition of the individual, including not only the physical and psychological self but also extending to all the persons, things, and institutions with which the individual has formed an identification. In a very real sense, people have as much a need to protect their family, their car, or their alma mater as they do to protect themselves. To lose them, or have them damaged or degraded, is painful to individuals because these needs have become a part of their world. When individuals strive to live up to their personal standards, they are striving to build up or preserve themselves. The drive to live within our personal value system is a drive for self-respect and self-acceptance.

## A Hierarchy of Organizational Needs

An organization is a group of people bound together in a formal relationship for the purpose of achieving organizational goals. As individuals have needs, so do organizations. While individual needs are the framework for behavior, organizational needs are the framework for combining and channeling resources into results.

Classical organizational theory deals with such characteristics of the organization as authority, responsibility, span of control, and reporting relationships. According to classical theory, organizational structure is created by functional and scalar division of work. This structure is communicated to its members by delegation of duties, responsibility, and authority, with the amount of each being relatively equal. Structure focuses on the job rather than on the person who performs it.

By examining an organization's needs, rather than its structure, we can further develop the basis for an effective program to improve productivity.

Describing a need as a self-generated demand or unfilled condition means that organizations have needs. Like the individual, those responsible for directing the organization behave in ways which they think will satisfy the organization's demands or needs. Also like an individual, the organization has a variety of needs, each competing for influence over the organization's focus and course of action.

Organizational needs combine in the form of a hierarchy, or ascending scale of priority. As the more basic needs are satisfied, the organization's leadership will focus on the higher-order needs. Should the organization's more basic needs not be satisfied, addressing the higher-order needs must be postponed. An organizational need priority of five levels is established as follows:

1. Demand
2. Resources
3. Direction
4. Effectiveness
5. Efficiency

At any given point in time the organization is concerned with all its needs, to varying degrees. Because organizations are operating in an ever-changing environment, managerial emphasis is fluid. It will help to better understand the organization if we look more closely at its needs.

## The Demand Need

The most basic of the organization's needs is the need of a demand for its products or services. Organizations are formed for the purpose of filling either an anticipated or an existing want. Needs conditioned by the environment either singularly or in combination condition a need resulting in a specific want. As long as the want is relatively simple and requires only limited and readily available resources, that want will probably be filled either by an individual or a number of individuals each working independently. An example of a basic want is the desire to have your lawn mowed. This want is the result of your need for acceptance being conditioned by your neighbors who take pride in the care of their homes and lawns and expect the same of you. As the mowing of the average lawn requires only basic resources, a lawn mower and someone to push it, your want can be satisifed by contracting the services of the youngster next door. The formation of an organization to satisfy this want is possible but not required.

An example of a more complicated want is your desire for a new car. You, like all of us, have a status need. Suppose, for example, that your job is selling real estate. You have noticed that prospective buyers seem to equate success, if not professional competence, to the type and model car the salesperson drives. Thus the environment has conditioned your need for status and resulted in the want for a new luxury car. Luckily for you, organizations have been formed for the special purpose of filling this more complicated want.

Regardless of whether the organization has been formed to provide a service or a product, the most basic of its needs is a demand for that product or service. That demand can either exist or be anticipated. In those instances where the organization was formed on an anticipated demand that failed to materialize, the organization's continuance is threatened; likewise threatened is an organization that competes for an existing demand but cannot get it. It matters not to the individual that food is available; only that some of the food can be claimed for his or her own. It matters not to an organization that there is a demand for its products or services; only that some of the demand can be directed to it.

## The Resource Need

As we are unlikely to find organizations without a demand, we are also unlikely to find organizations without resources to fill that demand. The organization exists for a purpose. The achievement of that purpose is dependent upon the availability of certain resources. An organization formed for the purpose of educating people, for example, has a need for the resources required to do such. These resources can be limited to teachers or expanded to include books, libraries, equipment, classrooms, and other related resources. While we may be able to educate with only books, or only teachers, it is a fact that available resources have an important bearing on the organization's ability to fulfill its purpose, as well as its prospects for growth.

Generally, the larger the organization and the more complicated its purpose, the more complex is its need for resources. The organization formed for the purpose of putting a man on the moon, for example, depended upon widespread and diversified resources requiring significant additional resources just for the purpose of coordination.

In recent years, the scarcity of certain resources has resulted in an inordinate amount of managerial time being consumed in the search for dependable supplies. With regard to those scarce resources, it can no longer be taken for granted that the organization's needs will be met without interruption. This development has tended to detract from the ability of organizations to achieve their purpose effectively.

## The Direction Need

When the organization's leadership cannot provide its members with an accurate sense of direction, the organization becomes a reactive system, simply responding to the forces acting upon it. In such a situation the organization functions as an amoeba, the small, one-celled animal that high school students enjoy watching under microscopes. The amoeba is very limited in what it can do. It simply drifts along in whatever direction it happens to be heading, until it collides with something. Faced with a new object in its environment, the amoeba either eats it, gets eaten itself, or simply turns and continues on its way. The simplistic pattern of functioning is analogous to the operation of an organization whose members are without direction. As a group, they drift.

When looking into the problem of how to make organizations more productive, the need for organizational direction becomes apparent. All organizations have, either stated or implied, a purpose for their being. Beyond the broad statement of purpose, organizations need more specific direction, and that direction must be dynamic in nature. Specific goals relating to the organization's purpose must first be developed. Once such goals are set, all available resources can be directed toward their achievement. Thereafter, changes in conditions both within the organization as well as outside it require that this direction be adjusted to ensure goal achievement. Without direction the organization cannot fulfill its purpose.

## The Need to Be Effective

All organizations have a need to be effective, or to accomplish results. Those results are achieved by managers bringing together and combining resources, then utilizing those resources so that the desired results are obtained. You will note that effectiveness has no consideration for cost. Practically speaking, there generally is some concern for cost when striving for results; but emphasis is on the results. If you have ever been involved with a "start-up" operation of any type, you will recall the progression of starting from scratch, first generating some momentum, then striving to achieve results, and lastly focusing on achieving those results in a more efficient manner. By initially striving for results without a concurrent consuming interest in cost, we recognize that there is a cost associated with becoming proficient at any productive task. The specific elements of that "cost of learning" are time, practice or repetition, and the possible waste of other resources such as materials. By making mistakes, we learn. In time the mistakes are reduced, if not eliminated, and the methods and procedures are debugged; most people, if not all, acquire a thorough understanding of what they are to do, and then and only then can the emphasis shift to efficiency.

## The Need for Efficiency

The highest-order need of any organization is efficiency. Only after satisfying all its other needs for the most part, can an organization focus on satisfying its need for efficiency. Efficiency relates not to results but to how well we achieve those results. Where effectiveness is concerned with generating outputs, efficiency focuses on minimizing the costs associated with producing those outputs.

You will recall that efficiency, as well as effectiveness, is a component of productivity.

As the organization has a need for efficiency, its leaders have the responsibility for maintaining a climate conducive to its achievement. To improve efficiency is to improve performance, or the relationship between output and the inputs required to generate that output. The amount of emphasis placed on competitive performance varies from one organization to another. Extreme emphasis on competitive performance within an organization produces consequences which are threatening to many of its members. This can result in powerful internal forces arising to combat that emphasis. On the other hand, no organization can realize its potential unless its members accept the need for high standards of performance and strive to achieve those standards within the limits of their abilities. The resolution of this apparent dilemma is dependent most upon management's ability to contribute toward individual need fulfillment within the work place.

## The Potential Compatibility of Individual and Organizational Needs

To some extent, all members of any organization seek to satisfy their need for achievement in their work. To satisfy this and other individual needs, the organization must be structured to provide the opportunity for individual success. While most members have a high need for achievement, others may have stronger social or esteem needs. Organizations whose managers have a good understanding of individual needs and their potential compatibility with the needs of the organization are in a good position to satisfy those other needs as well. Figure 4-1 illustrates both sets of needs.

The potential compatibility between individual and organizational needs

Figure 4-1. Individual and organizational needs.

becomes apparent as we look closely at the illustration, starting with the most basic and advancing to the higher-order needs.

## Number One Priority Needs

The individual's most basic needs are biological or physical: food, clothing, shelter, etc. Without these needs being satisfied, to at least a minimal degree, survival is not possible. Fulfillment of the individual's needs is dependent primarily on a paycheck from or through the organization. The organization's survival is dependent upon a demand for its product or service. In effect, unfilled wants enable the organization not only to survive but also to provide work for its employees. Members of organizations are generally aware of their dependence upon client or customer demand. In the case of a business organization, soaring demand taxes resources and may require that the individual work overtime, while reduced demand requires an adjustment of resources which could include layoffs. The organization serves the needs of both its members and itself by maintaining, if not increasing, demand for its products or services. Management has the responsibility for revising, on a continuous basis, its product and service offerings to better match current and anticipated demand. Only by fulfilling this responsibility can the organization's continuance, including its ability to provide employment to its members, be assured.

## Number Two Priority Needs

The individual's second most basic need is for safety or security. Every individual needs assurance that survival, both physical and economic, is not in jeopardy. The organization's second most basic need is for resources to be applied to fulfilling the demand for its product or service. An organization well endowed with resources is obviously better able to satisfy the security needs of its members. Individuals associated with a highly profitable business organization, for example, are more likely to have their security needs met than are the members of a bankrupt organization.

We previously mentioned that individual security was at least as much an internal condition as it was dependent upon external factors. Most organizations, despite what may be an abundance of resources, will have insecure members. While managers are seldom psychologists, having the ability to help resolve such internal conflicts, they can be sensitive to the impact of their actions on their employees. The individual need for security extends to having reasonable predictability of surroundings, enabling the person to be free of anxiety and feel at ease. Inconsistency on the part of the organization and its managers; the lack of communicated expectations and feedback related to individual performance; the policy of ignoring the worker, which includes lack of notification, if not consultation on, pending changes; and demonstrations of favoritism or discrimination all combine to create security stress among the organization's members. Enlightened managers will recognize these potential sources of individual need deprivation and dedicate themselves and the resources at their disposal to avoiding such problems. Emphasis here must be on prevention (avoiding situations that create security stress) rather than cure (after-the-fact correction).

## Number Three Priority Needs

When the individual has pretty much satisfied physical and safety needs, the focus shifts to satisfying social needs. Social needs include the individual's need to be included in the activities of others; needs for acceptance and memberships in one or more groups; and feedback from group members which confirms one's sense of belonging and significance.

After satisfying the need for demand, and resources to fill that demand, the organization's needs shift to providing direction aimed at combining and utilizing available resources. This is best accomplished by setting specific goals for the organization and with its members. Both individual and group goals should be set. When the goal-setting process includes all the organization's members, the stage is set for both providing direction to the organization and satisfying the individual's needs to belong as well.

In large part, the individual looks to the job situation to satisfy social needs. Sure, they may belong to organizations outside the work place; but because much of their time is taken up by work, the job either satisfies or fails to satisfy this need. Satisfaction of the social needs is dependent upon both peer group behavior and managerial behavior. The effective manager influences both.

Inattention on the part of the manager will seriously detract from an individual's social needs being satisfied. Nothing can crush a person's ego more quickly than being ignored. One of the most effective and economical ways to motivate any individual is to give five minutes of your undivided attention every once in a while. Talk with them, not at them, giving them a chance to express what is on their mind. Another effective method to satisfy the social needs is to periodically gather your employees together for a brief meeting. Use such meetings to express the organization's goals and concerns and to communicate the organization's dependence on their efforts. Each person is a member of the team and expected to contribute to the group effort. The very basic, but often forgotten, "howdy rounds," wherein the manager contacts each subordinate at least once early each morning, to say "Good morning," and again in the afternoon, to ask "How are things going?" not only helps satisfy the employees' social needs but also gives the manager an opportunity to confirm all is going as was planned—that everything is proceeding in the right direction. It is not uncommon for minor problems to develop into serious ones because the manager isn't in the area and cannot be advised. The howdy rounds guard against things getting too far out of line before you become aware of them.

In some organizations there exist rigid barriers between separate echelons, between different groups, and between various functions. No matter how good a person may be in such a situation, his or her growth is severely restricted because the efforts will not be noticed outside that person's particular work group. Accordingly, the individual is not accepted by the company as a whole and the need for social approval goes unsatisfied.

Considering the amount of time people spend in their work, it is tragic if we, as managers, do not treat them with courtesy and respect, fail to make them feel they belong, and neglect to tell them their contribution is important. To do so should be considered a primary responsibility of every manager within the organization.

## Number Four Priority Needs

An individual's next highest-order need is the ego or esteem need—the need for feeling that you are important; that you have made a contribution toward achieving worthwhile goals. The individual's desire to stand out, as a special person in some way or other, is especially significant and potent. The corresponding level need for the organization is to be effective; to do what it has intended to do, to achieve results. Organizations are dependent upon their members, working alone and in combination, to achieve results. Without individual effort there would be no results. The effective combination and coordination of individual efforts has a synergistic effect upon the quality and quantity of the results achieved.

A manager is responsible for achieving results. That responsibility includes building a framework for not only setting goals or achievement standards but also implementing a measurement system whereby individual contribution may be objectively evaluated. While most managers know that to criticize a person's performance in public is a bad practice, too many managers fail to consistently practice what they know. A manager should not be satisfied with second best and is obligated to continuously strive for the best efforts from employees. Subordinates are aware of what is possible and what should be expected. Should you be too easily satisfied, they will recognize that fact and, in the process, lose respect for both you and themselves. You may ask, "Without compromising my standards, how can I provide recognition to more than a few members of my work group?" First, even consistent top producers usually (making room for individual differences) do not have to receive outward praise or recognition every day. Second, recognition need not be confined to only the top all-around performer. Recognition can be given for good attendance, improvement in output, skill in training other employees, good housekeeping, error-free performance, team spirit or cooperation, and a host of other things. True, you are interested in end results, and these other things are not always end results; but by providing praise for what may be the lesser aspects of the job, you can motivate all-around improvement.

When one or more of your subordinates repeatedly fails to meet the minimum acceptable level of performance, you are obligated to criticize—constructively and in private. (The most successful managers use "individual capacity beyond the minimum acceptable level of performance," not a single "minimum acceptable level" of performance for the entire group, as a triggering point for constructive criticism. By expecting more in a constructive way, they consistently get more.) It is unrealistic to think you will never have to be abrasive to jolt a subordinate out of complacency and poor performance. From time to time you will have to take off the kid gloves, but that is not license to put on the brass knuckles. Sarcasm and belittling a person's character or abilities are destructive practices, generally tending to make poor performers worse.

## Number Five Priority Needs

The highest order of individual needs is the need for self-fulfillment, or achievement; and the corresponding order of organizational needs is the need for efficiency and success. As success is defined as the degree or measure of achieving a desired end result, the compatibility of the words *success* and *achievement* is apparent. But how do we go about satisfying both the individual's and the organization's highest-level needs? Satisfaction of the lower-level needs of both, of course, contributes toward that end, but in no way guarantees satisfaction of the highest-order needs. The difference between a good organization and a great organization is most often the ability of its management to satisfy its members' need for achievement. Important to that end is management's ability to unleash the creative abilities of the organization's members. Though an individual working alone can certainly be creative, the dynamics of group interaction may build enthusiasm for creativity among a wider range of people within the organization. Participative management makes everyone aware of organizational goals and what is expected from each member and provides feedback related to actual performance versus goal or expectation; it also provides each member the ideas of all other members to build upon. This generates excitement among the group for finding new and better ways to do things. When the resulting ideas are implemented, individual need satisfaction and the success of the organization are both at their highest.

To develop an operating climate most conducive to creativity and innovation, the manager must provide flexibility in the structuring of the organization. Some organizations suffer from overorganization. Their members suffer from overorganization. Those members must rigidly adhere to the organization chart and are tightly bound by policy and inflexible procedures. No room is left for individual contribution and creative effort. While policies and procedures are desirable, some room must be left to breathe, to experiment, and even to fail. By failing we learn, and by applying our gained knowledge we move further ahead.

Some managers relish the role of peacemaker. They will go to almost any lengths to reduce friction or resolve conflict of any sort. If we always choose to avoid conflict, so will our subordinates—even if it means restraining their achievement drives. Properly controlled, conflict and competitive spirit can contribute to the achievement of both individual and organizational goals and the fulfillment of needs. Particularly among managers, conflict and competition are to be expected. That is the price we must pay for having thoroughbreds rather than plow horses. Properly cultivated and controlled, conflict helps to open the channels of creativity.

## Summary

Satisfaction of our needs depends in large measure upon our jobs. Our physical, security, social, esteem, and self-fulfillment needs are all tied to our work environment. This is equally true of each person in our organization. Since most of us have to work and our work takes up a large part of the time available to us, there is no better place than on the job to seek satisfaction of our individual needs.

When managers understand that, and accept it both intellectually and emotionally, they can utilize it to build a highly productive organization. People are egocentric creatures. Each member of the organization sees the organization, coworkers, and management as they relate to her or him. An individual is the center of her or his universe. At best, people are partially objective. If, in their eyes, you put the organization and its work above them and the satisfaction of their needs, you demotivate them. On the other hand, if we can show them how the company and their jobs can be an outlet for release of their energies, and a source of satisfaction for their needs, they will be highly productive.

# 3

# Measuring
# Productivity

# 5
# Developing
# Appropriate Measurements

We are interested in measuring productivity basically for the reason that we require a relative indicator of the efficiency with which the organization has consumed resources in the course of achieving desired end results. Stated another way—we need to know how we are doing, managerially, as compared to our performance in prior periods. "Are we making improvement; or are we regressing? What is the magnitude of that improvement or regression? Are our programs effective?" Though productivity ratios themselves do not usually provide the underlying reasons for problems, they do, when properly compiled and reported on a timely basis and in an easily understood format, make management aware that a problem of a specific magnitude exists.

Before discussing productivity measurement and reporting further, it might be helpful to again review the definition of productivity. Exactly what are we intending to measure and report?

$$\text{Productivity} = \frac{\text{total output}}{\text{total input}} = \frac{\text{total results achieved}}{\text{total resources consumed}}$$
$$= \frac{\text{effectiveness}}{\text{efficiency}}$$

Productivity is defined as the ratio of total outputs to total inputs; or the ratio of results achieved to resources consumed; or the ratio of the effectiveness with which organizational goals are achieved to the efficiency with which resources

**51**

are consumed in the course of achievement. A basic and commonly used productivity measure is "output per hour":

$$\text{Productivity} = \frac{\text{output realized}}{\text{hours used to obtain the output}} = \frac{\text{output}}{\text{hour}}$$

Using a specific example, let's say 10 units of output were produced using 5 units of labor, then:

$$\text{Productivity} = \frac{10}{5} = 2.0$$

Let's also say that in a following period of time 12 units of output were produced in the same work situation, using 6 units of labor, then:

$$\text{Productivity} = \frac{12}{6} = 2.0$$

Though the output has increased, the amount of resources consumed has also increased, in this case in exact proportion to the increase in output; thus productivity remains the same. To improve productivity we must accomplish one or more of the following changes. Note: The base period referenced in the examples provided is:

$$\frac{\text{Output}}{\text{Input}} = \frac{10}{5} = 2.0$$

1. Maintain the same level of output while at the same time reducing the input or consumption of resources, i.e.:

$$\frac{10}{4} = 2.5$$

Note: Referring to the definition that productivity = effectiveness ÷ efficiency, in this example we have improved the efficiency of labor inputs; we have achieved the same result using fewer labor hours; thus productivity has increased from an output of 2.0 to 2.5 units produced per labor hour.
2. Maintain the same level of input while at the same time increasing the output, i.e.:

$$\frac{11}{5} = 2.2$$

Note: Again referring to the definition that productivity = effectiveness ÷ efficiency, in this example we have increased the effectiveness, or the magnitude of the results achieved or output, without increasing the labor inputs; thus productivity has increased from an output of 2.0 to 2.2 units produced per labor hour.

3. Increasing the level of output while at the same time decreasing the input, i.e.:

$$\frac{11}{4} = 2.75$$

Note: In this case we have increased the effectiveness, or magnitude, of results achieved while reducing the quantity of resources consumed. In so doing, we have significantly increased productivity from 2.0 to 2.75 units produced per labor hour.

## Ratios and Indexes

We have said that productivity is a relative measure in the sense its meaning is based on comparing the present productivity ratio with the ratio for a previous period referred to as the *base period*. Productivity ratios can also be compared to standards, and when they are, the standard then becomes the basis for comparison, or the base period. In either event, we need to know both the direction and the magnitude of the change—have we improved or regressed as compared to the base period, and what is the magnitude of change? Most commonly, the magnitude of change is expressed as a percentage: (current period — base period) ÷ base period. Communicating percentage change sometimes impairs understanding. An alternative is to calculate and communicate *index* numbers. An index number is simply the percentage change added to or subtracted from 100. Indexes can also be calculated directly from the basic data.

Index numbers have several advantages. They can be used to calculate or convert to other indexes. Percentage changes are easily derived from them. Indexes lend themselves to the charting of trend lines. They can be compared with government statistics, such as the productivity indexes produced by the Bureau of Labor Statistics.

The computation of index numbers requires that a period of time be designated as the base period. Most common, the base period is of a one-year duration. Caution must be exercised to ensure the base period is a "normal" period in the sense the volume of outputs is neither abnormally high or low. A period which includes abnormally low outputs due to a large influx of new, nonproficient employees, for example, would not be a good base period. Further, if indexes are compared, the two indexes must both be on the same base; that is, calculated from the same base period. Comparing two indexes having different base years is possible, but requires a conversion to a common base via additional calculation.

Table 5-1 illustrates the development not only of simple productivity ratios but also of other related ratios and index numbers.

**TABLE 5-1.** Calculating Ratios and Indexes from Basic Data

| | Base Period | | Following Period | |
|---|---|---|---|---|
| | Amount (1) | Index* (2) | Amount (3) | Index† (4) |
| 1. Output, units | 50,000 | 100 | 81,900 | 163.8 |
| 2. Hours | 5,000 | 100 | 6,500 | 130.0 |
| 3. Compensation | $30,000 | 100 | $42,250 | 140.8 |
| Ratios: | | | | |
| 4. Output per hour (line 1 ÷ line 2) | 10 | 100 | 12.6 | 126.0 |
| 5. Compensation per hour (line 3 ÷ line 2) | $6.00 | 100 | $6.50 | 108.3 |
| 6. Unit employment costs (line 5 ÷ line 4) | $0.60 | 100 | $0.516 | 86.0 |

*The index for the base period (column 2) is normally not shown as it is in this example, but instead is "understood" as being 100.
†The index for the following period (column 4) is derived as follows: (column 3 ÷ column 1) × 100. Indexes may also be calculated by dividing one index by another, as is shown in lines 4, 5, and 6.

## The Difficulty in Designing and Successfully Implementing Meaningful Measurements

Measuring productivity is easier said than done. For that reason many organizations do not have such measures, while some that do, unfortunately, do not have meaningful or complete measures. In an organization that produces the same product or provides the same service year after year, measurement is relatively simple. We quantify the goods produced or service provided during both the base and current periods. The sum of the current outputs is divided by the sum of the base period outputs to provide an output index. We quantify the resources consumed for both periods and similarly divide the current period inputs by the base period inputs to provide an input index. The productivity for the current period, in relationship to the base period, is measured by dividing the current output index by the current input index.

Even within an organization that produces a number of products or provides a variety of services, the different outputs can be added and the sum used as the measure of outputs, providing the products or services remain unchanged and they are used in exactly the same mix or proportions from period to period. Such is seldom the case. Products and services tend to be modified as time passes. New offerings are introduced as old ones are dropped. The product mix changes.

There are a number of other reasons that make it difficult to design, implement, and benefit from meaningful measurements.

## Measurements Tend to Be Too Broad

The official source of statistics for productivity within the United States is the Bureau of Labor Statistics (BLS) of the Department of Labor. The BLS publishes indexes of output per work hour for the total private U.S. economy and for the nonfarm and manufacturing and corporate sectors each quarter. It also publishes indexes for additional sectors, such as mining, transportation and utilities, and trade, at irregular intervals. Indexes for other sectors, such as services, construction, finance, real estate, and government, are not published due to deficiencies in the available data. The output component of available productivity indexes is computed from the U.S. Department of Commerce figures for gross national product for the total private economy and for each of the sectors. The input component of these indexes is based on a monthly survey of payroll records. Since this survey does not cover total employment in the private sector, and because there are gaps in the hours' information, some supplementary data is used to derive work-hour estimates for all persons involved in producing the output of the private economy. Such inputs include paid holidays, vacations, and sick leave. They are based on hours paid rather than hours actually worked and for this reason alone result in a period-to-period distortion.

Productivity as a concept and measurement has traditionally been a part of the economists' domain. Thus the comparisons have been based on outputs derived from total measures such as gross national product, or the total goods and services produced by the economy. This broad perspective has virtually no value to any single organization. Measurements are required that relate and are useful to the individual firm. Generalized measurements fall short of that mark.

Sometimes measurements implemented by an organization tend to be so broad that they communicate only that something is wrong without providing any clue as to even in what area the problem might lie. Measurements which are too broad-based detract from the performance of those who are contributing to the organization's goals without pinpointing those who are not. It is important not only that enough measurements be applied and at the right places but also that each level of management has the benefit of those specific productivity-related ratios best suited to their needs. While the first-line manager may have a real need for the detail provided by several measurements, each of limited scope, higher-level managers require fewer and more broadly based productivity ratios. If need be when problems arise, the higher-level manager can reference the microlevel ratios.

## Measurements Are Activity-Oriented Rather Than Results-Oriented

Sometimes within an organization, managerial focus drifts to the hustle and bustle of activities with diminished regard for results, such as a business, for example, where booking sales for the sake of booking sales takes precedent over booking sales to contribute to the organization's profit. In the former, pricing and profit margins are not considered; in the latter, they are. "Sales booked per salesperson's workday" is an activity-oriented measurement. "Contribution to profit per salesperson's workday" is a results-oriented measurement.

The trap of conducting and measuring activities for the sake of activities, rather than focusing on the results (or real outputs) we intend for those activities to generate, is a common problem. This potential problem can be avoided by focusing on the work processes in terms of the results the organization is trying to achieve, rather than on the activities it conducts.

### Inputs Are Oversimplified, Excluding Significant Factors Which Compromise the Measurements' Validity

Technically, productivity is the ratio of *total* outputs to *total* inputs. We previously have discussed productivity ratios which singularly relate output to any one of several inputs, such as labor, material, or capital. The fact that each ratio based on a singular input is influenced by the other inputs was also discussed. Those measures of productivity which relate outputs to all associated inputs are called *total factor productivity* measurements, to differentiate them from measures which relate outputs to a single input. While conceptually the total factor productivity measures make a lot of sense, it is extremely difficult to identify and capture all related inputs for any component output of the organization. This is readily achieved for the total output of any organization by calculating financial measures such as rate of return on assets.

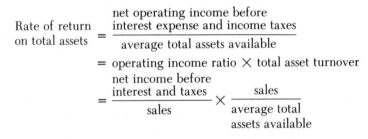

While this financial measure provides a valid indicator of total operating performance for any profit-oriented organization and is based on information from the balance sheet and income statements, such input information is generally not readily available for outputs of a much smaller scope.

While capturing all the inputs related to a given output of limited scope is not realistic, we must develop a sensitivity toward avoiding oversimplification of inputs that results in inaccurate measures, or measures which provide a false indicator. An example of the generation of such a false indicator would be to develop a measure of output per hour, wherein the only input considered would be the number of hours worked. If, for example, we were interested in the ratio of output per hour as an indicator of contribution to profit and we failed to recognize changing wage rates, we could generate a misleading measurement or indicator as follows:

If last year a given department produced 1,000,000 units which sell for $1.50 each; and required 50,000 labor hours at an average cost of $5.00 per hour for wages plus benefits

And this year the same department produced 1,100,000 of the same units which also sold for $1.50 each; and required 50,600 labor hours at an average cost of $6.40 per hour for wages plus benefits, then:

| | Output per Unit of Input | |
|---|---|---|
| | Without Regard for Labor Cost | With Regard for Labor Cost |
| Last year | 1,000,000 units | 1,000,000 units |
| | 50,000 labor hours | 50,000 labor hours × $5.00 |
| | or | or |
| | 20 units per hour | 4.0 units per labor dollar |
| This year | 1,100,000 units | 1,100,000 units |
| | 50,600 labor hours | 50,600 labor hours × $6.40 |
| | or | or |
| | 21.74 units per hour | 3.40 units per labor dollar |
| This year's productivity index | 108.7 | 85.0 |

While the measure that does not take into consideration the significant increase in labor costs yields an index of 108.7, the measure that factors in the increase in labor costs yields an index of 85.

Though total factor productivity, requiring the inclusion of all inputs related to the output, may be impractical, care must be exercised not to exclude from the input those factors which have, either directly or indirectly, an obvious and significant impact on the results the organization is striving to achieve.

## Organizations Are Hesitant to Provide the Resources Required for Measurement

Football is a sport based on interim goals (achieving 10 or more yards progress in advancing the ball toward the opponent's goal line within four attempts, or downs) and longer-range goals (advancing the ball beyond the opponent's goal line for a score). In the sport of football each of two opposing teams is allowed eleven players on the playing field at any time for a total of twenty-two players. In addition to the twenty-two players there are at least three persons, composing what is called the "chain gang," that do nothing but measure progress in advancing the ball. These three persons measure to determine whether the ball has been advanced the required 10 yards within four attempts. Every time this interim goal is accomplished, the achieving team is awarded four more attempts, within which they must either advance the ball another 10 yards or cross the opponent's goal line. Can you imagine what football, which is nothing more than a game, would be like without those resources being provided to measure progress. It is my guess that it would result in the game becoming much less interesting to both the players and the spectators, if not chaotic. It is doubtful that anyone would suggest that we economize and not continue to provide measurement resources for the game of football. Yet in business and service organizations there is often resistance to adding measurement resources to gauge progress in that more important game of reaching the organization's objectives. In other organizations, measurements are installed but are soon compromised, quite often because they make one or more managers uncomfortable.

As there is no free lunch, there cannot be a successful program to improve productivity without the provision of resources for measuring progress and the dedication of all managers to maintaining the integrity of all productivity indicators.

## Work Processes Are Complex and Difficult to Separate and Measure

Any organization of more than a few people is a complex web of people, equipment, and work processes. The flow of work through the organization may not be readily apparent to anyone but a trained observer. Frequently, the interdependence between people, processes, and functions is not fully understood even by long-term managers working on site. As there are certain points on the human body where the pulse can best be measured, so it is with the organization. By gaining an understanding of the work flow and the interdependence of people and processes, we can identify critical points at which meaningful measures can be most effectively applied. Those points are identified by reviewing the work flow and pinpointing those activities which have the greatest potential for becoming a "limiting factor"; that is, limiting the performance of other processes or other work groups. Even in sequential processes, such as assembly lines, some activities have a greater potential than do others to negatively impact the total organization's performance. Using an automotive assembly line as an example—one such activity is the starting of the car's engine prior to the car reaching the end of the assembly line. Should an engine not start, the car will have to be towed off the end of the assembly line and could cause the line to be shut down for a period of time, thus idling hundreds of assembly workers for a short period. In this example, the result we are interested in is that all car engines be started and running by the time the cars reach the end of the assembly line. Our measurement could be the ratio of results achieved (or engines started) to the objective (total number of cars processed).

Another critical point at which measurements can be effectively applied to complex processes are those points at which the efforts of many people and perhaps departments culminate. Such points could be called *milestones* in the organization's efforts to achieve its objectives. Again using an automotive assembly line as an example—the point in the assembly process at which the air-conditioning system is charged with refrigerant is such a milestone. The system components—compressor, evaporator, dehydrator, and hoses—must be assembled airtight before all air can be evacuated from the system and the system charged with freon. Similar to the engine start measurement, a ratio of systems successfully charged with refrigerant to systems attempted would be a meaningful productivity ratio.

## The Measurement System Encourages Short-Term Gains to the Detriment of Long-Term Results

There are many questionable ways to achieve short-term productivity gains, for example, quality control and training can be neglected. Too many employees, and sometimes even managers, are of the opinion that good quality and high productivity are mutually exclusive; you cannot have both at the same time. Contrary to popular belief, one complements the other. In numerous situations, I have been aware that employees have responded to productivity improvement programs with an ultimatum. "If management is looking for greater outputs, they had better be prepared for and willing to accept a deterioration in general quality of the product or services provided. On the other hand, if management is desirous of maintaining high quality standards, they had best back off on their request for improved productivity." Such an attitude is an indicator of management's inability to relate personal and organizational needs. To establish indicators for volume without establishing parallel indicators related to quality would be poor management. In the final analysis, management gets from its employees what the employees think is wanted. To measure output without providing equal resources dedicated to measuring quality communicates that management is interested more in increased volumes of output than it is interested in the quality of those outputs. Accordingly, improved productivity will be forthcoming at the expense of quality, in such a situation.

When confronted with the ultimatum of increased outputs or quality but not both, let us choose to appeal to the individual's ego needs or need for self-esteem. The public, in general, restricts the word *professional* to paid athletes and those occupied in a field of work requiring a high level of education and training. Though medical doctors, lawyers, and paid athletes may all be professionals by definition, not everyone that engages in those activities performs in a professional manner. In every field of work we can find people whose sound knowledge, and conscientious attitude, is manifested in the form of the speed *and* accuracy with which they perform their assigned duties. Most, if not all, employees would like to be recognized for performing in a professional manner and that connotes both speed *and* accuracy, not one *or* the other.

## The Measurement System either Fails to Delineate Responsibility or Emphasizes It in a Destructive Manner

In a constructive and nonthreatening manner, individual employees and, in turn, their managers must be held accountable for specific elements of the organization's performance, including the related productivity ratios. Without a doubt, buck-passing will be minimized when responsibility is unequivocally fixed. Responsibility accounting should be extended as far down in the organization as possible to produce the best results. This means having employees initial the paperwork that accompanies their work. The salesclerks should be asked to initial the sales slip, the order fillers should place their initials opposite each line on the order they have filled or attempted to fill, and the inspectors should initial the packing slip when they have inspected the order.

Some managers overemphasize accountability at the expense of motivation. Such managers substitute threats, real or implied, for encouragement and other intangible rewards. Managers whose thinking is overly dominated by such a punitive ethic will very likely destroy the motivation of their employees in the process of making certain no one "gets away with anything." The manager who bases accountability on the assumption that people will work properly if their internal system of values and sense of fairness are not violated can maintain a constructive, productive work environment.

## The Integrity of the Measurement System Is Compromised

The best method for maintaining the integrity of a measurement system is to reduce the opportunities for compromise. While the exertion of pressure on employees and managers for improved productivity may be both justified and desirable, it can have repercussions. As we will never know if we're truly honest until we've turned down a tempting offer to be dishonest, why take the chance of tempting managers to compromise the measurements related to their performance? Ideally, the taking of measurements should be assigned to an impartial but tough-minded person or group of persons who can relate to the importance of generating accurate indicators on a continuous basis.

Besides pressure for results, there are other factors in the work environment which increase the probability of measurements being compromised. The source documents may be so cumbersome or complicated that they encourage the persons assigned the responsibility for measurement to take error-inducing shortcuts. Further, the measurement system may provide no credit for coping with uncontrollable problems—i.e., defective material provided by a vendor.

Many factors combine in the work place to provide compromise-resistant measurements, including realistic goals, basic methods of measurement, measurement by an impartial party, goals and measurements used in a manner so as to elicit good performance from employees, rather than as a means to evaluate them as people, and an appeal to individual needs for fair play and self-esteem.

## The Measurement System Emphasizes Some Facets of the Organization's Performance at the Expense of Others

It is not uncommon, at a given point in time, for an organization to overemphasize a single facet of performance to the detriment of one or more other facets. Tours or inspections of a facility by the organization's top management too often precipitate such a problem. The organization's president or chairperson of the board fails to recognize that utterances akin to thinking out loud can easily be misconstrued as direction. The top-level executive who casually expresses the opinion that increased inventories of finished goods seem to stimulate sales and further wonders out loud "How many more widgets we could sell if we had them in finished goods inventory?" precipitates action. Before this executive leaves the premises, and without having given specific instruction to do so, the wheels are in motion to increase the schedule to produce more widgets. It doesn't matter that the demand for widgets has softened, or that we are shifting our resources away from more important matters; the divine order was interpreted as having been given.

Sometimes management's goals are faulty. Recognizing the scarcity of a certain raw material, for example, management sets a goal for recycling a certain amount of scrap each day or each month. The appropriate measurements are put into place. Now let's just imagine that you, as the first-line supervisor responsible, have been directed, in no uncertain terms, to meet this goal—or else. The reclaiming of a certain volume of scrap is the single most important element of your performance. Let's further imagine that you and those working with you improve your quality to the extent that not enough scrap is being generated to meet the reclamation goal. What might happen? You've got it! At the expense of everything else you start generating sufficient scrap to meet the goal. Silly! Sure it is silly, but don't think for a minute that similar instances of faulty judgment or overemphasis never occur. Another example is the city that establishes tons of garbage picked up per vehicle day as the productivity measurement related to its garbage pickup activities. To look good when judged by the movement of tons per vehicle day, the garbage crew schedules less frequent pickups. Their reported increased productivity is at the expense of sanitation and the public's health. Yet another example is a situation wherein the accounts receivable aging measurement tells us our customers are stretching out and delaying their payments to us for goods or services we have provided them. This measurement is then overemphasized to the extent that few prospective customers are given credit approval and the, at least, equally important measure of "sales entered" plummets.

Such misdirection of resources, measurements, and management attention is more likely to occur within organizations wherein upward communication is directly or indirectly discouraged.

## Criteria for Meaningful Measurements

An important step toward improving productivity in any organization is the design and implementation of meaningful measurements. Your organization may or may not have already crossed, or attempted to cross, this important bridge linking intellectual understanding with emotional involvement. If you have not as yet done so, the following can help get you started on the right foot. If you now have productivity measurements in place and working, you will want to compare those measures with the following criteria.

1. *Validity:* Accurately reflects changes in productivity
2. *Completeness:* Takes into consideration all components of both the output and the input for a given productivity ratio
3. *Comparability:* Enables the accurate measuring of productivity change between periods
4. *Inclusiveness:* Takes into account and measures separately the productivity of all activities
5. *Timeliness:* Ensures that data is provided soon enough for managerial action to be taken when problems arise
6. *Cost-effectiveness:* Obtains measurements in a manner that will cause the least interruption possible to the ongoing productive efforts of the organization

The more closely productivity measurements meet the above criteria, the more useful they are for improving productivity. Note the criteria do not have to be perfectly nor completely met for your measurement system to be of value.

### Validity

The most valid productivity measure is one that accurately reflects changes in real productivity. It is not uncommon for measurements to fall short of this basic requirement. Frequently, the basic unit of measurement is incorrect, resulting in a distorted, if not totally inaccurate, indicator of organizational productivity. Specific examples of this common shortcoming follow.

An order fulfillment or distribution center picks small items from inventory to fill customer orders. These orders vary in the number of items (or lines) ordered—a customer may place an order for a single item or for a number of different items. (Note in this example we are discounting the variance in quantity ordered of each item as more time is usually spent in locating a small item than in removing it from location, regardless of quantity.) Using "orders filled," in such a situation, as the common unit of measurement and the total number of orders processed or filled as the "output," the productivity ratio is, in this case, invalid. To measure and report "lines processed per hour" is a more valid measure than is "orders processed per hour." In this case, lines is a far superior common unit of measurement than is orders because lines recognizes and embodies the more critical variable, the number of items on any order. An order consisting of 17 lines, for example, would reasonably require more labor resources to process than would a 1-, 2-, or even a 16-line order because of the time required to move between a greater number of storage locations.

Table 5-2 illustrates an example of such an operation for two separate time periods, using orders as the output vs. lines as the output when comparing the output per hour for both periods.

**TABLE 5-2.** XYZ Distribution Center—Comparing Orders vs. Lines as Output per Hour

| Item | Base Period Quantity | Following Period Quantity | Index |
|---|---|---|---|
| 1. Number of orders processed | 5,000 | 6,000 | 120.0 |
| 2. Number of lines processed | 15,000 | 16,000 | 106.7 |
| 3. Total hours worked | 1,000 | 1,091 | 109.1 |
| 4. Total compensation paid | $6,500 | $7,091 | 109.1 |
| *Ratios:* | | | |
| 5. Order output per paid hour (1 ÷ 3) | 5.0 | 5.5 | 110.0 |
| 6. Line output per paid hour (2 ÷ 3) | 15.0 | 14.67 | 97.8 |
| 7. Compensation per hour (4 ÷ 3) | $6.50 | $6.50 | 100.0 |
| 8. Cost per order (4 ÷ 1) | $1.30 | $1.182 | 90.9 |
| 9. Cost per line (4 ÷ 2) | $0.433 | $0.443 | 102.3 |

Had we used "orders" as the common unit of measurement, we would think output per paid hour was *up* 10 percent and unit cost was *down* 9.1 percent. The more valid use of "lines" as the common unit of measurement provides an entirely different indicator—output per paid hour is *down* 2.2 percent and unit cost is *up* 2.3 percent.

Another example is a company that manufactures and assembles automobiles. Focusing on the assembly portion of such a business, where the many components are brought together and assembled into a drivable vehicle, is "number of cars assembled" a valid output measurement? While an Oldsmobile may be comparable to a Buick, is a Chevrolet comparable to a Cadillac? Let's focus our attention on an assembly operation that produces only Buicks. Is number of cars assembled a valid output measurement, considering that all the cars are Buicks? Even though all the vehicles assembled have the same product name, they differ. Some have air conditioning and some do not; some are standard models, while others are deluxe models; and some have power windows and some do not. In such a situation, rather than measure units assembled per hour, we must compare actual labor required to standard labor, or an engineered allowance. The basic automobile, without options, has an engineered labor standard for the assembly of each component and, in combination, for the entire basic car. Engineered standards are developed for each option that can be added. As options are added to the basic cars, the standards for those options

**TABLE 5-3.** Green Hornet Automotive Company—Developing a Valid Productivity Measure Based on Ratio of Actual to Standard Hours

| | Quantity | Standard Quantity | Actual Quantity | Actual Index |
|---|---|---|---|---|
| 1. Total number of cars assembled | 1000 | | | |
| 2. Number of cars equipped with deluxe trim | 300 | | | |
| 3. Number of cars equipped with air conditioning | 700 | | | |
| 4. Number of cars equipped with power windows | 500 | | | |
| 5. Basic unit assembly hours (no. 1 × 10.0) | . . . | 10,000 | 9,600* | 96.0* |
| 6. Deluxe trim option assembly hours (no. 2 × 1.0) | . . . | 300 | 310* | 103.3* |
| 7. Air-conditioning option assembly hours (no. 3 × 0.7) | . . . | 490 | 600* | 122.4* |
| 8. Power-window option assembly hours (no. 4 × 0.5) | . . . | 250 | 240* | 96.0* |
| 9. Total assembly hours (no. 5 + no. 6 + no. 7 + no. 8) | . . . | 11,040 | 10,750 | 97.4 |
| *Ratios:* | | | | |
| 10. Average assembly hours per car (no. 9 ÷ no. 1) | . . . | 11.04 | 10.75 | 97.4 |
| 11. Number of units assembled per hour (no. 1 ÷ no. 9) | . . . | 0.0905797 | 0.0930232 | 102.6 |

*This is an example simplified for the purpose of illustrating the concept of actual vs. standard hour measurement. In reality, actual automotive assembly hours are accumulated by work area or department, not by option. The asterisked information would not normally be available, while department actual vs. standard hours would be.

are added to the assembly time allowed for that particular car. If the allowed time (or standard) to assemble the basic car is 10 hours and the add-on allowances for deluxe trim, air conditioning, and power windows are 1.0, 0.7, and 0.5 hours, respectively, we can develop a valid productivity measurement based on the ratio of actual to standard hours. Table 5-3 illustrates such development of a valid productivity measure.

Measurement systems based on comparing actual hours worked to standard hours generated are particularly useful in situations where there exist many possible combinations of product or service offerings. The productivity index is 102.6 as compared to standard (base period), signifying a 2.6 percent improvement over standard.

## Completeness

Completeness refers to the thoroughness with which all outputs, or results delivered, and all inputs, or resources consumed, are measured and included in the productivity ratio. You will recall that total-factor productivity is defined as the ratio of *total* outputs produced to *total* inputs consumed. Further, mention was made that to capture all the components of inputs for less than the grand total of outputs for an organization (i.e., net sales) was, in most cases, impractical if not impossible. While the organization's balance sheet and income statements provide information of all inputs related to net sales, the grand total output, this can normally be done only on a monthly basis, the interval for preparation of the balance sheet and income statement. While the measurement and reporting of total factor productivity ratios on a monthly basis can serve as a meaningful indicator, especially for higher-level management, more frequent measurements are required for operating managers in each area. First-line supervisors, for example, would preferably have continuous measurements coupled with hourly productivity reports. It is virtually impossible to capture all components of input related to hourly, or daily, or even weekly outputs. Components of input, such as energy consumption and material consumption, are not easily captured for intervals of less than one month.

While on one hand there is an inability to capture all inputs, particularly for intervals of less than a month and as related to less than the grand total of outputs, there is a need for completeness in our measurements. The solution to this dilemma lies in recognizing what must be included, not for a perfect or totally complete measure but to provide a *meaningful* measure—one that produces productivity ratios and, in turn, indexes in which we can be reasonably confident. Too often, truly important and readily captured and quantified resources, such as indirect labor, are omitted from the total resources consumed. Table 5-4 illustrates the consequence of such an omission.

In this example, had we failed to include the indirect labor resources consumed—in the course of producing the widgets—in the input of our produc-

**TABLE 5·4.** Widget Manufacturing Company—Consequence of Omitting Indirect Labor from a Productivity Measure

| Item | Base Period Quantity | Following Period Quantity | Index |
|------|------|------|------|
| 1. Output, units | 100,000 | 102,000 | 102.0 |
| 2. Direct labor hours | 18,200 | 18,000 | 98.9 |
| 3. Indirect labor hours | 1,800 | 3,100 | 172.2 |
| 4. Total labor hours | 20,000 | 22,100 | 110.5 |
| *Ratios:* | | | |
| 5. Output per direct labor hour (1 ÷ 2) | 5.495 | 5.667 | 103.1 |
| 6. Output per total (direct + indirect) labor hours (1 ÷ 4) | 5.0 | 4.615 | 92.3 |

tivity ratio, our index would indicate we increased productivity by 3.1 percent. When we more accurately include indirect, as well as direct, labor in the input, the index tells us that, in reality, productivity is *down* 7.7 percent. This example covers an obvious omission. Let's look at another example wherein the omission is more subtle and relates to the output rather than the input.

A commercial truck is driven 325 and later 350 miles. It consumes 25 and 17.5 gallons of gas, respectively. Calculating miles driven per gallon of gasoline consumed as we do for our personal car, for the first trip the truck averaged 13 miles per gallon, while on the second trip it averaged 20 miles per gallon. On the basis of the miles-per-gallon calculation, we would say that on the second trip the truck utilized gasoline more efficiently in the accomplishment of its mission and was therefore more productive—right? Wrong. While miles per gallon may be a meaningful measure of productivity for your personal car, as the payload stays pretty much the same, such is not the case with a commercial truck. The payload may vary considerably between trips. To account for this significant and measurable change, we must talk in terms of ton-miles transported, rather than miles driven, when referring to the output. If on the first trip the truck carried a payload of 15 tons and on the second trip a payload of 9.5 tons, factoring this information into the measurement will provide an accurate indicator of relative productivity (see Table 5-5).

Were we to omit that element of output, payload, we would say the productivity of the second trip was 53.8 percent greater than the first trip. When adding payload to the output, as we should, we find the productivity of the second trip was 2.6 percent *less* than that of the first.

Completeness, within reason, is an important characteristic of good productivity measures. Accordingly, care must be taken to include all significant and readily measured components of both resources consumed (input) and results achieved (output) in the productivity ratio.

**TABLE 5-5.** Calculating a Meaningful Measure of Productivity for the Example of the Commercial Truck

|  | Base Period | Following Period | |
|---|---|---|---|
|  | First Trip | Second Trip | Index |
| 1. Incomplete output, miles driven | 325 | 350 | 107.7 |
| 2. Payload, tons | 15 | 9.5 | 63.3 |
| 3. Total output, ton-miles transported (1 × 2) | 4875 | 3325 | 68.2 |
| 4. Gasoline consumed, gallons | 25 | 17.5 | 70.0 |
| *Ratios:* | | | |
| 5. Miles driven per gallon (1 ÷ 4) | 13 | 20 | 153.8 |
| 6. Ton-miles transported per gallon (3 ÷ 4) | 195 | 190 | 97.4 |

## Comparability

Productivity is a relative measure. We measure, then compare today to yesterday, this month to last month, or this year to last year. Note that we are not comparing the productivity of one organization with the productivity of another. We are comparing the productivity of the same organization for two different time periods. The importance of productivity measurements lies in their ability to compare one period with another, or to an objective or standard, and thereby determine if we are utilizing available resources more or less efficiently as we achieve desired end results. The key is to make certain that the data we are using is comparable. We previously mentioned the importance of including not only hours worked but also the prevailing wage for each period in our productivity ratios. Ratios of output per hour are generally less meaningful than are ratios which factor in wage rates, such as output per labor dollar paid.

**The principle of equivalents.** Organizations which produce a mix of products, rather than a single product, or provide a mix of services, rather than a single service, generally experience greater difficulty in generating comparable productivity ratios. Comparing this month's productivity to last's will probably be meaningless if there has been a shift in product or service mix between the two periods. Table 5-6 illustrates calculating productivity without regard for a change in the mix of products produced.

Without regard for the change in product mix between the two periods, and the fact that each product requires different amounts of labor resources to produce, we would say that the output per labor hour at the ABC Company has increased by 11.8 percent, comparing the second period to the first.

To recognize and account for the change in product mix between the two

**TABLE 5-6.** ABC Company—Comparison of Output per Hour *without* Regard for the Different Labor Requirements to Produce Various Products

| Item | Base Period Quantity | Second Period Quantity | Index |
|---|---|---|---|
| 1. Output, A units | 8 | 30 | 375.0 |
| 2. Output, B units | 24 | 8 | 33.3 |
| 3. Output, C units | 16 | 14 | 87.5 |
| 4. Output, total units | 48 | 52 | 108.3 |
| 5. Hours worked, total | 160 | 155 | 96.9 |
| *Ratios:* | | | |
| 6. Total output per hour (4 ÷ 5) | 0.30 | 0.3355 | 111.8 |

periods, we must alter our method of calculating productivity to include the labor resources required to produce each product. In many cases, standard labor hours for each product may not exist. This presents no problem, providing we know how many labor hours were used to produce each product in the base period and we have access to payroll records which will tell us the total labor hours used in the second period. With such information we can calculate average labor hours per unit in the base period and apply those same per-unit averages to the second period's product mix. Table 5-7 illustrates the productivity calculations which recognize the change in product mix between periods.

The application of the concept of equivalents, ensuring that we are comparing apples to apples (and not plums) between the two periods, enables us to measure productivity more accurately. Without regard for the different labor resources required to produce each product, it appears that productivity gains were realized. With regard for the change in mix of products produced in the second period and for the different amounts of labor required to produce each product, we see that, in fact, productivity in the second period dropped by 21.9 percent.

**Constant dollar value.** In our effort to ensure that productivity ratios between periods are comparable, we must be sensitive to the impact of both changes in the cost of resources consumed and changes in the prices (or value) of outputs. In an inflationary economy, costs and prices continuously escalate. If prices rise, the total value of the outputs will rise, even if nothing else changes, and the resultant productivity index will indicate a false increase. If either costs and/or prices are subject to change over a period of time, the differential will result in the related productivity measures being inaccurate. If our productivity measurement system incorporates dollar values, then we must adjust the figures to compensate for any change in values between periods. Such adjustments can

**TABLE 5-7.** ABC Company—Comparison of Output per Hour *with* Regard for the Different Labor Requirements to Produce Various Products

| | Base Period | | | | Second Period | | | | |
| | | | Labor Hours | | | | Labor Hours | | |
| Item | Quantity (1) | Total (2) | Average per Unit* (3) | Weighted Units† (4) | Quantity (1) | Total (2) | Average per Unit‡ (3) | Weighted Units§ (4) | Index |
|---|---|---|---|---|---|---|---|---|---|
| 1. Output, A units | 8 | 16 | 2.0 | 16 | 30 | ? | 2.0 | 60 | 375.0 |
| 2. Output, B units | 24 | 96 | 5.0 | 120 | 8 | ? | 5.0 | 40 | 33.3 |
| 3. Output, C units | 16 | 48 | 1.5 | 24 | 14 | ? | 1.5 | 21 | 87.5 |
| 4. Output, total units | 48 | ... | ... | 160 | 52 | ... | ... | 121 | 75.6 |
| 5. Hours worked, total (from payroll records) | ... | 160 | ... | ... | ... | 155 | ... | ... | |
| 6. Combined output per hour (column 4 ÷ line 5) | ... | ... | ... | 1.00 | ... | ... | ... | 0.781 | 78.1 |

*Column 2 ÷ column 1.
†Column 3 × column 1 (base period).
‡Same as base period.
§Column 3 × column 1 (second period).

be made by using applicable indexes for the value of the output and/or for the cost of inputs. Unfortunately, national price indexes are unlikely to be applicable to any specific firm, and it is unlikely that the firm has developed and maintained a price index of its own. If the firm has such indexes, great. If they do not have such indexes, constant dollar values can be obtained by multiplying the number of units produced in each period by the unit price in the base period.

**Calculating price indexes and deflated value for material, labor, and total inputs, and for total output.** Company XYZ combines labor and material to produce a product. For the same period in two different years, Table 5-8 indicates the inputs that were used to provide the different outputs. By com-

**TABLE 5-8.** Raw Data Pertaining to Inputs and Outputs

| Item | Period One, Year 1 | | | Period One, Year 3 | | |
|---|---|---|---|---|---|---|
| | Unit Value, in $ (1) | Quantity (2) | Weighted Value, in $* (3) | Unit Value, in $ (4) | Quantity (5) | Weighted Value, in $† (6) |
| *Input:* | | | | | | |
| 1. Materials | 0.35 | 250 lb | 87.50 | 0.45 | 300 lb | 135.00 |
| 2. Labor | 6.00 | 8 h | 48.00 | 6.75 | 8 h | 54.00 |
| 3. Total inputs | . . . | . . . | 135.50 | . . . | . . . | 189.00 |
| *Output:* | | | | | | |
| 4. Total output produced | 0.20 | 750 units | 150.00 | 0.22 | 900 units | 198.00 |

*Column 1 × column 2.
†Column 4 × column 5.

paring the weighted inputs with the weighted output for both periods, based upon the costs and selling price prevailing in each period, we can calculate the indexes and productivity ratios as illustrated by Table 5-9.

Without factoring out changes in either costs or selling price, we know that the value of outputs produced in period one of year 3 was 32 percent greater than the value of outputs produced in the same period of year 1. Further, our productivity ratios indicate that the value of material consumed and the value of labor consumed in year 3 was 16.9 percent greater and 14.8 percent less, respectively, than in the same period of year 1. In total, the value of resources consumed to produce an output of 32 percent greater value was only 5.7 percent more than the value of resources consumed in the same period of year 1.

Being aware that the cost of both material and labor has changed from year 1 to year 3, as well as the selling price per unit, we can deflate the value of year 3 resources consumed and output produced to year 1 values as illustrated by Tables 5-10 and 5-11.

**TABLE 5·9.** Comparison of the Weighted Inputs with the Weighted Output for Both Periods

| Item | Period One, Year 1<br>Weighted Value @ Costs/ Price Then Prevailing | Period One, Year 3<br>Weighted Value @ Costs/ Price Then Prevailing | Index |
|---|---|---|---|
| 5 Material input | $ 87.50 | $135.00 | 154.3 |
| 6. Labor input | 48.00 | 54.00 | 112.5 |
| 7. Total inputs | 135.50 | 189.00 | 139.5 |
| 8. Total output | 150.00 | 198.00 | 132.0 |
| *Ratios:* | | | |
| 9. Material input per output (5 ÷ 8) | 0.5833 | 0.6818 | 116.9 |
| 10. Labor input per output (6 ÷ 8) | 0.320 | 0.2727 | 85.2 |
| 11. Total inputs per output (7 ÷ 8) | 0.9033 | 0.9545 | 105.7 |

By deflating the costs and selling price prevailing in year 3 and then comparing those deflated costs to year 1 (base-year) values, we find that:

• Though the cost per pound of material increased from year 1 to year 3, deflated material cost per unit produced remained the same; that is, the unit consumption of material per unit production of output was exactly the same in period one of both years.

**TABLE 5·10.** Calculating Deflated Costs, and Prices

| Item | Period One, Year 1 | | | Period One, Year 3 | | | Value Based on Costs/ Prices Prevailing in Year 1, in $‡ |
|---|---|---|---|---|---|---|---|
| | Value, in $<br>(1) | Quantity<br>(2) | Actual Value, in $*<br>(3) | Value, in $<br>(4) | Quantity<br>(5) | Actual Value, in $†<br>(6) | (7) |
| *Input:* | | | | | | | |
| 12. Materials | 0.35 | 250 lb | 87.50 | 0.45 | 300 lb | 135.00 | 105.00 |
| 13. Labor | 6.00 | 8 h | 48.00 | 6.75 | 8 h | 54.00 | 48.00 |
| 14. Total input | . . . | . . . | 135.50 | . . . | . . . | 189.00 | 153.00 |
| *Output:* | | | | | | | |
| 15. Total output produced | 0.20 | 750 units | 150.00 | 0.22 | 900 units | 198.00 | 180.00 |

*Column 1 × column 2.
†Column 4 × column 5.
‡Column 1 × column 5.

**TABLE 5-11.** Deflated Index Calculations

| Item | Weighted Value of Period One Expressed in Year 1 Costs/Prices, in $ | | Deflated Index, Year 3 |
| | Year 1 (1) | Year 3 (2) | (3) |
| --- | --- | --- | --- |
| *Input:* | | | |
| 16. Materials | 87.50 (line 12, col. 3) | 105.00 (line 12, col. 7) | 120.0 |
| 17. Labor | 48.00 (line 13, col. 3) | 48.00 (line 13, col. 7) | 100.0 |
| 18. Total inputs | 135.50 (line 14, col. 3) | 153.00 (line 14, col. 7) | 112.9 |
| *Output:* | | | |
| 19. Total output produced | 150.00 (line 15, col. 3) | 180.00 (line 15, col. 7) | 120.0 |
| *Ratios:* | | | |
| 20. Deflated cost of material per unit of output | 0.1167 (line 16, col. 1 ÷ line 4, col. 2) | 0.1167 (line 16, col. 2 ÷ line 4, col. 5) | 100.0 |
| 21. Deflated cost of labor per unit of output | 0.0640 (line 17, col. 1 ÷ line 4, col. 2) | 0.0533 (line 17, col. 2 ÷ line 4, col. 5) | 83.3 |
| 22. Deflated cost of total inputs per unit of output | 0.1807 (line 18, col. 1 ÷ line 4, col. 2) | 0.1700 (line 18, col. 2 ÷ line 4, col. 5) | 94.1 |
| 23. Deflated gross profit margin | 0.0967 [(line 19, col. 1 − line 18, col. 1) ÷ line 19, col. 1] | 0.1500 [(line 19, col. 2 − line 18, col. 2) ÷ line 19, col. 2] | 155.1 |

- While the cost per hour of labor increased from year 1 to year 3, deflated labor cost per unit in year 3 decreased 16.7 percent below the year 1 level.
- Combined deflated labor and material cost per unit produced in year 3 was 5.9 percent below the same cost for year 1.
- Had neither the costs nor selling price increased from year 1 to year 3, the gross profit margin in year 3 would have exceeded the gross profit margin in year 1 by 55.1 percent.

The above example illustrates that if given quantities and per-unit costs and selling prices related to a certain unchanging product(s) produced or service(s) provided in two periods, we can either deflate the later period's values to the earlier (or base) period's costs and prices (as was done above) or we can inflate the earlier period's value to reflect the later period's costs and price(s). By doing either, we have factored out all changes in costs and selling price, enabling us to make an apples-to-apples comparison of productivity in the two periods.

Unfortunately, the required data is often not available; or if available, the products or services have been changed; or the number of various products or services makes it difficult to complete the calculation. What is seemingly a great approach can seldom be applied in real life for the reasons just mentioned.

Constant dollar productivity indexes are generated for the purpose of determining, without regard for changes in costs and prices that may have occurred, how efficiently resources were consumed in each of two different periods to produce the actual level of outputs in each. In the example just covered, had there been no changes in either costs or selling price, the company's gross profit margin would have increased by 55.1 from 9.67 percent in year 1 to 15 percent in year 3. But there were increases in both per-unit cost and per-unit selling price. The 20 percent improvement in output per hour and the 10 percent increase in per-unit selling price, in combination, were not enough to offset the increases in per-unit labor and material costs. In reality, the gross profit margin slipped from 9.67 percent in year 1 to 4.55 percent in year 3 [(line 15 column 3 − line 14 column 3) ÷ line 15 column 3 vs. (line 15 column 6 − line 14 column 6) ÷ line 15 column 6]. While the pounds of material used per unit of output remained the same, the cost per pound increased by 28.6 percent. While the number of units produced per labor hour increased by 20 percent, the increased hourly cost of labor exactly offset the related productivity gain. While total per-unit cost increased by 16.2 percent, per-unit selling price was raised by only 10 percent. Thus there was the erosion of gross profit margin, despite a substantial improvement in the efficiency with which labor was utilized to produce the outputs.

Constant dollar calculations, such as the above, enable us to factor out changes in both costs and prices and thereby quantify real changes in productivity measurements in dollars between periods. However, as the primary objective of most businesses relates to profit, there is little consolation in knowing that although productivity improvements may have been realized, the profit margin has been eroded by increasing costs which could not be fully offset by increased selling prices. Such is too often the case.

## Inclusiveness

It is not uncommon for productivity measurements to focus on production or manufacturing activities, and then only upon a limited number of elements within the total manufacturing activity. The scope of activities measured within manufacturing should be enlarged beyond the usual labor and material measurements to include quality, equipment, and facility. Further, the use of productivity measurements should be expanded to nonmanufacturing activities within the organization, including purchasing, inventory management, production control, data processing, personnel, finance, customer service, and sales. Productivity measurements encompassing a wide range of activities within all functions of the organization sensitize all managers to the importance of continually working to improve effectiveness while using available resources more efficiently. In such an environment, managers quickly come to realize that initiating improvements is the sum and substance of their job. Emphasis shifts from maintaining the status quo to finding a better way. Productivity becomes a common focal point, rather than only the focus of those in production or manufacturing.

## Timeliness

For productivity measurements to serve as an effective managerial tool, as they are intended, they must be communicated to the responsible manager on a basis as near to real time as practical. Can you imagine the participants of a sporting event, such as a basketball game, not having access to the score until after the game is over? Of course not. Knowledge of the score throughout the game has an effect upon how we will proceed. To be deprived of that knowledge as we seek to contribute to the achievement of the organization's objectives limits our ability to respond to problems and situations of which we may not be aware. Whereas continuous, or real time, productivity measurements may not be practical, the system would preferably be designed to recognize and communicate, to those managers directly responsible, significant exceptions or deviations from plan on at least a daily basis—time lag not to exceed eight working hours.

## Cost-Effectiveness

Productivity measurements must be made with regard for the related costs, both direct and indirect. The resources dedicated to taking the measurements must be viewed as any other resource and utilized as efficiently as possible in the process of providing the required measurements. Further, a sensitivity must be developed and maintained regarding the possible interference to, or interruption of, the ongoing productivity efforts of the organization by the measurement process.

Productivity measurements are established for the purpose of improving organizational results via increased managerial awareness and improved control. Managers, not uncommonly, view the involvement of themselves and their employees in the measurement process as consuming too much time. They blame someone above them for "forcing them to waste time on measuring that would best be devoted to getting the work itself done." Obviously, there is an element of truth to such a statement—any addition to existing resources assigned to getting the work done *should* enhance results. However, the question is, Does the benefit of providing more resources to perform the work outweigh the cost of the manager probably not being as aware as he would otherwise be (with the measurements), thereby diminishing managerial control?

To resist the implementation of meaningful measurements is characteristic of what John Wareham, management recruiter, calls the "tap-dancing manager."[1] Tap dancers cannot function as effective managers because they lack the cutting edge, the focus, and the results orientation required. Tap dancers are more style than substance and will go to any extreme to avoid a structure wherein their performance can be objectively evaluated.

Since measuring is a nonproducing cost item, managerial judgment must be exercised to ensure it is used in a consistent manner and in proportion to the value of the data derived. In essence, a cost-benefit analysis must be applied to the function of measuring.

## Summary

The need to measure and thereby improve productivity is found in nearly every work activity of most organizations. Comparing both past and present productivity levels of various work activities within the organization is a key step toward realizing productivity improvement. Productivity improvement is dependent upon valid and complete measurements applied to a broad range of the organization's activities.

There exist several obstacles to the implementation of meaningful productivity measurements, including the complexity of work processes, the reluctance to provide the required measurement resources, and others. Meaningful measurements require resources, plus an unwaivering management commitment, but provide the basis for realizing the organization's potential to reach its stated objectives via increasing managerial awareness.

[1]John Wareham, *Secrets of a Corporate Headhunter*, Atheneum, New York, 1980, p. 133.

# 6 Design Aids

The system for measuring productivity in all but very small and uncomplicated organizations will most likely require a number of measurements of varying types to be taken at different intervals. Before a meaningful measurement system can be designed and implemented, an awareness must be gained as to the present status of productivity measurements within the organization and their validity. Also, the organization's purpose or goals must be fully understood and internalized. The measurements must be designed and implemented with regard to both where you now are and where you want to go.

## The Productivity Measurement Audit

As a starting point toward designing a system of productivity measurements for your organization, the following questionnaire, the Productivity Measurements Audit, is provided. This questionnaire is designed to assist you in investigating and evaluating existing measurements as well as gaining further insight into what has happened in the past regarding productivity measurements within your organization. It is strongly recommended that you personally audit or inspect the current existing conditions before answering each question.

Productivity Measurements Audit

| Questions to Be Answered | Indicate Answer Here: | | If "Yes," Proceed to Question: | If "No," Proceed to Question: |
|---|---|---|---|---|
| | Column 1 | Column 2 | | |
| 1. Is productivity now being measured in any of your organization's activities? | _____ Yes | _____ No | 4. | 2. |

Productivity Measurements Audit *(continued)*

| Questions to Be Answered | Indicate Answer Here: | | If "Yes," Proceed to Question: | If "No," Proceed to Question: |
|---|---|---|---|---|
| | Column 1 | Column 2 | | |
| **2.** Was productivity ever previously measured within the organization? | _____<br>Yes | _____<br>No | **3.** | **5.** |
| **3.** If productivity measurements were implemented but later discontinued, indicate the reasons for discontinuance below:<br>Benefits derived failed to justify cost? | _____<br>No | _____<br>Yes | | |
| Measurements consumed too much time? | _____<br>No | _____<br>Yes | | |
| Measurements generated conflict between management and employees? | _____<br>No | _____<br>Yes | | |
| Measurements generated conflict between employees? | _____<br>No | _____<br>Yes | | |
| Measurements lacked the support of higher management? | _____<br>No | _____<br>Yes | | |
| Other reasons (specify):<br>_____<br>_____<br>_____ | | _____<br>Yes | **5.** | **5.** |
| **4.** To which of the following can existing productivity measurements be related?<br>Profit? | _____<br>Yes | _____<br>No | | |
| Service? | _____<br>Yes | _____<br>No | | |
| Quality? | _____<br>Yes | _____<br>No | | |
| Indirect plant labor? | _____<br>Yes | _____<br>No | | |

Productivity Measurements Audit *(continued)*

| Questions to Be Answered | Indicate Answer Here: Column 1 | Column 2 | If "Yes," Proceed to Question: | If "No," Proceed to Question: |
|---|---|---|---|---|
| Direct plant labor? | Yes | No | | |
| Office labor? | Yes | No | | |
| All employees? | Yes | No | | |
| Equipment? | Yes | No | | |
| Materials? | Yes | No | | |
| Facility? | Yes | No | | |
| Sales? | Yes | No | | |
| Credit and collections? | Yes | No | | |
| Scheduling? | Yes | No | | |
| Inventory management? | Yes | No | | |
| Purchasing? | Yes | No | | |
| Receivables? | Yes | No | | |
| Transportation? | Yes | No | | |
| Other (specify): | | | | |
| _____ | Yes | | | |
| _____ | Yes | | 5. | 5. |
| 5. Do engineered work standards exist within the organization? | Yes | No | 6. | 7. |
| 6. Indicate in which areas engineered work standards are currently being applied: Plant? | Yes | No | | |
| Office? | Yes | No | | |
| Other (specify): | | | 7. | 7. |
| _____ | Yes | | | |

Productivity Measurements Audit *(continued)*

| Questions to Be Answered | Indicate Answer Here: | | If "Yes," Proceed to Question: | If "No," Proceed to Question: |
| --- | --- | --- | --- | --- |
| | Column 1 | Column 2 | | |
| 7. Do specific expectations other than work standards exist within the organization? | _____ Yes | _____ No | 8. | 14. |
| 8. Indicate in which areas specific work standards are currently being applied: Plant? | _____ Yes | _____ No | | |
| Office? | _____ Yes | _____ No | | |
| Other (specify): _____ | _____ Yes | | 9. | 9. |
| 9. Is individual compensation based, in part, on either productivity or profitability: Among plant personnel? | _____ Yes | _____ No | | |
| Among office personnel? | _____ Yes | _____ No | | |
| Among managers? | _____ Yes | _____ No | | |
| Other (specify): _____ | _____ Yes | | 10. | 10. |
| 10. Are people within the organization ever responsible for measuring elements of their own productivity? | _____ No | _____ Yes | | 11. |
| If yes, which ones? Inputs? | | _____ Yes | | |
| Outputs? | | _____ Yes | 11. | |
| 11. Are all employees routinely counseled when their productivity slips below an acceptable level? | _____ Yes | _____ No | 12. | 12. |

| Questions to Be Answered | Indicate Answer Here: Column 1 | Column 2 | If "Yes," Proceed to Question: | If "No," Proceed to Question: |
|---|---|---|---|---|
| 12. Does the operating head of the organization review productivity measurements at least once each month? | _____ Yes | _____ No | | 13. |
| If yes, does he or she review such measurements at least once each week? | _____ Yes | | 13. | |
| 13. Do existing measurements generally meet the following criteria: *Validity:* Do they actually gauge real changes in productivity? | _____ Yes | _____ No | | |
| *Completeness:* Do they take into consideration all significant components of toal inputs and total outputs? | _____ Yes | _____ No | | |
| *Comparability:* Do they enable the accurate comparison of productivity between periods? | _____ Yes | _____ No | | |
| *Inclusiveness:* Are activities other than production/ manufacturing/order filling being measured? | _____ Yes | _____ No | | |
| *Timeliness:* Are measurements reported soon enough for appropriate managerial action to be taken when required? | _____ Yes | _____ No | | |
| *Cost-effectiveness:* Are measurements performed in a cost-effective and noninterruptive manner? | _____ Yes | _____ No | 14. | 14. |

80

| Questions to Be Answered | Indicate Answer Here: Column 1 | Column 2 | If "Yes," Proceed to Question: | If "No," Proceed to Question: |
|---|---|---|---|---|
| **14.** Does your organization tend to look upon resources committed to measurement as being wasted? | _____ No | _____ Yes | 15. | 15. |
| **15.** Are all resources dedicated to productivity measurement periodically quantified and evaluated on a cost-benefit basis? | _____ Yes | _____ No | 16. | 16. |
| **16.** With what frequency are productivity measurements now being reported to the responsibile manager(s): Every hour? | _____ Yes | _____ No | | |
| Every day? | _____ Yes | _____ No | | |
| Every week? | _____ Yes | _____ No | | |
| Every month? | _____ Yes | _____ No | | 17. |
| Other (specify): _____ | _____ Yes | | 17. | |
| **17.** Is the company's financial statement always prepared and distributed within seven working days after the end of the month? | _____ Yes | _____ No | 18. | 18. |
| **18.** With only rare exception, do period expenses match period sales as reported on the financial statement? | _____ Yes | _____ No | 19. | 19. |
| **19.** Is the magnitude of all variances—actual expenses to budgeted expenses or to a standard—expressed in dollars on the financial | | | | |

Productivity Measurements Audit *(continued)*

| Questions to Be Answered | Indicate Answer Here: | | If "Yes," Proceed to Question: | If "No," Proceed to Question: |
|---|---|---|---|---|
| | Column 1 | Column 2 | | |
| statement for both the month and for the year to date? | | | 20. | Complete |
| | Yes | No | | |
| 20. Is detail related to unfavorable variances usually provided with the financial statement? | | | | Complete |
| | Yes | No | | |

After completing the above questionnaire:

Add the total number of responses in column 1, and enter here → _____ A

Add the total number of responses in column 2, and enter here → _____ B

Add the grand total number of responses in both columns (column 1 + column 2) and enter here → _____ C

Divide the total number of responses in column 1 (A above) by the grand total number of responses (C above), and enter here → _____ D

If **C** is greater than 40 and **D** is greater than 75 percent, it indicates that managers within the organization are generally interested in measuring productivity. The greater the value of **D** beyond 75 percent, the more meaningful are existing measurements.

If, on the other hand, **C** is less than 40 and **D** is less than 75 percent, then the good news is that you will not have to worry about changing a number of current measurements because current measurements are few in number. Besides being few in number, existing measurements are most likely not very meaningful. More questions have possibly been generated by the questionnaire than have been answered. Leading the list of such questions is, Why, specifically, has little effort been expended to date to install measurements and improve productivity? (A following questionnaire will help you in answering that question.)

The summarized results of the measurement audit, and its meaning as it relates to existing productivity measurements, are of lesser value, in all probability, than is the information provided in the course of answering each question. Ideally, before answering the questions, you personally audited or inspected the current conditions relating to each question. You also spoke with the people involved, both employees and managers, and received some inputs related to prevailing attitudes. You have gained further insight into how people working in all areas of the organization generally feel about productivity and its measurement. That insight can help you identify possible limiting factors—those factors that threaten or limit your productivity program, including the design and implementation of meaningful measurements.

## The Audit of Prevailing Attitudes Related to Productivity Improvement

No single factor impacts organizational climate to a greater degree than does managerial attitude—more specifically, the attitudes of upper to top management. If your goal is to improve results, including increasing productivity, then your success is dependent upon your ability to change the operating climate of the organization, which, in turn, is dependent upon top management's attitude toward change. You cannot expect favorable changes in results if you are unable or unwilling to change the existing conditions which, in the past, have contributed to those results.

A common characteristic of truly effective leaders is a continual striving for excellence. This attitude manifests itself in the behavior of such a leader. Risk, or becoming vulnerable to making a mistake, is of far less concern than is improving the organization's effectiveness. Such a leader generates an ideal climate for improving productivity.

The answers to the following questionnaire, the Organizational Climate–Management Attitude Audit, will, because it deals more with such intangibles as attitudes, be relatively more subjective. To answer it properly requires both an understanding and sensitivity toward the direction provided by upper management within your organization.

### Organizational Climate—Management Attitude Audit

| Questions to Be Answered | Column 1 | Column 2 |
|---|---|---|
| 1. Is managerial focus more on "how" things will be done, or on "whether" things will be done? | "How" | "Whether" |
| 2. Is "empathy" or "excellence" stressed more by managers? | "Excellence" | "Empathy" |
| 3. What is the most common response to well-prepared and complete proposals aimed at realizing operating improvements: a "decision" ("yes" or "no") or | | |

## Organizational Climate—Management Attitude Audit

| Questions to Be Answered | Column 1 | Column 2 |
|---|---|---|
| repeated requests for "further anaysis"? | "Decision" | "Further analysis requested" |
| 4. Are responsibilities generally well-defined and clearly communicated to those both directly and indirectly involved? | Yes | No |
| 5. Do all managers have specific performance-related goals, and are they held responsible for achieving them? | Yes | No |
| 6. Within the last year, has any employee been penalized financially due specifically to low productivity? | Yes | No |
| 7. Within the last year, has any employee been terminated due specifically to low productivity? | Yes | No |
| 8. Other than sales commissions, is the compensation of any employee dependent upon quantified results produced? (Discretionary bonuses not requiring quantitative substantiation to be excluded.) | Yes | No |
| 9. Do employees ever participate, at any level, in planning or decision making? | Yes | No |
| 10. Are managers held strictly responsible for cost control and budget achievement? | Yes | No |
| Total responses in each column: | | |

Though the questions on the preceding questionnaire are quite basic, the manner in which they are answered provides valuable insight into the operating climate of your organization. The fewer the responses in column 2, the better is the organizational climate for improving productivity. Less than seven responses in column 1 requires that you take a long, hard look at the existing climate. It is an indicator that the organization is not results-oriented and that there exists an attitude not conducive to change.

Some successful organizations have an operating climate exactly opposite that which is generally accepted as necessary for growth. Yet they flourish. The fact that such an organization continues to flourish and grow reinforces the attitude that the way the business is run, including the operating climate it creates, is not only the right way but also the "only way." Typically, such an organization's success is due primarily to a unique product or service, or to being in the right place or right market at the right time. While you can't knock the success of such organizations as compared to less successful organizations, you have to be critical when comparing that success to the organization's potential for even greater success. Given a charter, outlined by the organization's purpose, a specific situation, and a set of resources, a manager's job is to realize the organization's potential—not just to get results but to maximize those results within the constraints of available resources. There are managerial errors of "commission" and there are managerial errors of "omission." An error of commission is based on action taken, while an error of omission is based on failure to initiate action; in this case, failure to initiate action aimed at generating a work environment conducive to realizing the organization's growth potential.

Whether your organization is successful or unsuccessful or anywhere in between, your potential for improving productivity is ultimately more a function of intangible resources (i.e., managerial attitudes and operating climate) than of tangible resources (i.e., number of people, availability of materials, and amount of money). The stage must be properly set before productivity improvement can begin. If the proper climate does not exist within your organization, you will have to alter the climate as a prerequisite to introducing change. Realistically, you cannot change prevailing attitudes completely before you introduce a productivity improvement program; but you can, depending on your position, either solicit support or initiate action aimed at properly setting the stage. Using material previously presented in this book, you can appeal to individual needs to launch the program successfully. More on that later.

## Expense Rates

A common objective of business organizations is to generate a profit. Profit is the difference between total sales revenues and total expenses. The relationship between sales and expenses is critical to the profit-oriented organization's success. It is obviously better to generate $10 in sales using $2's worth of labor than it is to generate the same $10 in sales using $3's worth of labor. All other expenses being equal, the former provides a dollar more profit than does the latter. We can build on the basic relationship between sales, expenses, and profit to provide effective, profit-oriented measurements called *expense rates*. Expense rates are simply the ratio of expenses to net sales.

$$\text{Expense rate} = \frac{\text{period expense}}{\text{period net sales}}$$

If our net sales were $10 and to achieve those sales we had spent $2 for labor, then our labor expense rate is 20 percent or 0.20.

$$\text{Labor expense rate} = \frac{\text{period labor expense}}{\text{period net sales}}$$

$$= \frac{2}{10}$$

$$= 0.20$$

If our net sales were $10 and to achieve those sales we had spent $3 for labor, then our labor expense rate is 30 percent or 0.30.

The lower the expense rate for any given level of sales, the greater is the productivity—assuming no increase in per-unit selling price and no decrease in per-unit cost of resources or expenses. Both the advantages and disadvantages of incorporating expense rates in a system of productivity measurements are as follows:

### Use of Expense Rates in a System of Productivity Measurements

| Advantages | Disadvantages |
| --- | --- |
| 1. Required data for the calculation is readily available. | 1. Is dependent upon a financial statement for data—can normally only be calculated on a monthly basis. |
| 2. Expense rates are directly related to the objective of many organizations—profit. | |
| 3. Expense rates factor out changes in sales volume from period to period. | 2. Does not recognize any change from period to period in product or service mix, or costs, or selling prices. |
| 4. As past financial statements are usually on file, the past history of expense rates can be easily generated to provide recent trends. | |
| 5. As data is available and calculation is basic, the cost of generating expense rate measurements is nominal. | |
| 6. Is a total factor approach—the cost of all inputs and value of all outputs are considered. | |

Though far from perfect, expense rates can be an integral part of a meaningful productivity measurement system. Table 6-1 is a basic example of the calculation of expense rates and comparison of those rates between periods.

**TABLE 6-1.** Calculation and Comparison of Expense Rates

| | Base Period | | Following Period | | |
| --- | --- | --- | --- | --- | --- |
| Item | Dollars (1) | Expense Rate* (2) | Dollars (3) | Expense Rate† (4) | Index‡ (5) |
| 1. Gross sales | 160,500 | . . . | 185,000 | | |
| 2. Returns and adjustments | 2,500 | . . . | 4,000 | | |
| 3. Net sales | 158,000 | . . . | 181,000 | | 114.6 |
| 4. Material | 58,000 | 0.36709 | 63,000 | 0.34807 | 94.8 |
| Direct labor | 13,000 | 0.08228 | 14,000 | 0.07735 | 94.0 |
| Indirect labor | 12,000 | 0.07595 | 12,000 | 0.06630 | 87.3 |
| Controllable overhead | 14,000 | 0.08861 | 15,000 | 0.08287 | 93.5 |
| Noncontrollable overhead | 13,000 | 0.08228 | 14,500 | 0.08011 | 97.4 |
| Administrative expenses | 20,000 | 0.12658 | 21,500 | 0.11878 | 93.8 |
| Engineering expenses | 5,000 | 0.03165 | 5,500 | 0.03039 | 96.0 |
| Selling expenses | 12,000 | 0.07595 | 16,000 | 0.08840 | 116.4 |
| Other expenses | 1,000 | 0.00633 | 2,000 | 0.01105 | 174.6 |
| Total expenses | 148,000 | 0.93671 | 163,500 | 0.90331 | 96.4 |
| Pretax profit | 10,000 | 0.06329 | 17,500 | 0.09669 | 152.8 |

*Expense rate = column 1 ÷ line 3.
†Expense rate = column 3 ÷ line 3.
‡Index = [(column 4 − column 2) ÷ column 2] ± 100.

Though sales increased by 14.6 percent over the base period, the total expenses incurred to generate those increased sales decreased by 3.6 percent. Pretax profit increased by 52.8 percent over the base period. Note that column 5 in Table 6-1 quantifies our productivity improvement, or regression, for each category of expense. For those expenses whose index in column 5 is below 100, there has been improvement in productivity, the exact magnitude of which is equal to 100 − the index indicated in column 5. Using line 4, material expense, as an example, the index indicated in column 5 is 94.8 percent, telling us that we have consumed only 94.8 percent of the resources we would have consumed had the base period rate of consumption been applied to the following period's results (net sales). Thus the rate of improvement (100 − 94.8) is +5.2; in other words, a 5.2 percent improvement in the utilization of material per dollar of net sales output. Had the result of the calculation (100 − indicated index) been negative, regression, rather than improvement, would have been indicated.

With regard to expenses, a number below 100 indicates improvement over the base period and a number over 100 indicates regression as compared to the base year. With regard to either sales or profit, a number over 100 indicates improvement and a number under 100 indicates regression.

The most serious flaw in using expense rates to generate productivity measurements is that neither changes in costs, nor in selling prices, nor in the mix of outputs are recognized. Dependent upon the amount of change in these factors within any given organization, this flaw can range in degree of seriousness from negligible to very serious. The organization that has radical swings in the mix of its outputs and/or significant changes in the cost-price relationship should steer away from expense rates. On the other hand, organizations not subject to meaningful changes in the mix of their outputs or significant changes in the cost–selling price relationship will find expense rates a convenient tool for developing meaningful productivity measurements.

## Standards

In its quest for increased profitability via improved productivity, management can have powerful tools in the form of standards and budgets representing what should be accomplished. Our expectations of specifically what should be accomplished in the present and in the future are often based only on our experience, or past performance. This is akin to equating the familiar with the best way, which often is not the case. Although the study of past performance is a useful starting point, our expectations should not be just an extension of past experience. The past may have been characterized by gross inefficiencies. Possible changes in methods, products, personnel, equipment, and technology also limit the validity of comparisons with the past. Performance should be judged in relation to a current goal that takes all present factors into consideration, a goal that is attainable but can only be reached by a skilled and dedicated effort, and then with a reasonable degree of difficulty. Concern with the past is a historical, not a managerial, function. Management's attention must focus on what costs and profits should be, not on what they have been.

When we mention "standards of performance," it is not uncommon for the phrase to be interpreted as meaning only "work standards," or being limited only to labor inputs. The focus on standards for our usage includes labor but also includes material. As it can be determined that an hour of labor should produce a certain quantity of outputs, it can also be determined that a certain amount of material should be required to produce a certain quantity of outputs. Further, when we speak of standards, we are referring to currently achievable standards. Expectations are set high enough so that employees regard their achievement as difficult, but possible. Allowances are made for normal shrinkage, waste, and breakdowns.

The primary purpose of standards is to provide a basis for evaluating performance against a set benchmark or goal. A standard is a measure of accomplishment that should be attained in a specified activity, under specified methods and conditions which affect the activity. In setting standards, determination of an equitable relationship between the volume of goods or services produced and the labor and materials utilized in the process is of prime importance. It is in arriving at this equitable relationship that the proper output requirement for a fair day's work is determined.

Ideally, the establishing of standards would be preceded by a methods analysis to determine the "best way"; and the standard would then be based on the methods incorporated in that best way. Realistically, the available time and resources may limit your methods review and changes to correcting obvious problems, rather than finding and implementing the best way. In any event, method changes tend to open people's minds to a request for improved productivity. If you request more, without in some way modifying the method, chances are your actions will be viewed as an attempt to wring blood out of the proverbial turnip. On the other hand, common sense supports increased expectations as being reasonable, or at least as being *more* reasonable, when accompanied by a methods revision.

The industrial-engineering approach provides the most refined and precise standards. Whether or not to use this approach in developing standards is dependent upon available resources and the projected cost. If you have industrial engineers on staff and available, it would be best that you use them to develop your standards. If you do not have such specialized resources available and are concerned with the cost of hiring engineers to develop labor and material standards, the following procedures are suggested to assist you in establishing meaningful standards.

## Developing Material Standards

In most companies, the acquiring of materials or merchandise entails different control decisions than their use. The purchasing manager for a manufacturing company is concerned with obtaining raw materials at a favorable price. The production manager, on the other hand, focuses on using those materials efficiently. The purchasing manager for a distributor of products produced by others is concerned with buying these products at the best possible price. The operations manager is responsible for minimizing losses from theft, spoilage, and the like.

Assessing the performance of individual managers is facilitated by separating the items which are subject to the manager's direct influence from those which are not. Generally, this requires that we separate purchase price from quantity factors. While price factors are subject to uncontrollable external influences such as economic conditions, availability, and unforeseeable increases, it remains desirable that we hold the person responsible for purchasing accountable for the price at which materials are acquired. The arbitrary price standard would simply be the current price plus perhaps an allowance for inflation in anticipation of price increases. The specific type of material and its most recent availability and pricing trends can be factored into the material purchase price standards.

As there exists a different degree of pricing volatility between different types of materials, it is more practical to recognize those differences by varying the add-on allowances or the purchase price standard, dependent upon the category of material. Table 6-2 depicts a productivity report for a purchasing manager based upon material purchase price standards.

Per Table 6-2, the actual cost per unit of material A was 10 percent below standard, resulting in a total savings of $25; the actual cost per unit of material B was 10 percent above standard, resulting in a total loss on the quantity pur-

**TABLE 6-2.** Material Purchase Price—Actual vs. Standard—Variances (in Dollars), and Purchasing Productivity Indexes

| Actual Quantity (1) | Material Purchased (2) | Cost per Unit, in $ | | Total Cost, in $ | | Cost Index (5 + 6) × 100 (7) | Total Cost Variance, in $* (5 − 6) (8) |
|---|---|---|---|---|---|---|---|
| | | Actual (3) | Standard (4) | Actual (1 × 3) (5) | Standard (1 × 4) (6) | | |
| 500 lb | Material A | 0.45/lb | 0.50/lb | 225 | 250 | 90 | −25 |
| 2000 gal | Material B | 1.10/gal | 1.00/gal | 2200 | 2000 | 110 | +200 |
| 1000 pc | Material C | 1.93/pc | 2.00/pc | 1930 | 2000 | 96.5 | −70 |
| | All materials | . . . | . . . | 4355 | 4250 | 102.5 | +105 |

*Minuses indicate favorable variances, pluses unfavorable variances.

chased of $200; and the actual cost per unit of material C was 3.5 percent below standard, resulting in a total savings on the purchase of $70. The cost, or purchase price, of all purchases combined was 2.5 percent greater than allowed by the standard, for a total dollar loss to standard of $105.

With regard to usage or consumption, material standards are based on minimum requirements plus an allowance for waste or scrap. In the production of products, the minimum material requirements are listed in the bills of material. Should bills of material not be available, or available but outdated, it is strongly suggested top priority be given to the engineering function for providing updated bills. Bills of material are generally easier to produce for highly engineered products which require detail and assembly drawings. Bills of material for nonengineered products are generally more difficult to produce but can be generated by reviewing the manufacturing processes and analyzing the finished product. In either case, the allowances provided for waste or scrap can only be quantified after reviewing the processes, determining the process capabilities, and pinpointing any other relevant factors, such as potential material contamination, for example.

As Table 6-2 relates to material purchase price or cost standards, Table 6-3 relates to material usage or consumption standards.

**TABLE 6-3.** Material Consumption—Actual vs. Standard—Variances (in Dollars), and Usage Productivity Indexes

| Item | Quantity (1) | Material Components of Output | Standard Consumption per Unit of Output (2) | Total Standard (1 × 2) (3) | Actual Total Consumed (4) | Actual per-Unit Cost, in $ (5) | Actual (4 × 5) (6) | Standard (3 × 5) (7) | Consumption Index [(6 + 7) × 100] (8) | Consumption Variance, in $ (6 − 7) (9) |
|---|---|---|---|---|---|---|---|---|---|---|
| A | 1000 | S | 0.2857 lb | 285.7 lb | 304 lb | 0.52/lb | 158.08 | 148.20 | 106.7 | +9.88 |
| | | T | 6.0 pc | 6000 pc | 6014 pc | 1.15/pc | 6,916.10 | 6,900.00 | 100.2 | +16.10 |
| | | U | 0.01 gal | 10 gal | 9.8 gal | 27.50/gal | 269.50 | 275.00 | 98.0 | −5.50 |
| | | V | 1.65 sq ft | 1600 sq ft | 1590 sq ft | 1.75/sq ft | 2,782.50 | 2,800.00 | 99.4 | −17.50 |
| | | W | 2.0 pc | 2000 pc | 2005 pc | 2.05/pc | 4,110.25 | 4,100.00 | 100.3 | +10.25 |
| | | X | 0.06 lb | 60 lb | 58 lb | 18.75/lb | 1,087.50 | 1,125.00 | 96.7 | −37.50 |
| | | Y | 1.0 pc | 1000 pc | 1000 pc | 0.58/pc | 580.00 | 580.00 | 100.0 | 0 |
| | | Z | 4.0 pc | 4000 pc | 3946 pc | 2.71/pc | 10,693.66 | 10,840.00 | 98.7 | −146.34 |
| | | Total | … | … | … | … | 26,597.59 | 26,768.20 | 99.4 | −170.61 |

You will note in Table 6-3 that the actual consumption of some components of finished product A exceeded the standard allowance, while the actual consumption of other components was less than the allowed standard. In total, actual consumption of all materials was 0.6 percent less than the standard allowance for a savings of $170.61.

The responsibility for purchase price variances usually rests with the purchasing manager. Purchase price variances, however, are sometimes the result of poor forecasting rather than a failure to buy at specified prices. Some control is exercisable over price variances by getting several quotations, buying in more economical lots, taking advantage of cash discounts, and selecting the most economical mode of delivery. Failure to meet price standards may be the result of unanticipated demand or a sudden shift in production schedules. Such situations may require the purchasing manager to buy at uneconomical prices and/or to request delivery by air freight. In such cases, the responsibility for purchase price variances may rest with either the sales manager or the manager of production scheduling rather than with the purchasing manager.

The responsibility for quantity variances usually rests with production or operations management. When quantity variances are recognized a follow-up or analysis is required to pinpoint the specific cause(s). Some common causes of quantity variances are defective material, poor workmanship, new or untrained employees, improper handling, and faulty equipment or tooling. One method of controlling quantity variances is to issue material in the exact quantities required, per the bill of materials, to produce a specified number of acceptable units. As manufacturing proceeds, additional materials may be obtained only by submitting a special excess materials requisition, from which the material usage variance is compiled. The only other reliable method of recognizing and quantifying material usage variances requires frequent physical inventories of all materials. That basis for quantifying consumptions or usage variances is the following calculation, which can be applied to any time period, but preferably a one-month period.

Beginning inventory + purchases

$$= \text{total available inventory} - \text{consumption allowed per standard}$$
$$= \text{"should be" ending inventory based on standard consumption}$$
$$\text{vs. "actual" ending inventory per physical inventory}$$

The standard consumption in the above calculation is derived by multiplying the quantity produced of each product during the period by the per unit of production standard per the bills of material. Partially completed products, or work in process, at the time the physical inventory is taken must be recognized, and the related material components credited to the ending inventory. The difference between the "actual" and "should be" ending inventories is the consumption (or material usage) variance.

The above-mentioned monthly physical inventories of component materials is necessary only in the absence of a control based on bills of material at the point of material issuance. Ideally, the variance reports resulting from the physical inventories will provide the quantified variance for each separate material component. Should a large number of material components, coupled with limited resources, prohibit a timely, detailed report of consumption variance, the combined variance, in dollars, can be calculated and reported. While this net variance does not pinpoint specific problem materials, it does quantify overall performance.

### Developing Labor Standards

If you have engineered labor standards, or the resources for developing engineered labor standards, you have only to integrate those standards into your productivity measurement system. If you lack both engineered labor standards and the resources to develop such standards, another approach, better suited for the lay person, will have to be taken.

A good starting point for the untrained person to begin developing labor standards is in those work functions that have a substantial amount of repetitive work. Standards are more quickly established for such work, and the experience gained will be beneficial in more complex future applications. The intent of the following procedure for developing labor standards is to avoid reliance upon historical data via a programmed and objective evaluation of exactly what is being done. At best, the resulting standards will approximate engineered standards. More important, it should force casting off the bonds of "what is" and "what has been," in favor of recognizing "what could be." An outline of the specific steps to be taken to develop labor standards follows:

1. Observe the existing method. Become familiar with what is being done; who is doing it; why they are doing it; how, or the specific method; steps, procedures, tools, and equipment used; and the work environment.
2. Evaluate the current method in terms of:
   a. Deviation from prescribed procedure
   b. Obvious opportunities for improvement
   c. Negative impact upon other activities and/or upon end results
3. Identify the most beneficial opportunities of methods improvement; focus available resources on improving those methods first.
4. Using work-sampling techniques, set a labor standard. Continuously evaluate actual performance vs. standard performance, thereby providing a quantitative measurement of labor productivity.

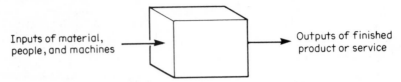

**Figure 6-1.** The productive processes of industrial engineers can be thought of as a black box.

Steps 1 through 3, above, relate to observing, evaluating, and, if possible, improving the design of the productive process. Step 4 focuses on quantifying expectations related to labor inputs. All four activities are within the realm of the industrial engineer. Steps 1 through 3 encompass that segment of industrial engineering known as methods engineering, while step 4 is referred to as either standards or work measurement engineering.

The organization is composed of buildings, equipment, and people. The organization is constantly affected by internal and external environmental changes. The organization must continuously adjust to these changes if it is to reach its objectives. Industrial engineering's thrust is to design the facility, methods, and procedures in a manner that will enable the organization to meet its objectives. Industrial engineers are concerned with the complex aggregate of people, machines, facilities, and materials and how they can best be combined to produce the desired results. The productive processes might be thought of as a black box of as yet unspecified contents, as is illustrated by Figure 6-1.

The industrial engineer's job is to specify the contents of this black box—the specific methods, procedures, and controls required to meet the organization's objectives.

## Methods Engineering

People play the most critical role in the successful operation of any organization. As people costs—recruitment, training, salaries, wages, insurance, and benefits—rise, management becomes all the more interested in the productivity of its personnel and justifiably so. In addition to the performance of manual tasks, people play an important role in the effective utilization of other resources, such as materials and equipment. Even in situations characterized by a high degree of mechanization or automation, people are needed to "sense" deviations from schedules and specifications and variations in conditions, so that corrective action may be taken. People are the communications link between the problem-sensing, decision-making, and action functions in almost all situations. The human element is, and will remain, a critical link in the total system requiring that *more* attention be given to integrating and utilizing a person with maximum effectiveness. The prevailing methods and procedures either contribute to or detract from realizing the maximum effectiveness from your personnel. Our use of methods engineering will evolve around organized application of common sense in observing, evaluating, and improving productive processes within the organization.

As you strive to apply *common sense* to reviewing and possibly improving existing methods, you should seek to generate an environment characterized by *common purpose* and making best use of *common knowledge*. Specifically, those operations being reviewed should be reviewed with the full knowledge and cooperation of the responsible area manager. The evaluation of the existing methods and generation of possible alternative methods ideally would combine the ideas and experience of both the area manager and the key people working in the area. The critical ingredient in designing and successfully implementing meaningful change is cooperation. Accordingly, all action taken from the observing and through the evaluating and improving stages must be designed to generate cooperation and participation among all persons concerned.

**1. Observation.** To facilitate comprehension and understanding of what is actually going on with regard to any process within the organization, it is mandatory that any official records or written descriptions of what is supposed to be happening be supplemented with actual observation. Too often what should be going on is not what is actually going on for various possible reasons. Perhaps there has been much turnover, and new personnel have not been properly trained in the prescribed method. Perhaps equipment, on which the prescribed method was based, has been replaced by equipment of a different type and capacity. If written records or descriptions of prescribed methods are available, be sure to study them. Such information, when available, can get you off to a fast start as you actually observe what is going on.

As you observe what is going on, strive for the overview of the whole system. While the focus of attention may be on key processes, it is essential to understand what transpires from beginning to end. Only in this manner can you gain an understanding of the interdependence between various activities. Getting the overview is oftentimes difficult to accomplish. Relationships between activities or operations may be difficult to establish, dependent upon your familiarity and experience. Industrial engineers have developed several descriptive aids to help in establishing exactly what is going on. One such aid is called the *flowchart*. The flowchart is to the industrial engineer and manager what the play diagram is to the football coach. It is difficult to imagine the football coach operating without benefit of the familiar play diagram and successfully introducing a new play using only verbal or written descriptions of each player's assignment. It is equally difficult to imagine a manager successfully comprehending an entire operation without the benefit of the flowchart. The flowchart uses five distinct symbols, each having a specific meaning, as is illustrated by Figure 6-2.

These symbols are incorporated in a format, as is illustrated by Figure 6-3,

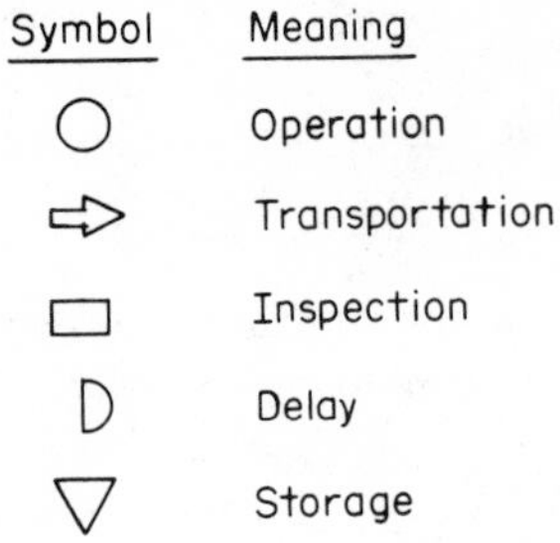

**Figure 6-2.** The five distinct symbols of a process flowchart.

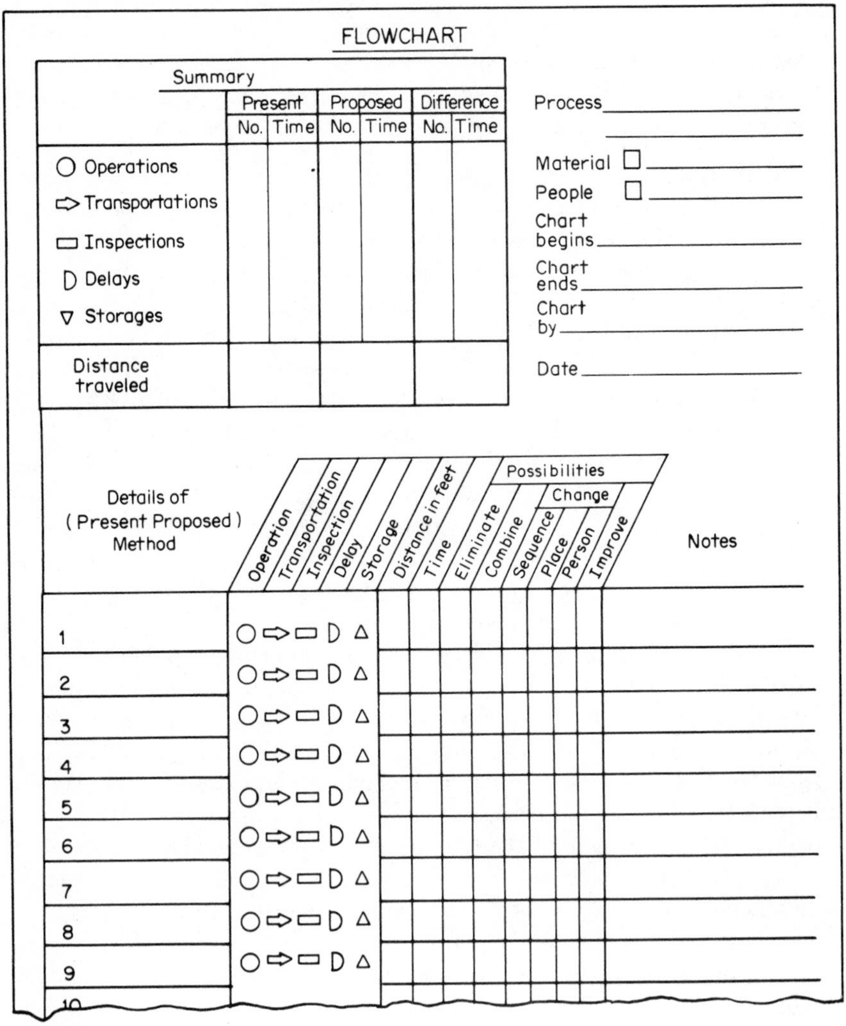

**Figure 6-3.** A preprinted flowchart format.

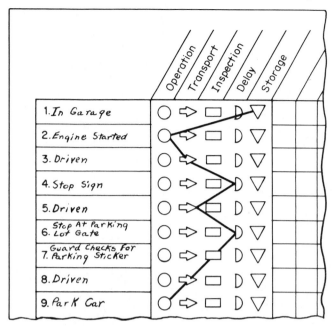

**Figure 6-4.** Flowchart of a car being driven to work in the morning.

which is often preprinted and used to facilitate methods improvements, as well as identifying what is going on.

The body of the flowchart is filled in after observation and recognition of:

**1.** All events
**2.** The sequence of those events

The flow of work is the result of listing all events in sequential order and attaching a hand-drawn line between the symbols representing each event. For example, Figure 6-4 charts a car being driven to work in the morning.

The flowchart depicts the car being in storage, its engine started, being driven from the garage or storage place, stopping at a stop sign, continuing toward its destination, stopping again at the entrance to the company's parking lot, the parking lot guard or attendant inspecting the vehicle for an authorized parking sticker, the car being driven into the lot, and parked; all in that sequence.

"Flow" does not mean the direction of movement, but rather the sequence in which the successive steps of the process follow one another. The times and distances associated with the various events should also be noted in the space provided on the form. When it is required to show activities being performed either concurrently or by the same employee at the same work station, the symbols for such activities are combined by drawing one symbol within the other.

In the previous example, the pause at the parking lot gate to enable the attendant to confirm an authorized parking sticker might be classified as a single activity by placing the symbol for delay, D, within the symbol for inspection, $\square$, as follows: $\boxed{\text{D}}$. Combined elements of activities are not uncommon. Two basic examples are an employee performing an operation on a product while visually inspecting the product for defects and a secretary typing a letter while on "hold" on the telephone.

Before observing the operation, it is a good idea to review historical data providing information related to problems generated in the processing of work. Such problems can manifest themselves in many ways, including:

Poor customer service
Substandard quality
Excess scrap
High costs

With this information in mind, you can search for possible clues as to the causes as you observe what is going on.

**2. Evaluation.** After observing and comprehending what is actually going on, focus shifts to evaluating what has been seen. Deviations from written procedure are automatically suspect and must be evaluated in detail. The current actual method can be either better or worse than the prescribed method. Should the current actual method be better than the prescribed method, then the written procedure should be revised to reflect the current method. Should the current method be worse than the prescribed method, an effort must be made to determine why the variance in method exists. Does the prescribed method present problems to the people responsible for doing the work? If so, what is the specific nature of those problems, and how can they be overcome.

First and foremost, the evaluation process should be characterized by an open mind. A fine balance is required between the attitude that there is always a better way and the reality of the cost, both tangible and intangible, of implementing change. Change for the sake of change is expensive and disruptive. Even change aimed at providing improved results should be subjected to a cost-benefit analysis. When observation suggests that either time, effort, or materials are being wasted, management is obligated to seek out and implement a better way.

Specific questions that will aid in the evaluation process follow.

**Can something be eliminated?** Does there exist a duplication of effort? Could one or more of the elements be eliminated without an adverse impact on the desired end result?

**Can any of the elements be combined?** Is the same activity being performed in two or more places? Would economies of scale be realized by combining this activity into one area? While performing one element of the activity, could the employee simultaneously perform another element, thereby saving time and effort?

**Can the sequence of events be changed?** Can bottlenecks and delays be reduced, if not eliminated, by changing the sequence in which activities are performed?

**Can the place be changed?** By changing the location in which one or more elements are performed, can you provide a net benefit to the whole of the related activity?

**Can we change who performs the work?** Could the work be processed more efficiently by another person or another group? Do assigned tasks match individual skills?

**Can improvements be made?** Does there exist an opportunity to enhance either the effectiveness or the efficiency with which results are now being accomplished? Specific opportunities can be identified by reviewing the:

- *Flowchart:* Does the sequence make sense? Can delays be designed out?
- *Records and reports:* Do you have the right information, in the hands of the right people, at the right time? Can reports be discontinued without consequence?
- *Forms design:* Does the design of forms fit user requirements? Are forms simple and not prone to generating error? Do forms highlight exceptions?
- *Work-place design:* Does the work place itself detract from performance? Can wasted time be converted into productive time by rearrangement?

**3. Improvement.** While the observation and evaluation processes focus on existing conditions, the improvement process begins with the pinpointing of opportunities for improvement and continues through the implementation of improvement-oriented action. The work situation is a complex web of people, methods, machines, and materials. Compounding the complexity of comparing the potential values of identified improvement opportunities is the influence of external factors upon the organization. Studies have shown that high-achieving managers exhibit a common ability to attach relative importance to each of many activities as they relate to the achievement of organizational goals, and to focus on those that have the greatest potential for improvement. The following four steps shift your focus from the microlevel to the macrolevel for the purpose of identifying those areas within which method improvements will provide the quickest and greatest results.

**Focus on costs.** Whether your company is a profit or nonprofit organization, focusing on areas of high cost can help you identify activities with the greatest potential for improving organizational results. By better controlling costs within the profit-oriented organization, you will increase your profit. By better controlling costs within a nonprofit organization, you will be able to provide more services for every dollar spent. Cost has the quality of being a universal measurement which responds to improvements in the methods by which the organization generates its outputs. Generally, when methods are improved, costs go down. This is not to imply that either the quality of those outputs or the services with which they are delivered should be compromised for the purpose of reducing costs. Focus must be on identifying areas of greatest expense and pinpointing within those areas specific actions which can reduce the expenditure, per unit of output, without adversely affecting either quality or service.

Cost reduction is important to both flourishing and faltering organizations. The need for cost reduction is more often associated with faltering organizations, wherein survival is directly dependent upon reducing expenses. Either no need, or a lesser need, for cost reduction is generally associated with the organization whose sales and profits are both rising. In both situations, but especially in the latter, it requires a truly professional manager to recognize and capitalize on cost reduction opportunities.

**Identify the sources of customer dissatisfaction.** The most basic need of all organizations is the demand for its products or services. The organization's continued existence is dependent upon satisfying its customer's or client's requirements. When attempting to pinpoint methods improvement opportunities which have the potential of generating the greatest benefits for the organization, a good place to start is with those that generate the greatest benefits for your customers or clients. That effort would logically start with specific sources of complaint but must extend to those weaknesses which have not, as yet, been presented as complaints. It is not uncommon for organizations to avoid any effort to bring hidden weaknesses into open view. The old adage let a sleeping dog lie prevails. Organizations are surprised when their customers or clients take their business elsewhere for no apparent reason. Most often the reason is that there exists a dissatisfaction that was never voiced as a "complaint." If you don't satisfy your customers or clients, you can rest assured your competition will be more than eager to try.

**Look closely at activities which have remained unchanged for a long period of time.** In this age of rapid technological advancement, those activities that have not incorporated methods changes for a period of years are at least suspect. They are probably ripe for improvement. Don't be surprised if after identifying such improvement opportunities and presenting possible specific changes, you are told, "We tried that once and it didn't work." Resistance to change, in varying degrees, is a universal inhibitor of progress. No one approach can break down that resistance, but sometimes a concise statement of the problem and its impact on the organization can put those involved in a better frame of mind for generating their own methods improvements.

**Assess outside influences on both your activities and the demand for your products or service.** The market for your product or service influences what you do and, to a lesser extent, how you do it. Other external factors, such as governmental regulations, influence the methods by which your outputs are generated.

Increasingly, governmental regulations are influencing the methods used in business and industry. Such constraints have to be an integral part of your thinking as you embark on changing methods.

Henry Ford successfully pioneered the mass production of automobiles offering the public "any color they wanted as long as it was black." While this was exactly what the situation called for in the 1920s and 1930s, the limited color policy threatened the company with extinction after World War II. Methods had to be altered to provide a choice of colors to consumers. Where previously any fender of a certain model could be assembled to any car of that model, that flexibility was lost with the introduction of a variety of colors.

The format illustrated by the Checklist for Recognizing Methods Improvement Opportunities is provided for the purpose of assisting you in your efforts both to pinpoint methods improvement opportunities and to initiate methods improvements prior to setting labor standards.

### Checklist for Recognizing Methods Improvement Opportunities

Operation Observed_____ Date Observed_____

Place Observed_____ Duration of Observation from_____to_____

Observed and Evaluated by_____

#### Summary of Operating Conditions at Time of Observation

| Category | | Classification Type | Number | | Comments |
|---|---|---|---|---|---|
| | | | Available | Being Utilized | |
| RESOURCES | People | | | | |
| | Materials | | | | |
| | Equipment | | | | |
| | | Type | Quantity | Quality | Comments |
| OUTPUT | Finished Product or Service | | | | |

## Checklist for Recognizing Methods Improvement Opportunities
### *(continued)*

| PROBLEMS NOTED | Specify problem(s), possible cause(s), and suggested change(s): |
|---|---|
| | |

| | Yes | No | Does Not Apply | Comments |
|---|---|---|---|---|
| *Layout-related checklist:* | | | | |
| 1. Can walking distances be reduced? | ☐ | ☐ | ☐ | 1. _____ |
| 2. Are waits or delays apparent? | ☐ | ☐ | ☐ | 2. _____ |
| 3. Is access to tools, equipment, and materials adequate? | ☐ | ☐ | ☐ | 3. _____ |
| 4. Are materials and tools available generally in the same location each cycle? | ☐ | ☐ | ☐ | 4. _____ |
| 5. Can conveyors be used to facilitate transport? | ☐ | ☐ | ☐ | 5. _____ |
| 6. Are materials stored in containers from which they can be easily removed? | ☐ | ☐ | ☐ | 6. _____ |
| 7. Can stops, guides, or other devices be used to better position work? | ☐ | ☐ | ☐ | 7. _____ |
| 8. Can materials, people, and/or equipment now in multiple locations be combined into fewer locations to advantage? | ☐ | ☐ | ☐ | 8. _____ |
| 9. Can two or more tools be combined? | ☐ | ☐ | ☐ | 9. _____ |
| 10. Can a device hold the material as it is being worked on? | ☐ | ☐ | ☐ | 10. _____ |
| 11. Can a clamp, vise, magnet, or vacuum do the holding? | ☐ | ☐ | ☐ | 11. _____ |
| 12. Can a drop disposal be utilized? | ☐ | ☐ | ☐ | 12. _____ |
| 13. Can difficult-to-grasp parts be located on a sponge rubber mat to facilitate grasping? | ☐ | ☐ | ☐ | 13. _____ |
| 14. Can incoming and/or outgoing materials be accumulated to advantage? | ☐ | ☐ | ☐ | 14. _____ |
| 15. Can containers and/or parts be color-coded? | ☐ | ☐ | ☐ | 15. _____ |
| 16. Can a written work procedure and related drawings be placed at the work station? | ☐ | ☐ | ☐ | 16. _____ |

| | Yes | No | Does Not Apply | Comments |
|---|---|---|---|---|
| *Equipment-related checklist:* | | | | |
| 17. Can controls be simplified? | ☐ | ☐ | ☐ | 17. _____ |
| 18. Are handles, knobs, and levers properly located and the correct type? | ☐ | ☐ | ☐ | 18. _____ |
| 19. Can start-up and shutdown procedures be scheduled so as to increase operating time? | ☐ | ☐ | ☐ | 19. _____ |
| 20. Can bells or flashing lights be installed to signal malfunction? | ☐ | ☐ | ☐ | 20. _____ |
| 21. Can recorders be attached to quantify downtime? | ☐ | ☐ | ☐ | 21. _____ |
| 22. Can operations be performed on a moving assembly line or conveyor rather than in a static work station? | ☐ | ☐ | ☐ | 22. _____ |
| 23. Can controls be activated by foot or leg action? | ☐ | ☐ | ☐ | 23. _____ |
| 24. Can manual operations be mechanized? | ☐ | ☐ | ☐ | 24. _____ |
| 25. Can machine feed be made automatic? | ☐ | ☐ | ☐ | 25. _____ |
| 26. Can equipment be automated? | ☐ | ☐ | ☐ | 26. _____ |
| 27. Can equipment start-up, operating, and shutdown procedures be posted nearby? | ☐ | ☐ | ☐ | 27. _____ |
| *Procedure-related checklist:* | | | | |
| 28. Can work elements be eliminated? | ☐ | ☐ | ☐ | 28. _____ |
| 29. Can work elements be combined? | ☐ | ☐ | ☐ | 29. _____ |
| 30. Can work elements be simplified? | ☐ | ☐ | ☐ | 30. _____ |
| 31. Can the sequence of work elements be changed to advantage? | ☐ | ☐ | ☐ | 31. _____ |
| 32. Can sliding be used rather than carrying? | ☐ | ☐ | ☐ | 32. _____ |
| 33. Can the number of times something is handled be reduced? | ☐ | ☐ | ☐ | 33. _____ |
| 34. Can impulse counters, either mechanical or electrical, be installed to measure outputs more accurately and efficiently? | ☐ | ☐ | ☐ | 34. _____ |
| 35. Can the work be paced by continuous inputs? | ☐ | ☐ | ☐ | 35. _____ |
| 36. Can the learning curve be affected by improved training procedures? | ☐ | ☐ | ☐ | 36. _____ |
| 37. Can employees be cross-trained to advantage? | ☐ | ☐ | ☐ | 37. _____ |

Checklist for Recognizing Methods Improvement Opportunities
*(continued)*

| | Yes | No | Does Not Apply | Comments |
|---|---|---|---|---|
| 38. Can the quality of inputs be verified prior to the beginning of processing? | ☐ | ☐ | ☐ | 38. _____ |
| 39. Can work be batch-processed to advantage? | ☐ | ☐ | ☐ | 39. _____ |
| 40. Could overtime be reduced to advantage by working two or three shifts? | ☐ | ☐ | ☐ | 40. _____ |
| 41. Can scheduling be better controlled to both reduce downtime and improve customer service? | ☐ | ☐ | ☐ | 41. _____ |
| 42. Can measures be taken to reduce scrap and rework? | ☐ | ☐ | ☐ | 42. _____ |
| 43. Can scrap be reclaimed? | ☐ | ☐ | ☐ | 43. _____ |
| 44. Can the cost of materials be reduced without consequence? | ☐ | ☐ | ☐ | 44. _____ |

**4. Setting the standard.** After having observed, evaluated, and perhaps improved the operation, you are ready to set the related standard(s) or quantify your expectations. Standards serve as the goal against which actual performance can be measured and evaluated. Standards can be developed via statistical means based upon past performance. Obviously, this method is not preferred, as it perpetuates the status quo by incorporating all the system's existing weaknesses. Standards can also be developed by two separate methods, both based on direct observation and factoring out apparent controllable problems. The first of these two methods based on direct observation is *stopwatch time study*. This method requires a trained industrial engineer. The second of the two methods based on direct observation is called *work sampling*. Work sampling generally does not require the training and expertise of an industrial engineer. The programmed procedure can be followed by the layperson to produce standards which approximate time study standards. The work-sampling procedure is objective in nature in that it is based on actual observation and factors out controllable problems.

Work sampling estimates the time devoted to performing a certain activity based upon random observations over a period of time, each observation being of very brief duration. Work sampling recognizes only two states, "working" and "idle," on any job for the entire workday. In conducting a work-sampling survey, the employee is observed at randomly selected times and noted as being either working or idle. The times the observations are made are randomly selected from the period of time worked, excluding breaks, lunch periods, and other authorized nonworking times such as a wash-up period. The observations, besides being at random times, should be great in number to increase the confidence level in the survey's findings. Classifying an employee as idle should be restricted to only those delays that are avoidable. Nonavoidable delays, such as equipment failure and material shortages, should be tallied as working. Based upon records pertaining to output or good units produced, random observations determine what portion of the available time is, on the average, being wasted. With the observer rating or comparing the employee's work place to a visualized norm, a specific standard or level of expectations is generated. For example, should you desire to set a standard for a given activity via work sampling, the following procedure could be utilized:

1. Specify both the total amount of time and the periods of time during the day that employees working this activity are expected to be on the job and working. If the starting time is 8:00 A.M.; quitting time 4:30 P.M.; a 30-minute lunch period is provided from noon to 12:30 P.M.; two 15-minute breaks are allowed, one beginning at 10:00 A.M. and the other at 2:30 P.M.; a 5-minute wash-up period is provided from 4:25 P.M. to 4:30 P.M.; and the employee receives 8 hours pay, then:

$$\text{Total hours paid} = 8$$
$$\text{Total hours worked} = 7.417 \ (8 - 35/60)$$

Percentage of paid hours employee is
expected to be on the job and working $= 0.927125 \ (7.417 \div 8)$
Allowed idle periods $=$ 10:00 A.M. to 10:15 P.M. (break)
12:00 P.M. to 12:30 P.M. (lunch)
2:30 P.M. to 2:45 P.M. (break)
4:25 P.M. to 4:30 P.M. (wash up)

Expected periods of time that the
employee will be on the job working $=$ 8:00 A.M. to 10:00 A.M.
10:15 A.M. to noon
12:30 P.M. to 2:30 P.M.
2:45 P.M. to 4:25 P.M.

2. Randomly select specific times, during those periods that the employee is expected to be on the job and working, at which you will observe the employee at the assigned work station. Obtain three containers, such as small cardboard boxes. Label the first container "work hour" and place nine pieces of paper, each one with a different number written on it, from 1 through 9, in the box. Label the second box "minutes (first digit)." Place six pieces of paper, numbered 0 through 5, in that box. Label the third box "minutes (second digit)." Place ten pieces of paper, numbered 0 through 9, in the third box. Blindly select a single piece of paper from each box in the sequence work hour, minutes (first digit), and minutes (second digit). Record each

**TABLE 6-4.** Choosing Observation Times by Random Drawings

| Order Drawn | Work Hour | Minutes (1st Digit) | Minutes (2d Digit) | Time | Sequence* |
|---|---|---|---|---|---|
| | | **Numbers on Pieces of Paper Randomly Selected** | | **Corresponding Observation** | |
| 1 | 1 | 5 | 8 | 8:58 A.M. | 2 omit |
| 2† | 3 | 0 | 2 | 10:02 A.M. | (break) |
| 2 | 7 | 4 | 7 | 2:47 P.M. | 4 |
| 3 | 1 | 3 | 6 | 8:36 A.M. | 1 |
| 4 | 6 | 2 | 9 | 1:29 P.M. | 3 |
| . | . | . | . | . | . |
| . | . | . | . | . | . |
| . | . | . | . | . | . |
| 30 | 9 | 1 | 5 | 4:15 P.M. | 5 |

*The sequence in which observations are to be made is in chronological order; the sequence noted on this example relates only to the sets of numbers drawn and excludes the twenty-five sets of numbers drawn which were not listed.
†Observation times randomly selected which fall within allowed idle periods must be redrawn.

number in the sequence drawn. Replace the numbers in the boxes they came from before drawing another set of three. Should you choose to make thirty observations, draw thirty sets of numbers, recording the numbers of each set as they are drawn. Table 6-4 illustrates a possible set of outcomes resulting from such a drawing. Note that the confidence level, which the observations represent, increases with the number of observations made. Ideally, perhaps 100 observations should be made over a 3-day period.

3. At the precise time resulting from the random selection of numbers, observe the employee who is the focal point of the study and indicate via a tally mark on a card either working (including instances of unavoidable idleness) or idle (avoidably idle). Accumulate the data resulting from the observations on a single card.

4. Based upon one or more extended observations, and all other very brief observations, rate the employee's work pace to the norm (100 percent). For example, should the employee generally be working at a pace you consider to be 10 percent below the normal pace, the employee's rating would be 90 percent, or 0.90 (100 percent − 10 percent). On the other hand, should the employee generally work at a pace you consider 15 percent faster than the normal pace, then the employee's rating would be 115 percent, or 1.15 (100 percent + 15 percent).

5. Using all pertinent data, calculate the standard time. If, for example, a work-sampling study shows that 15 percent of the total observations were avoidable delays, the employee, when working, was judged or rated to be functioning at 90 percent of the normal work pace, and if 400 good units were produced by that employee in that work period in exchange for 8 hours pay, then:

$$\text{Work standard} = \frac{\left(\begin{array}{c}\text{paid} \\ \text{hours}\end{array} \times \begin{array}{c}\text{percent of observations} \\ \text{where employee was working}\end{array} \times \begin{array}{c}\text{work-pace} \\ \text{rating}\end{array}\right)}{\text{number of good units produced}}$$

$$= \frac{8 \times 0.85 \times 0.90}{400} = \frac{6.12}{400}$$

$$= 0.0153 \text{ hours per good unit produced}$$

$$\begin{array}{c}\text{Expected number of good units} \\ \text{produced per 8-hour workday}\end{array} = \frac{\text{paid hours}}{\text{standard hours per good unit produced}}$$

$$= \frac{8 \text{ hours}}{0.0153 \text{ standard hours per unit}}$$

$$= 522 \text{ good units}$$

While standards based directly or indirectly on stopwatch studies provide greater detail, and are generally more accurate, standards based on work-sampling studies usually are preferable to statistically derived standards based only on past performance. When refined measurements of work elements and cycles are *not* required and when overall impressions are most useful, the work-sampling technique is very adaptable to the generation of labor (or work) standards.

Experience with work sampling has pinpointed specific applications where it is particularly useful for obtaining work measurement data on which labor standards can be based.

- When physical layout and other working conditions facilitate flash observations, work sampling provides labor standards substantially the same as obtained by other study methods.
- While geared to the aggregate or total time values for specific work, elements within a job can be obtained when the element represents 5 percent or more of the whole time population sampled.

## Flexible Budgets

### Difference between Standards and Budgets

If standards are "currently attainable" rather than "ideal," there is no conceptual difference between standards and budgets. The term *standard cost*, as it is commonly used, is a *unit* concept. The term *budgeted cost*, as it is most widely used, is a *total* concept. If the standard cost of material is $5 per unit, the budgeted cost of material is the number of units to be produced multiplied by the $5-per-unit cost. A standard is a per-unit budget.

## The Flexible Budget

As a general term, the word *budget* includes any formalized quantitative plan. Budgets may include all the organization's activities—i.e., material purchases, direct labor, production scheduling, and credit and collections. A *flexible budget*, sometimes referred to as a variable budget, provides for more flexibility than do other types of budgets. All other budgets have two common characteristics:

- They are usually prepared for only one level of activity. A typical budget is a single plan encompassing sales, production, and cash requirements to meet a specific targeted volume, i.e., 2 million units or $20 million net sales.
- They are a static basis for comparison. All results are compared to the original plan, regardless of deviations from plan. For example, if actual sales are 2,500,000 units, or $25,000,000, rather than the planned respective volume of 2,000,000 units, or $20,000,000, all reference is to the obsolete plan.

In contrast, flexible budgets have the following distinguishing features:

- They are prepared for a range of activity, rather than a single level of activity.
- They provide a dynamic basis for comparison because they are automatically adjusted to actual changes in volume.

All managers have two major obligations: (1) to be effective; that is, to meet the schedule, to get the job done; and (2) to produce any given output efficiently. The problem with static budgets is that they fail to distinguish between these two facets of managerial performance. The concept of comparing performance at one activity level with a plan that was developed at another activity level leaves something to be desired from a control viewpoint; that is, from the perspective of judging how efficiently a manager has produced any given level of outputs. Let's examine a typical situation and apply to that situation both a static and a flexible budget. (See Table 6-5.) Based on what happened last year, coupled with a combination of several subjective factors, Ramrod Electronics' management has developed the static budget illustrated by Table 6-5 for this year. The first month's report comparing actual with budgeted performance is illustrated by Table 6-6.

As compared to the static budget, last month's pretax profit exactly equaled the budgeted amount. Note that the static budget is based on a fixed level of activity, in this case 11,000 units produced, or $605,000 gross sales, and makes no adjustment for the actual level of activity, 12,500 units produced, or $650,000 gross sales.

The flexible budget approach is based on a knowledge of cost behavior patterns at various levels of activity. Some costs are *fixed* in that they will remain essentially the same, regardless of the activity level. Other costs are *variable*, or

**TABLE 6-5.** Ramrod Electronics, Inc.—Static Budget Based on Last Year's Actual Performance

|  | Last Year's Actual Monthly Average | This Year's Static Monthly Budget |
|---|---|---|
| Units produced | 10,000 | 11,000 |
| @ average selling price/unit | $    50 | $    55 |
| Gross sales | $500,000 | $605,000 |
| Less: Returns and adjustments | 10,000 | 15,000 |
| Net sales | $490,000 | $590,000 |
| Less: |  |  |
| Direct labor | $100,000 | $125,000 |
| Direct material | 215,000 | 240,000 |
| Controllable overhead (supplies, repairs, utilities, etc.) | 20,000 | 30,000 |
| Noncontrollable overhead (rent, depreciation, taxes, etc.) | 40,000 | 45,000 |
| Administrative expenses | 25,000 | 30,000 |
| Selling expenses | 35,000 | 40,000 |
| Total expenses | $435,000 | $510,000 |
| Pretax profit | $ 55,000 | $ 80,000 |

directly related to activity level, and will rise or fall in direct proportion to the change in output volume. Still other costs are neither truly fixed nor truly variable, but rather exhibit some of the characteristics of both. Rent is a good example of a fixed cost. Regardless of activity level (at least up to the point the outputs can be produced in the same facility), the rent will stay the same. Direct

**TABLE 6-6.** Ramrod Electronics, Inc.—Actual vs. Static Budget Performance

|  | Monthly Budget | Last Month Actual | Variance* | Index |
|---|---|---|---|---|
| Units produced | 11,000 | 12,500 | 1,500 | 113.6 |
| @ average selling price/unit | $    55 | $    52 | $    (3) | 94.5 |
| Gross sales | $605,000 | $650,000 | $45,000 | 107.4 |
| Less: Returns and adjustments | 15,000 | 20,000 | (5,000) | 133.3 |
| Net sales | $590,000 | $630,000 | 40,000 | 106.8 |
| Less: |  |  |  |  |
| Direct labor | $125,000 | $157,500 | (32,500) | 126.0 |
| Direct material | 240,000 | 240,000 | . . . | 100.0 |
| Controllable overhead | 30,000 | 30,000 | . . . | 100.0 |
| Noncontrollable overhead | 45,000 | 47,500 | (2,500) | 105.6 |
| Administrative expenses | 30,000 | 30,000 | . . . | 100.0 |
| Selling expenses | 40,000 | 45,000 | (5,000) | 112.5 |
| Total expenses | $510,000 | $550,000 | (40,000) | 107.8 |
| Pretax profit | $ 80,000 | $ 80,000 | . . . | 100.0 |

*Figures in parentheses indicate an unfavorable variance.

labor and direct material are good examples of variable costs. As the activity level increases or decreases, the requirements for both labor and material change proportionately. All other things being equal, if the activity level goes up 10 percent, then the amount of direct labor and direct material required will also go up 10 percent. An example of a mixed cost is utilities. A certain portion of the requirement for electrical power is fixed, but as the activity level increases, more power will be needed to run more machines and, perhaps, to provide lighting for more work hours each workday.

Since fixed costs do not fluctuate with changes in activity level, static budgets are adequate for planning and controlling fixed costs. Flexible budgets are designed to be applied to either mixed or variable costs. In many organizations, no distinctions are made between fixed, variable, or mixed costs. The application of the flexible-budgeting concept to all costs, regardless of their nature, though not technically proper, can provide management incentive with no real consequence. If we treat all costs as "variable," then we are in effect rewarding management with favorable variances for achieving a volume of outputs exceeding the plan or budget, while providing a penalty for not achieving the

**TABLE 6-7.** Ramrod Electronics, Inc.—Flexible Budget Based on Last Year's Actual Performance

| | Last Year's Actual Performance | | This Year's Flexible Budget | | |
|---|---|---|---|---|---|
| | Average Monthly Expense | Expense Rate* | Units and $ Each Month Based on Plan | Expense Rate* | Expense Rate Index |
| Units produced | 10,000 | . . . | 11,000 | . . . | 110.0 |
| @ average selling price/unit | $    50 | . . . | $    55 | . . . | 110.0 |
| Gross sales | $500,000 | . . . | $605,000 | . . . | 121.0 |
| Less: Returns and adjustments | 10,000 | (0.02 gross sales) | 15,000 | (0.024793 gross sales) | 124.0 |
| Net sales | $490,000 | . . . | $590,000 | . . . | 120.4 |
| Less: | | | | | |
| Direct labor | $100,000 | 0.2040816 | $125,000 | 0.2118644 | 103.8 |
| Direct material | 215,000 | 0.4387755 | 240,000 | 0.4067796 | 92.7 |
| Controllable overhead | 20,000 | 0.0408163 | 30,000 | 0.0508471 | 124.6 |
| Noncontrollable overhead | 40,000 | 0.0816326 | 45,000 | 0.0762711 | 93.4 |
| Administrative expenses | 25,000 | 0.0510204 | 30,000 | 0.0508474 | 99.7 |
| Selling expenses | 35,000 | 0.0714285 | 40,000 | 0.0677966 | 94.8 |
| Total expenses | $435,000 | 0.8877551 | $510,000 | 0.8644067 | 97.4 |
| Pretax profit | $  55,000 | 0.1122449 | $  80,000 | 0.1355933 | 120.8 |

*Expense rate = expense ÷ net sales.

**TABLE 6-8.** Ramrod Electronics, Inc.—Actual vs. Flexible Budget Performance

| | Last Month Actual | Budgeted Expense Rate | Net Sales | Flexible Budget* | Variance, Last Month's Actual to Flexible Budget† | $ Index |
|---|---|---|---|---|---|---|
| | | | | Flexible Budget | | |
| Units produced | 12,500 | . . . | . . . | 12,500 | | |
| @ average selling price/unit | $ 52 | . . . | . . . | $ 52 | | |
| Gross sales | $650,000 | . . . | . . . | $650,000 | | |
| Less: Returns and adjustments | 20,000 | 0.024793 | 650,000 | 16,115 | $ (3,885) | |
| Net sales | $630,000 | . . . | . . . | $633,885 | 3,885 | |
| Less: | | | | | | |
| Direct labor | $157,500 | 0.2118644 | 630,000 | $133,475 | (24,025) | 118.0 |
| Direct material | $240,000 | 0.4067796 | 630,000 | $256,271 | 16,271 | 93.7 |
| Controllable overhead | $ 30,000 | 0.0508471 | 630,000 | $ 32,034 | 2,034 | 93.7 |
| Noncontrollable overhead | 47,500 | 0.0762711 | 630,000 | 48,051 | 551 | 98.9 |
| Administrative expenses | 30,000 | 0.0508474 | 630,000 | 32,034 | 2,034 | 93.7 |
| Selling expenses | 45,000 | 0.0677966 | 630,000 | 42,712 | (2,288) | 105.4 |
| Total expenses | $550,000 | 0.8644067 | 630,000 | $544,576 | (5,424) | 101.0 |
| Pretax profit | $ 80,000 | 0.1355933 | 630,000 | $ 85,424 | (5,424) | 93.2 |

*Flexible budget = budgeted expense rate × net sales. However, for returns and adjustments, the flexible budget is calculated from gross sales ($650,000), not net sales ($630,000).
†Figures in parentheses indicate an unfavorable variance.

planned volume. As profit is significantly impacted by changes in volume in most organizations and particularly those with high fixed costs, a strong results-oriented case can be made for treating all costs as variable for flexible-budgeting purposes. Table 6-7 applies the flexible budget concept to the previous example, Table 6-6.

The calculation of expense rates provides us with a set expenditure allowance for any activity level. The budgeted or allowed expenditure for any category of cost is easily calculated by simply calculating the budgeted expense rate times the actual net sales. Table 6-8 looks at the previous actual vs. static budget comparison from a flexible, rather than static, budget perspective.

Where the actual vs. static budget comparison (Table 6-6) communicated that the management of Ramrod Electronics had achieved the exact pretax profit expected, the actual vs. flexible budget comparison (Table 6-8) tells us that, when considering sales, allowed expenditures exceeded plan and the pretax profit was $5424 less than it should have been.

Seldom do actual outputs exactly match the plan or budget, making flexible budgets an important tool for evaluating managerial performance.

## Summary

While measurement commonly presents the greatest obstacle and hinders efforts to quantify productivity so that it can be better managed, there does exist an assortment of tools which can be effectively applied to the design of productivity measurement systems. Management is best aided by prepared standards and budgets representing what should be accomplished. Such performance standards should be based on other than perpetuating past performance because past performance incorporates inefficiencies and ignores the organization's performance potential.

The evaluation of managerial performance is best accomplished by the comparison of actual results with budgeted expectations. The resulting variances can be classified as either "price" or "quantity" variances, quantity relating to usage or efficiency of consumption. Generally, the quantity variances are more influenced by management action than are variances in prices of materials or wages. While not perfectly controllable, price variances must still be an assigned managerial responsibility and should be measured and reported as are quantity variances. Only by including both price and quantity in its system of measurements can management accurately gauge progress and recognize problems.

Material standards can be generated by adding an allowance for waste or scrap to the quantity of material required per the bills of material for items produced. Both material and labor standards are dependent upon the methods employed to produce the desired results. Ideally, methods should be reviewed and either verified as being substantially correct or, if the obvious source of wasted resources, changed prior to establishing standards. The development of labor standards is normally an industrial-engineering function. In the absence of industrial-engineering resources, work-sampling procedures can be used to generate reasonably accurate labor standards.

The concepts of expense rates and flexible budgets are easily applied to most organizations. Expense rates change our perspective from a specific number of total expense dollars to a percentage of net sales allowance that can be applied to any level of sales. Flexible budgets are geared to changing levels of activity rather than to a single, static level as are conventional budgets. Flexible budgets can incorporate expense rates and tell us how much expenses should have been incurred for any level of output. Flexible budgets provide a more accurate measure of managerial performance than do static budgets simply because they are based on the actual activity level rather than a planned activity level. Where static budgets incorporate forecasts, flexible budgets incorporate reality.

# 7 Quality Considerations

Up to this point, our focus with regard to measurements has been on quantity, the quantity of inputs and the quantity of outputs. It is conceivable, if not predictable, that managerial emphasis on *only* quantity can negatively impact the quality of the organization's outputs. Recognizing the possibility of quantity being achieved at the expense of quality, and further recognizing that specific action must be aimed at establishing and maintaining a balance between the quantity and quality of outputs, astute management incorporates quality measurements into its overall system of measurements. While outputs can be readily quantified by counting, or weighing, or by some other means of measurement, it is generally more difficult to evaluate the quality of outputs. To paraphrase an old saying, "Quality is in the eyes of the beholder." Most often it is a subjective, rather than objective, evaluation based primarily on personal preferences and feelings. Ideally, the organization will equate quality to customer satisfaction. Customer satisfaction is important as it is the basis for the generation of goodwill, which manifests itself in the form of repeat business and glowing referrals being provided to prospective customers or clients. A leading manufacturer of appliances estimates that 1 in 3 dissatisfied customers will complain to the company but each person who is dissatisfied with the product or service provided will advertise that complaint to at least fifteen friends and acquaintances. One of the big-three auto makers has one case on record where the irate owner of a luxury car cost the company no fewer than 100 lost sales in a single year.[1]

A problem lies in the fact that the organization cannot realistically be all

[1]Edward M. Stiles, *Handbook for Total Quality Assurance*, Prentice-Hall, Englewood Cliffs, N.J., 1977, p. 3.

**113**

things to all people. To attempt total customer satisfaction would not only be cost prohibitive but would also generate unrealistic expectations among clients and customers, which in the long run would have a devastating impact on goodwill and reputation. Any attempt to measure quality must be accompanied with recognition of the fact that all products and all services are designed for limited usage or application. Those restrictions must be communicated outright to the customer or client.

As numbers quantifying output are useful for purposes of managerial control only when compared to a standard or specific reference point, so it is with qualitative measurements. Quality standards must be developed to provide meaning to quality measurements.

## The Two Primary Elements of Quality

Equating quality with customer satisfaction, the quality of the organization's outputs as perceived by the consumer is nothing more or less than providing them with *what* they want *when* they want it.

Quality = what is wanted + when it is needed

The "what" in this equation implies providing the customer or client with outputs which *accurately* match specifications and expectations. The "when" implies providing the customer or client with what is needed on a *timely* basis. Therefore:

Quality = accuracy + timeliness

To provide the customer or client with exactly what is wanted but after the need has expired is as unfortunate as to provide other than what is needed but on a timely basis: both equally fail to generate the desired customer satisfaction. Both accuracy and timeliness, in combination, are required if you are to produce quality outputs in the sense that you are generating customer or client satisfaction.

## The Trend in Quality Demands

There are three quality trends that must be recognized by the management of any organization operating in today's competitive marketplace.

**1. Both customers and clients have been increasing their quality expectations very sharply.** As competition increases, this tendency is likely to be further amplified. New technology has made possible a myriad of new product and service offerings. The complexity of those new offerings has increased significantly. As products and services have become generally more complex, the probability of error or malfunction has often increased. While increased complexity caused by rapidly advancing technology has impacted our organization's ability to produce a reliable product or service, it has also impacted the customer or client. It has become increasingly difficult for the customer or client to accurately judge the quality of the organization's outputs at the time he or she receives them. Technological advances, the increased complexity of product and service offerings, and a wave of increased consumerism have acted in combination to sensitize consumer attitudes and expectations related to the quality and reliability of purchased products and services.

**2. New technology and increasing consumer expectations of quality have made long-standing practices and procedures marginal, if not outmoded.** New technology and increasing consumer expectations have reduced the allowable margin for error. Where previously quality efforts have focused upon operators in the form of inspection and *control*, focus, out of necessity, has shifted to managerial responsibility and *preventing* errors at the source. Automation has increased the need for mechanization of previously manual inspection and test equipment. The machined part that could once be satisfactorily checked with a pocket scale or a hand-held micrometer must now be more carefully measured with an air gauge. Materials that previously could be accepted on the basis of only a visual inspection, must now be subjected to refined physical and chemical analysis.

**3. Many organizations face a serious squeeze between increasing costs and customer or client resistance to price increases.** This facet produces two distinct pressures on quality. First, the greater the pressure exerted by total costs, the more vigorous are the measures management must take to reduce them. Such measures often lead to increased mechanization and automation and place more critical demands on quality. Second, the drive to reduce costs must sharpen the organization's system of measurements and result in increased and constant awareness of the quality of outputs and better identification of quality costs. Quality costs, in general, are growing at an alarming rate within most organizations. Such costs, if not identified and better controlled, can result in the difference between profit and loss.

Quality affects both the organization's current and future income. With superior quality, the organization can secure a bigger share of the market and will stand a better chance of successfully raising its prices. On the other hand, it costs valuable resources to build quality, to control it, and to pay for its failures. Finding and maintaining the proper balance between the cost of quality and its resultant value, in the form of reduction in overall cost resulting from conformance to standards, are not easy tasks, but they can be facilitated by quality measurements.

## Five Factors Affecting Quality

The quality of the outputs produced by any organization is dependent upon five basic factors, as is illustrated by Figure 7-1. Those factors are design, equipment, materials, scheduling, and performance. In combination, they determine both the accuracy or acceptability of outputs and the timeliness with which those outputs are provided.

### 1. Design

The quality of outputs is dependent not only upon the design of the product but also upon the design of the systems required to produce those outputs. Improved quality through design does not necessarily mean higher costs.

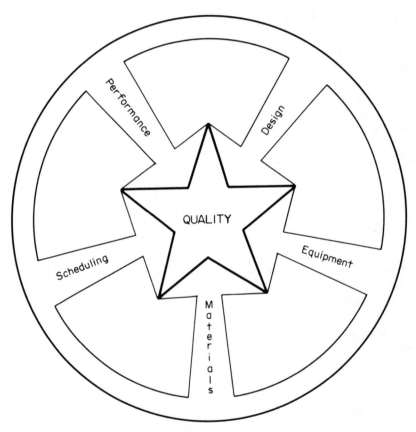

**Figure 7-1.** Quality of output is based on five factors.

Human ingenuity often finds ways by which designs can be made better and cheaper. For example, designs can be simplified so that fewer parts are required, or less expensive materials can be used without consequence, or the outputs can be accomplished using fewer operations.

For consumer goods and services, two factors usually govern the quality of design. The first factor is the market in which the organization is trying to compete. Is that market a luxury market, a middle-of-the-road market, or is it an economy market? The second factor influencing design is based on what the direct competition is doing. A lower quality than that provided by a competitor at the same price will result in fewer repeat customers. On the other hand, producing quality which is far superior to that of the competition, while charging the same price, will normally result in higher costs and shrinking profit margins.

## 2. Equipment

The ability with which the provided equipment, tools, and machinery can accurately and reliably produce the desired outputs has an important impact on quality. The selection of equipment and tools capable of both holding design tolerances and providing the required outputs in sufficient quantity to favorably impact costs is critical to the organization's success. If the processing equipment selected can accurately and reliably meet established design tolerances, then reasonable costs and acceptable quality can be expected. If the processing equipment selected cannot accurately and reliably meet design tolerances, then high costs, scrap, and a sizable investment in rework operations are inevitable outcomes.

## 3. Materials

Materials of many types are used by organizations in the generation of outputs. It is essential that the characteristics of those materials conform with specifications or requirements. The best design—coupled with superior equipment, a highly skilled and motivated work force, and a schedule providing adequate process time—oftentimes is incapable of overcoming the negative impact upon the quality of outputs caused by faulty or substandard materials. Visualize, if you will, the following situation: a periodic and supplementary audit of the torque on fasteners holding together critical components of automotive front suspensions finds that some of the bolts, though not overtorqued, are broken. Broken bolts could result in the loss of steering control and possibly collisions and personal injury. Management has the problem of determining when the faulty bolts first were used and possibly faces a recall campaign that could result in an additional expense of hundreds of thousands of dollars, not to mention the impact of the negative publicity resulting from the recall—all because faulty materials found their way into production.

## 4. Scheduling

Equating quality with customer satisfaction, including receipt of what is needed on a timely basis, scheduling has a tremendous impact on quality. Scheduling can obviously affect the timeliness with which outputs are delivered. Less obviously, poor scheduling can adversely affect the conformance of outputs to standard. Recognizing promised delivery dates and that insufficient time is provided for proper processing, operating management may, depending on the pressures applied to meeting that date, take shortcuts which result in substandard quality being shipped to the customer.

## 5. Performance

Human performance has an important bearing upon the quality of outputs produced. Performance is dependent upon two factors: skill and motivation.

Performance = skill + motivation

Skill is a function of two factors: training and experience

Skill = training + experience

Motivation is also a function of two factors: attitude and environment.

Motivation = attitude + environment

A positive attitude; a results-oriented environment with genuine concern for both employees and customers; the design and implementation of meaningful training programs; and management that provides performance-related feedback to its employees, as well as striving to maximize each individual's contribution to the achievement of the organization's objectives, all combine to have a significant influence on the quality of outputs produced.

Design, equipment, materials, scheduling, and human performance are distinct factors which individually and in combination determine the process capability, or the inherent ability to produce quality outputs in sufficient quantity so as to control production costs and enable a reasonable profit margin while meeting customer expectations. The prevailing operating conditions within the organization also influence the process capability. The concept of process capability is not limited to shop operations. It can be applied to administrative areas of cost control, clerical functions, office machine operations, maintenance functions, and scheduling, to mention just a few.

## Quality Effectiveness Considerations

### The Quality Program

The primary consideration when designing, implementing, and maintaining a quality program is to ensure the program's effectiveness. Some typical measures of the quality effectiveness of an organization are:

- The number of defects generated
- The frequency and severity of customer complaints
- The production yield
- Quality audit scores or indexes

The steps in developing a quality program aimed at improving effectiveness are as follows:

1. Define quality characteristics desired based on customer expectations.
2. Set quality standards based on the level of expectations.
3. Design and implement a quality appraisal program.
4. Design and implement a quality training program.
5. Design and implement a system of quality measurements and reports.

### Defining Quality Characteristics

The first step in the design phase is to determine and define in detail the quality characteristics desired by the customer. This involves a review of customer requirements as stated on the purchase order, drawings, technical specifications, and other applicable documents. Other possible sources of information are company catalogs and advertising brochures, as well as the insight of marketing personnel. Customer surveys are another means of obtaining valuable information related to both customer expectations and the quality practices of competitors. For the end product or service, criteria must be established that incorporate both the organization's and the customer's viewpoints. When there exists a wide disparity between these two viewpoints, an immediate effort must be made to resolve such differences. Should resolution not be possible, it would be foolish to continue the business relationship as customer dissatisfaction is imminent and will adversely affect the company's reputation. The criteria should be defined or rated in terms of importance for the purpose of decision making. The ranked criteria, or characteristics listed by degree of importance, provide the direction required to design a meaningful quality program.

## Setting Quality Standards

After the quality characteristics have been defined, the next step is to determine the desired quality levels and relate them to the process averages and the inspection methods to be used. The cost of attaining and maintaining a certain level of quality must be estimated and compared to the cost of potential failures. If there exists a significant variation between the actual and desired quality levels provided by any given process, a need for improvement in the process is indicated rather than extensive sorting by inspection.

When evaluating the costs associated with rejects or failures, the fact that defects when caught in the early stages are less costly than defects not recognized until later should be kept in mind.

Figure 7-2 represents what is sometimes referred to as the *funnel principle*. The cost of rejects increases with time as is indicated by the cost line and shaded area beneath the line. The nearer to the start of the process the defect is recognized, the lower is the cost of rejection. As the product or service progresses through the process, more resources are invested. The greater the amount of resources invested, the greater is the cost of rejection. The greatest cost is experienced when the customer is the source of rejection. In that event, the loss is potentially the cost of processing resources, plus the cost of processing the related complaint, plus the intangible cost of the resulting loss in goodwill.

Quality standards which specify the acceptable level of certain characteristics must be developed. Such standards will serve as the reference point, or the "should be," for comparisons of "is" vs. "should be." Wherever possible, standards must be based on measurable or objective criteria, rather than upon subjective judgments. Should length be important, then the related standard should be expressed in millimeters, inches, feet, or some other common unit of measurement. Should weight be an important characteristic, then the related stan-

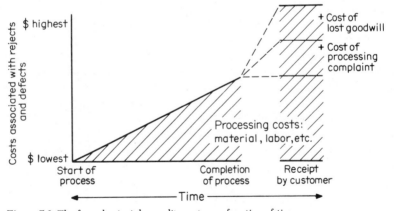

Figure 7-2. The funnel principle: quality costs as a function of time.

dard should be expressed in grams, ounces, or pounds. But what about other characteristics, such as the color and gloss of painted surfaces? Such characteristics are more difficult to measure objectively. Sample paint chips exhibiting the correct color and gloss can be provided to serve as the reference point for comparisons. Approved samples of other subjective but desirable characteristics could also be provided. The fewer the subjective judgments made with no tangible references or basis for comparison, the more accurate will be the evaluations of "is" vs. "should be."

## Designing the Appraisal Program

After having defined the quality characteristics and developed the related standards, the next step in the development of a quality program is to define the appraisal program. This definition should include the planned locations at which inspections will take place, the equipment needed, the inspection methods to be utilized, written job instructions, procedures, reporting formats, criteria for the maintenance of inspection records, and any other special requirements. The development of a flowchart or other sequential document can be a great aid in this process.

Inspection points are those physical points in the production process at which appraisal of material, products, or services is made. Typically, inspection will start with a receiving inspection function, continue through the entire process, and conclude with a finished product, and sometimes even a shipping inspection. Inspections are performed either at static stations where the product comes to the inspector for appraisal or by roving inspectors who go to the product at various stages of the processing cycle. Either all that is produced is inspected or only some of the product is inspected, in which case the limited number of inspections is viewed as "representative of all products produced." The former is referred to as a "100 percent inspection" plan, the latter as a "sampling" plan. Studies have shown that 100 percent inspection is only 65 to 98 percent effective, dependent upon the skill level of the inspector, the nature of the product being inspected, the subjectivity of the appraisal, and inspector fatigue. For example, the inability to concentrate over long periods of time results in the inspector both rejecting good products and missing real defectives. When sampling is compared with 100 percent inspection, it has several advantages, including:

• Due to the fewer number of inspections performed, sampling is less costly.
• Sampling places the responsibility for 100 percent inspection, or "sorting," squarely where it belongs, upon the person who performs the production operation.
• As fewer products are inspected, fewer are exposed to inspection-handling damage.

• Sampling results in fewer inspectors needed and thereby simplifies recruiting, training, and supervision.

Inherent disadvantages of sampling plans are:

• There is a risk that greater numbers of bad products will get out.
• More time and effort is devoted to planning and documentation and less to physically inspecting.
• If the sampling plan itself is faulty, erroneous conclusions will be reached at greater potential cost to the company.

The sampling used in industrial applications takes many forms, from a spot-checking technique, to the lot-by-lot technique of acceptance sampling based on statistical tables.

**Spot checking.** This is the phrase usually applied to sampling procedures that are hit or miss. The number of parts to be inspected and the size of the lot to be sampled are generally determined in an arbitrary manner under spot-check procedures. On some occasions, too many inputs or outputs are inspected, resulting in unnecessary expense. On other occasions, too few inputs or outputs are inspected, resulting in either an abnormal amount of defective inputs being placed into the production process or an excessive number of defective outputs being delivered to the customer. When spot checks incorporate well-regulated and well-defined procedures based on consistently inspecting a certain percentage of available inputs and/or outputs in a random fashion, the results of those inspections are meaningful and can provide adequate control.

**Acceptance sampling.** There are three types of statistical-sampling plans: single, double, and multiple. In a single-sampling plan, one sample is drawn from the lot and a decision to either accept or reject the lot is based on the results of that single sample. Double-sampling plans are more complicated; on the initial sample, a decision is made to either (1) accept the whole lot, (2) reject the whole lot, or (3) take another sample. Should a second sample be required, the combined results of the first and second samples are the basis for acceptance or rejection. A multiple-sampling plan is a continuation of double sampling in which three, four, or more samples, as desired, are taken. The size of individual samples in the multiple process is generally smaller than in either the single or double process. The technique is the same as with double-sampling plans.

In contrast to the hit-or-miss nature of spot-checking plans, statistical-sampling procedures are quite reliable. They are based upon well-defined probability principles which have been translated into charts and formulas suitable for use in the construction of sampling plans to meet the individual needs of any particular situation. A series of sampling schedules, with different percentages of defective values to meet varying conditions, are provided in these tables.

Different sampling plans express quality targets in different forms, among them being "average outgoing quality limit" (AOQL), "acceptable quality level" (AQL), and "lot tolerance percent defective" (LTPD). Each of these quality targets is designed to serve a somewhat different purpose.

Of the many statistical-sampling tables and plans that have been developed, some have been published in a form which makes them available for general use. The most popular of these published plans are:

- Dodge-Romig tables
- Military Standard 105A[2]

## Designing the Quality Training Program

The generation, by an organization, of products or services of consistently high quality requires a high degree of effectiveness in at least three characteristics of company personnel:

- *Quality attitudes:* Essential here is the genuine belief by the company's employees in the importance of the quality of outputs, the timeliness with which those outputs are generated, and a general concern for satisfying the customer or client needs.
- *Quality knowledge:* Critical in this regard is both a keen awareness of quality requirements and a good understanding of everything needed to meet those requirements.
- *Quality skills:* Important here are the ability levels, both mental and physical, displayed by employees in the process of attempting to fulfill their quality responsibilities.

In the development of an effective quality training program, emphasis must focus on the practical rather than the theoretical. To generate and maintain employee interest, the material presented should display information in a manner which relates to current or anticipated problems in the employee's work situation. Theory is fine for those who aren't responsible for results but will turn off the employees who can't relate the theory to real problems they are experiencing. Accordingly effective quality training programs are quality-problem centered, rather than quality-theory centered. Following are several principles on which any effective quality training program must be based:

**Principle number one.** Keep the program down to earth and centered upon real problems within the company.

[2]For a detailed appraisal of these plans, see Harold Dodge and Harry Romig, *Sampling Inspection Tables,* Wiley, New York, 1959; and *MIL-STD-105A, Sampling Procedures and Table for Inspection by Attributes,* United States Government Printing Office, 1950.

**Principle number two.** Emphasize the required balance between cost of quality and the value of quality. Quality has value in that superior quality results in greater market share, firmer pricing, and other benefits related to increasing income. Although it costs money to achieve quality and to control it, the costs of nonconformance are potentially greater. The balance is achieved when customer expectations are met at minimum cost.

**Principle number three.** Quality must be built in to any product or service. It can never be "inspected in." Accordingly, focus must be on prevention rather than correction—that is, doing it right the first time. Inspectors and other quality control personnel must be viewed as the customer or client's in-house representatives. Quality responsibility rests with designers, operators, and management, more than with inspectors.

**Principle number four.** Quality requires a team effort. The customer or client judges the company by its service and its products. In the final analysis, it matters not why the customer or client takes business elsewhere. All employees are equally affected by poor quality or poor service. It serves the best interest of each individual employee to contribute to the total quality effort, not just the person's own work area, in any and every way possible.

**Principle number five.** Due to rapidly advancing technology, increasing competition, greater governmental regulation, rising consumer expectations, and an ever-changing work place, quality training must be viewed as a continuing process.

**Principle number six.** Quality training is important for all functions and levels of the organization. Programs must be tailored for individual or departmental needs to be meaningful. The quality needs of the operator differ from the needs of the department manager. Engineering's quality needs vary from the quality needs of accounting.

The responsibility and authority for quality training usually rests within the quality control component of the organization. Many companies integrate persons from other than the quality function as speakers or instructors in their quality training programs. To do so communicates common interest and coordination related to the overall quality effort.

To ensure the credibility of the training programs, it is essential that all programs be consistent with each other and with the actual operating practices and policies of the organization.

## Quality Measurements and Reporting

Quality programs are aimed at both controlling and improving the quality of outputs. Both control and improvement are dependent upon a feedback cycle. Figure 7-3 illustrates that cycle. The control and improvement of quality are dependent upon measurements to quantify the effectiveness of the quality

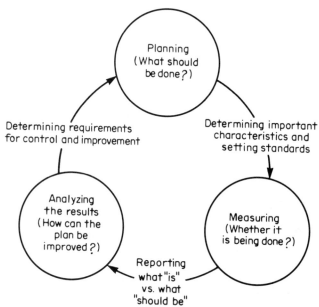

**Figure 7-3.** The feedback cycle of quality control and improvement.

effort and upon reports to accurately communicate, on a timely basis, what actually is as compared to what should be.

Quality measurements may be classified in terms of processes:

**Preprocess measurements.** Such measures may be required for the purpose of controlling the materials or parts entering the process. Preprocess measurement and reporting focuses on making management aware of the quality of goods and services which are inputs to the organization's processing system. Such information is valuable in the sense the inputs could cause costly downtime, adversely affect the ability to produce quality outputs, and, if missed or not corrected, result in customer complaints.

**In-process measurements.** Control resulting from in-process measurement is based on measures of the required quality characteristics as the product is being produced. Such in-process measurements provide signals indicating the need to change, regulate, or stop the process for the purpose of ceasing the generation of faulty outputs.

**Postprocess measurements.** These are based on a measurement of the quality characteristics of the completed product. Such measurements can be either prior to shipment, in which case they provide both an early indicator of what the customer will receive and a last chance to correct defects, or they can be after shipments in the form of feedback from customers.

**TABLE 7·1.** In-Plant Quality Report

**IN-PLANT QUALITY REPORT**

Product _Widgets_    Date _10/23_

Location produced _Plant 711_

Report compiled by _O.K. Kelly_

| | | Daily | | | | | Month to date | | | | |
|---|---|---|---|---|---|---|---|---|---|---|---|
| | | Number | | % inspected | % goal | Sampling index | Number | | % inspected | % goal | Sampling index |
| | | Inspected | Processed | | | | Inspected | Processed | | | |
| **S A M P L E  S I Z E** | Receiving | 80 | 160 | 50 | 50 | 100.0 | 1400 | 2400 | 58.3 | 50 | 116.6 |
| | In-process Mfg. area | 150 | 1000 | 15 | 20 | 75.0 | 2550 | 20,000 | 12.75 | 20 | 63.8 |
| | In-process Assembly area | 12 | 100 | 12 | 15 | 80.0 | 240 | 1750 | 13.71 | 15 | 91.4 |
| | In-process Paint area | 13 | 105 | 12.38 | 15 | 82.5 | 265 | 1700 | 15.59 | 15 | 103.9 |
| | Final Preshipment | 10 | 97 | 10.3 | 10 | 103.0 | 170 | 1650 | 10.3 | 10 | 103.0 |
| | Total | 265 | 1362 | 19.5 | | | 4625 | 27,500 | 16.8 | | |

| | | Number | | % OK | % goal | Quality index | Number | | % OK | % goal | Quality index |
|---|---|---|---|---|---|---|---|---|---|---|---|
| | | OK | Inspected | | | | OK | Inspected | | | |
| **P E R C E N T  O K** | Receiving | 77 | 80 | 96.3 | 98.0 | 98.3 | 1385 | 1400 | 98.9 | 98.0 | 100.9 |
| | In-process Mfg. area | 138 | 150 | 92.0 | 99.0 | 92.9 | 2500 | 2550 | 98.0 | 99.0 | 98.0 |
| | In-process Assembly area | 11 | 12 | 91.7 | 97.0 | 94.5 | 235 | 240 | 97.9 | 97.0 | 100.9 |
| | In-process Paint area | 9 | 13 | 69.2 | 98.0 | 70.6 | 251 | 265 | 94.7 | 98.0 | 96.6 |
| | Final Preshipment | 9 | 10 | 90.0 | 96.0 | 93.8 | 158 | 170 | 92.9 | 96.0 | 96.8 |
| | Total | 244 Ⓐ | 265 Ⓑ | Total defects Ⓑ − Ⓐ | 21 Ⓒ | | 4529 Ⓐ | 4625 Ⓑ | Total defects Ⓑ − Ⓐ | 96 Ⓒ | |
| | | | | % defective Ⓒ ÷ Ⓑ | 7.9% | | | | % defective Ⓒ ÷ Ⓑ | 2.1% | |

| | Specific defect | Area having prime quality responsibility | Number | | Effectiveness index | Area having prime quality responsibility | Number | | Effectiveness index |
|---|---|---|---|---|---|---|---|---|---|
| | | | OK | Inspected | | | OK | Inspected | |
| **T O P  D E F E C T S** | Quantity rec'd. short | Vendors | 77 | 80 | 96.3 | Vendors | 1390 | 1400 | 99.3 |
| | Part #163.650 cracked | Stamping | 146 | 150 | 97.3 | Stamping | 2533 | 2550 | 99.3 |
| | Misassembled | Assembly | 11 | 12 | 91.7 | Assembly | 236 | 240 | 98.3 |
| | Poor packaging | Packaging | 9 | 10 | 90.0 | Packaging | 165 | 170 | 97.1 |
| | Dirt in paint | Paint | 11 | 13 | 84.6 | Paint | 260 | 265 | 98.1 |
| | Paint off color | Paint | 13 | 13 | 100.0 | Paint | 258 | 265 | 97.4 |
| | Total of the above | Percent of total defects this date | | 52.4% | | Percent of total defects month to date | | 50.0% | |

It obviously serves the best interest of the organization to focus measurement activities on those quality characteristics deemed critical to achieving customer satisfaction. Care must be exercised so as not to waste valuable resources measuring and reporting characteristics that have little or no bearing upon customer satisfaction. Less obvious is the need to measure sample sizes against predetermined levels required to generate a certain confidence level, when sampling is used in lieu of 100 percent inspection.

Each individual form of output will have its own set of critical quality characteristics which should be measured and reported. Likewise, the reporting format used must be designed for the individual situation. Table 7-1 is an example of a reporting format for quality effectiveness.

You will notice that Table 7-1 communicates, in the form of indexes, the "is" vs. "should be" related to sample size, quality level, and the quality effectiveness of each individual work area in the processing system. The report focuses on in-plant quality and includes preprocess-receiving inspection, in-process inspection, and postprocess-preshipment inspection information. Data related to both daily and month-to-date inspection activity and results is summarized. Information pinpointing the most frequent specific defects is an integral part of this reporting format. In a single-page format, all information related to in-plant quality effectiveness is provided.

Examples of reporting formats for quality effectiveness related to timeliness of order processing and customer complaints are shown in Tables 7-2 and 7-3, respectively.

## Quality Efficiency Considerations

All factors influencing quality are dependent upon an investment of organizational resources to improve the quality of outputs. This is not to imply that an organization should not strive for the best quality in its competitive field, but rather that it should not strive to be so far ahead of its competition that profit margins are adversely affected.

## Measuring Quality Costs

In the final analysis, the value of programs and efforts, aimed at improving or maintaining the quality of outputs, must be based on their contribution to the primary objective of the organization—which is profit for most businesses. The efficiency of most organizations is measured in terms of dollars. Therefore, as with production, engineering, sales, and other activities, the cost of quality must be known. The cost of quality is not different than other costs. It can be pro-

**TABLE 7·2.** Processing Timeliness Reporting Format

**PROCESSING TIMELINESS REPORT**

Date _____

Product _____

Location _____

Report Compiled by _____

| | | Daily | | | | | Month to Date | | | | |
|---|---|---|---|---|---|---|---|---|---|---|---|
| | | Number | | % chk'd | % goal | Sampling index | Number | | % chk'd | % goal | Sampling index |
| | | Timeliness chk'd | Processed | | | | Timeliness chk'd | Processed | | | |
| **S A M P L E** | Receiving | | | | | | | | | | |
| | In-process ___ area | | | | | | | | | | |
| **S I Z E** | In-process ___ area | | | | | | | | | | |
| | In-process ___ area | | | | | | | | | | |
| | Final preshipment | | | | | | | | | | |
| | Total | | | | | | | | | | |

| | | Frequency-process time-workdays-in to out | | | | | | Actual weighed avg. E. T. | Frequency-process time-workdays-in to out | | | | | | Actual weighed avg. E. T. |
|---|---|---|---|---|---|---|---|---|---|---|---|---|---|---|---|
| | | Same day | 1 day | 2 days | 3 days | 4 days | 5+ days | | Same day | 1 day | 2 days | 3 days | 4 days | 5+ days | |
| **P R O C E S S** | Receiving | | | | | | | | | | | | | | |
| | In-process ___ area | | | | | | | | | | | | | | |
| **T I M E** | In-process ___ area | | | | | | | | | | | | | | |
| | In-process ___ area | | | | | | | | | | | | | | |
| | Final preshipment | | | | | | | | | | | | | | |
| | Total each column | | | | | | | | | | | | | | |

| | | Average order process time in workdays | | | Oldest unprocessed order in workdays | | | Average order process time in workdays | | | Oldest unprocessed order in workdays | | |
|---|---|---|---|---|---|---|---|---|---|---|---|---|---|
| | | Goal | Actual | Index | Goal | Actual | Index | Goal | Actual | Indes | Goal | Actual | Index |
| **E F F E C T I V E N E S S** | Receiving | | | | | | | | | | | | |
| | In-process ___ area | | | | | | | | | | | | |
| | In-process ___ area | | | | | | | | | | | | |
| | In-process ___ area | | | | | | | | | | | | |
| | Final preshipment | | | | | | | | | | | | |
| | Total all areas | | | | | | | | | | | | |

**TABLE 7-3.** Customer Complaint Reporting Format

CUSTOMER COMPLAINT REPORT

Product _____

Date _____

Report compiled by _____

| Responsibility for complaint | Month | | | | | | Year to date | | | | | |
|---|---|---|---|---|---|---|---|---|---|---|---|---|
| | Total number | | % complaints to shipments | | Complaint index | | Total number | | % complaints to shipments | | Complaint index | |
| | Complaints last month | Shipments previous month | Goal | Actual | | | Complaints thru last month | Shipments thru previous month | Goal | Actual | | |
| Design | | | | | | | | | | | | |
| Vendor | | | | | | | | | | | | |
| Manufacturing | | | | | | | | | | | | |
| Packaging | | | | | | | | | | | | |
| Traffic | | | | | | | | | | | | |
| Carrier | | | | | | | | | | | | |
| Sales | | | | | | | | | | | | |
| Unknown | | | | | | | | | | | | |
| Total | | | | | | | | | | | | |

| Most frequent specific complaints received | Responsibility | Month No. of complaints | | | | Year to Date No. of complaints | | | |
|---|---|---|---|---|---|---|---|---|---|
| | | Goal based on actual shipments in previous month | Actual for last month | Index | | Goal based on actual shipments thru previous month | Actual thru last month | Index | % of total complaints rec'd |
| | | | | | | | | | |
| | | | | | | | | | |
| | | | | | | | | | |
| | | | | | | | | | |
| | | | | | | | | | |
| | | | | | | | | | |
| | | | | | | | | | |
| | | | | | | | | | |

grammed, budgeted, measured, and analyzed to achieve the objective of improved quality at lower quality costs.

Quality costs cut across department boundaries and involve all activities of the organization—manufacturing, purchasing, engineering, and customer service, to mention a few. Some costs are readily identifiable, such as the wages or salaries of quality control personnel and the cost of inspection instrumentation. Other costs are less apparent or easy to capture, such as the costs associated with scrap, rework, and customer returns. In addition, there are costs related to customer dissatisfaction and loss of customer loyalty which are difficult, if not impossible, to measure. Producing outputs that have a high level of quality is not enough. The cost of achieving that quality must be carefully managed so that the long-range impact of quality costs does not negatively impact the organization's profits.

## Direct Quality Costs

In defining general categories of direct quality costs, we have those costs that are attributed to either prevention, appraisal, internal failure, or external failure. The cost of prevention would be defined as those costs incurred to minimize later defects or failures. The cost of appraisal would include costs incurred in performing appraisal functions such as inspections, tests, calibrations, and sortings. The cost of internal failures includes the costs of scrap and rework. The cost of external failures includes the costs of warranty and customer returns. Each of the four main categories of quality cost contains several elements as follows:

### Prevention

- *Quality training:* The cost of designing, implementing, operating, and maintaining formal training programs related to quality
- *Procedures and manuals:* The cost involved in developing and communicating quality procedures, inspection standards, and so forth
- *Vendor surveys:* The cost of resources consumed in the process of finding and selecting qualified vendors
- *Design and development of equipment:* The cost of personnel and other resources dedicated to the design and development of measurement and other quality control equipment
- *Quality personnel:* The cost of personnel involved in quality planning, equipment design, and similar activities other than those personnel involved in the appraisal or response to failure processes

### Appraisal

- *Vendor inspections:* The cost of time and travel associated with performing inspections or audits at a vendor's plant
- *Receiving inspection:* The costs associated with inspecting and testing incoming purchased materials
- *In-process inspection:* The cost of inspecting and testing the product as it is in the process of being produced
- *Finished-goods inspection:* The cost of inspections and testing after the product is produced but prior to shipment to the customer
- *Equipment calibration and maintenance:* The costs associated with the maintenance and calibration of equipment used to measure and/or control quality

- *Process control:* The cost of all process control activities performed to quality-supplied instructions by other than quality control personnel
- *Quality reports:* The costs associated with generating periodic quality reports communicating the findings of appraisal activities
- *Materials:* The cost of material consumed as part of the appraisal activities, including the costs of products or samples destroyed through tests, utility costs, and the costs of supplies

## Internal failure

- *Scrap:* The net loss of labor, material, and overhead resulting from defective products that cannot be economically repaired or used
- *Rework:* The cost of correcting defective outputs so that they meet specifications
- *Failure analysis:* The costs incurred to determine the cause of product or service failures
- *Supplier-caused losses:* The cost of unrecoverable losses due to failure of supplier-provided material
- *Reinspection:* The extra costs associated with reinspecting reworked materials
- *Downgrading:* The cost reflecting the price differential between the normal selling price and the reduced price because the product did not meet standard

## External failure

- *Complaints:* The costs associated with resolving customer complaints
- *Returned goods:* The costs associated with the handling and replacement of returned products
- *Repair:* The costs resulting from the repair of returned products
- *Warranty:* The cost of replacing or repairing products that fail during the warranty period
- *Liability:* The cost incurred as the result of product liability litigation

When management increases expenditures related to prevention and appraisal, it does so in the hope that the savings derived from fewer failures will more than offset that greater investment. At some point, the combined total cost of quality is at its lowest point. That point is referred to as the *quality cost optimization point* and is illustrated by Figure 7-4.

## Indirect Quality Costs

In addition to the direct operating costs, the indirect quality costs and their impact on the total cost curve must be taken into consideration. Indirect quality costs can be divided into three categories:

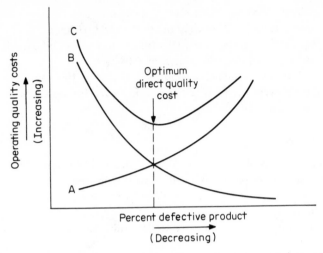

**Figure 7-4.** Direct operating quality costs. A, cost of prevention and appraisal; B, cost of failures (internal plus external); C (= A + B), total direct operating quality cost.

**Customer penalty.** This category includes cost penalties incurred by the customer. Specific examples are equipment downtime, nonreimbursed repair costs (i.e., postwarranty period), and transportation costs.

**Customer dissatisfaction.** The customer is either satisfied or dissatisfied. The greater the degree of dissatisfaction, the higher the associated costs or the greater the probability that future business will be taken elsewhere.

**Loss of goodwill or reputation.** These costs represent the compound effect of dissatisfied customers communicating that dissatisfaction to others and thereby reducing the number of viable prospects for future purchase of any product or service provided by the company.

Indirect quality costs are, at least in part, difficult, if not impossible, to measure accurately. They do, however, have a negative impact, of sometimes uncertain magnitude, on the total quality cost curve. (See Figure 7-5.) Note that as compared to the optimum direct quality cost, the optimum point for overall quality cost (direct + indirect) has shifted to the right on the graph. This shift denotes the need to reduce the rate of defective product. A lower rate of product defect can be achieved by increasing the prevention and appraisal expenditures. This will result in the lowering of the failure rate, both internal and external. The lowering of the external failure rate has a positive impact on indirect costs.

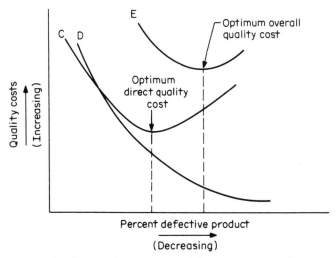

Figure 7-5. Direct and indirect quality costs. C, total direct operating quality cost; D, indirect quality cost; E (= C + D), total quality cost.

## Collecting and Compiling Quality Cost Data

The cost data required to generate an operating quality cost report is sometimes available within the existing accounting system. If available, then it is only a matter of compiling the different elements of quality cost and placing them in the categories previously mentioned. When such data is not available, it may be possible to make valid estimates of quality costs based on knowledge, experience, and the factoring of available cost data. Such estimates are time-consuming, and because they are "estimates," regardless of accuracy, they tend to lack the credibility required to counter effectively the self-serving opinions offered by your management team. Ideally, if the quality cost data is not presently available within the accounting system, you can convince whomever is in charge of the benefits to be derived from classifying and periodically compiling all such costs.

## Analyzing Quality Costs

After either estimated or, preferably, actual quality costs have been obtained, it is necessary to analyze those costs for the purpose of identifying the appropriate course of action. The process of analysis consists of examining each cost element in relation to either labor hours, other costs, sales revenues, or the quantity of outputs produced.

**Labor hours.** The quality cost per hour of direct labor is a common index. Information on direct labor hours worked is usually readily available. The validity of comparing quality cost per hour of direct labor measurements between two periods is, of course, dependent upon the operation remaining essentially the same. If, for example, automation was introduced after the base period, such a comparison between following periods and the base period would be deceiving. Sometimes direct labor *dollars* are used as the basis for comparison rather than hours. In that event, quality cost per direct labor dollar is a dollar-to-dollar relationship within the same period, thereby eliminating the inflation factor. Though inflation is factored out in such a dollar-to-dollar comparison, a change such as the previously mentioned automation, if incorporated after the base period, would result in the same erroneous impression as when using hours as the basis for comparison.

**Costs.** Quality cost per dollar of total manufacturing or operational expense is another common quality cost index. Total manufacturing or operational expense consists of direct labor, indirect labor, and manufacturing or operational overhead. As with the previous measurement base, a change such as automation would impact the validity of interperiod comparisons. Because more than just direct labor cost is involved, the negative impact of a change such as automation would be diminished, somewhat.

**Sales.** Quality cost per dollar of net sales, or the quality cost expense rate, is the most common type of quality cost index. This measurement base and the resulting index are affected by changes in selling price and/or product mix. Using previously discussed methods, such changes can be factored out for a more accurate comparison of indexes between periods.

**Unit.** Quality cost per unit of output is an excellent index, providing dissimilar products and their associated quality costs are kept separate and multiple indexes are generated.

Each of the above-mentioned measurement bases and the resulting indexes have advantages and disadvantages. For that reason, the implementation of two or more measurement bases and indexes is recommended for any given situation.

## Operating Quality Cost Report

The primary purpose of a quality cost program is to identify profit improvement opportunities while maintaining conformance to customer expectations. An effective quality cost system provides the means to recognize such opportunities. It directs managerial action toward those specific situations offering the greatest opportunities for profit improvement. The basic tool for providing such direction is the operating quality cost report. Such reports should be compiled and distributed periodically, the exact time interval depending upon the situation and the need. These reports should include the expenditures for each element of quality cost as related to whatever measurement base(s) used. Comparing the actual costs with budgeted costs or goals provides the cost index. Table 7-4 is an example of one possible format for such a report.

**TABLE 7-4.** Operating Quality Cost Report

Period _9/1_ Through _9/30_    Year to Date through _9/30_

| Operating Quality Cost Categories | Actual cost | Goal | Variance * | Cost index | Actual cost | Goal | Variance * | Cost index |
|---|---|---|---|---|---|---|---|---|
| Prevention costs | $1,700 | $2,000 | $300 | 85.0 | $17,000 | $18,000 | $1,000 | 94.4 |
| Appraisal costs | 7,000 | 6,000 | (1,000) | 116.7 | 61,000 | 54,000 | (7,000) | 113.0 |
| Internal failure costs | 3,000 | 5,000 | 2,000 | 60.0 | 25,000 | 45,000 | 20,000 | 55.6 |
| External failure costs | 8,000 | 3,000 | (5,000) | 266.7 | 57,500 | 27,000 | 30,500 | 213.0 |
| Total quality costs | 19,700 | 16,000 | (3,700) | 123.1 | 160,500 | 144,000 | (16,500) | 111.5 |
| Ratio of Operating Quality Costs to Net Sales (Expense Rate) | | | | | | | | |
| Prevention | .00515 | .00526 | .00011 | 97.9 | .00630 | .00526 | (.00104) | 119.8 |
| Appraisal | .02121 | .01579 | (.00542) | 134.3 | .02259 | .01579 | (.00680) | 143.1 |
| Internal failure | .00909 | .01316 | .00407 | 235 | .00936 | .01316 | .00390 | 70.4 |
| External failure | .02424 | .00789 | (.01635) | 307.2 | .02130 | .00789 | (.01341) | 270.0 |
| Total all categories | .05969 | .04210 | (.01759) | 141.8 | .05944 | .04210 | (.01734) | 141.2 |
| Ratio of Specific Significant Costs to Net Sales (Expense Rate) | | | | | | | | |
| In-process inspection | .01310 | .01000 | (.00310) | 131.0 | .01270 | .01000 | (.00270) | 127.0 |
| Final inspection | .00500 | .00200 | (.00300) | 250.0 | .00615 | .00200 | (.00415) | 307.5 |
| Returned goods processing | .01200 | .00600 | (.00600) | 200.0 | .01450 | .00600 | (.00850) | 241.7 |
| Ratio of Operating Quality Costs to Unit of Good Output | | | | | | | | |
| Prevention | .02576 | .03030 | .00454 | 85.0 | .03146 | .02632 | (.00516) | 119.6 |
| Appraisal | .10606 | .09091 | (.01515) | 116.7 | .11296 | .07895 | (.03462) | 143.1 |
| Internal failure | .04545 | .07576 | .03031 | 60.0 | .04630 | .06579 | .01949 | 70.4 |
| External failure | .12121 | .04545 | (.07576) | 266.7 | .10648 | .03947 | (.06701) | 269.8 |
| Total all categories | .29848 | .24242 | (.05606) | 123.1 | .29722 | .21053 | (.08669) | 141.2 |
| Net sales | $330,000 | $360,000 | $(30,000) | 86.8 | $2,700,000 | $3,420,000 | $(720,000) | 78.9 |
| Output of good units | 66,000 | 76,000 | (10,000) | 86.8 | 540,000 | 684,000 | (144,000) | 78.9 |

*Variance legend : (unfavorable), favorable.

In Table 7-4, the measurement bases of "net sales" and "units of good output" were arbitrarily chosen. Other bases such as "total manufacturing cost" or "total direct labor hours worked" could have been selected in lieu of net sales or units of good output, respectively.

### The "Significant Few"

What is often referred to as a *Pareto distribution* is a distribution wherein a few specific items represent an inordinate amount of the total cost. Figure 7-6 depicts such a distribution.

This distribution is sometimes also referred to as the *80-20 distribution;* 80 percent of the total dollar cost or loss is attributable to only 20 percent of the total items or characteristics. Once those "significant few" have been identified, specific programs can be designed and implemented aimed at reducing their costs. In Table 7-4, in-process inspection costs, final inspection costs, and the costs associated with processing returned goods, in total, account for 68.8 and 95.3 percent of the total unfavorable expense rate variance (ratio to net sales) for the month and year-to-date, respectively.

### Trend Analysis

Monthly quality cost reports, even when they incorporate year-to-date data, leave something to be desired as far as providing information for long-range planning. Trend analysis fulfills that need. Data for the trend analysis is taken directly from the monthly quality cost reports. To minimize the normal varia-

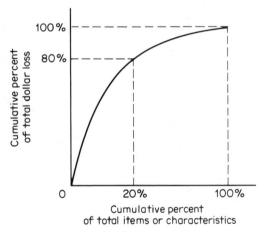

**Figure 7-6.** A Pareto distribution.

tions which manifest themselves in the form of month-to-month fluctuations, monthly data can be compiled into either quarterly or annual data, whichever best serves the purpose of the analysis. Figure 7-7 is an example of such trend analysis graphs.

Quality costs are an important managerial tool. They provide:

• An objective method of assessing the overall effectiveness and efficiency of the quality program
• A means for pinpointing problem areas, determining action priorities, and establishing need programs
• Information that can be used to more accurately price products and bid on jobs

Producing items that have a high quality level is not enough. The cost of achieving that quality must be carefully managed to ensure there is no erosion of the company's profits.

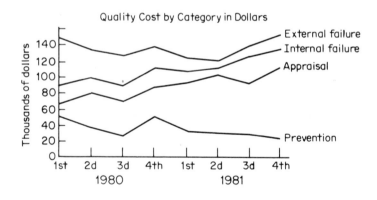

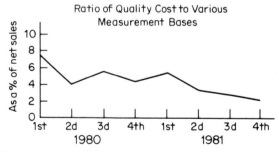

**Figure 7-7.** A sequence of trend analysis graphs.

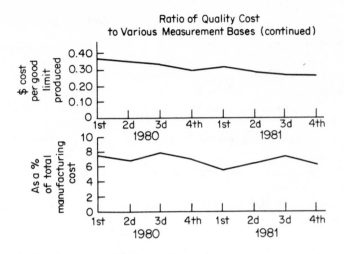

## Ratio of Quality Cost
### to Various Measurement Bases (continued)

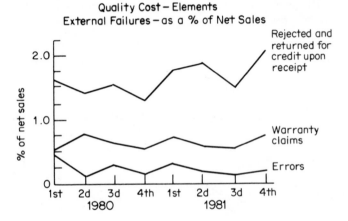

## Quality Cost – Elements
### External Failures – as a % of Net Sales

## Quality Cost by Product as a %
### of Product Net Sales

**Figure 7-7.** A sequence of trend analysis graphs *(continued)*.

## Summary

Quality is synonymous with customer satisfaction. Customer satisfaction is dependent upon the organization providing what is wanted when it is wanted. Increasingly, customer expectations are rising. Technological change and the increasing complexity of products and services, as well as organizations being squeezed between rising costs and customer resistance to price increases, present sizable obstacles to today's management. For management to be successful in today's operating environment, it must continually strive to find and maintain the balance between the cost of quality and the value quality has to the organization in the form of increased market share and other profit-related benefits.

The "what is wanted" element of customer satisfaction is best defined by determining the specific quality characteristics required. The "when it is needed" element stresses the importance of timeliness in order processing and delivery. The specific level of quality required is communicated via quality standards. When referring to more tangible quality characteristics, quality standards should be expressed in measurable terms. When referring to less tangible characteristics, standards should be communicated via approved samples which can serve as a basis for comparing what is with what should be.

Measurements related to the effectiveness with which the organization produces quality outputs are important to the organization's success. The desired quality characteristics serve as the basis for determining what is to be measured. The effectiveness with which quality of outputs is achieved determines customer satisfaction.

Measurements related to the efficiency with which the organization utilizes resources in the processing of quality products are equally important to the organization's success. Valuable resources are consumed to produce quality, to control it, and to pay for its failures. As standards are set for quality characteristics, standards must also be set for the consumption of resources used in producing those quality characteristics. Management should strive for optimum quality costs or that defect rate at which the cost of prevention and appraisal equals the cost related to product failures, both within and without the organization.

Quality emphasis has shifted over the last several years from sorting to prevention. Methods have also changed from 100 percent inspection to statistically based sampling.

The manner in which quality measurements are reported has an important bearing on their value to the organization and the achievement of both quality and profit goals.

# 4

# Management by Goalz

# 8

# A Managerial Philosophy

Management by objectives is a well-known phrase to most managers. I have found the word *objectives* to be viewed by many managers as being stilted. To overcome what I feel is built-in resistance to the formality of the word, I started substituting the word *goals* for *objectives* many years ago. Further, as an attention grabber, I started spelling the word *goals* with a *z* rather than an *s*. As I am not a very formal person, goalz suits me just fine and, in my opinion, tends to make people feel more comfortable. Who is going to be intimidated by a phrase ending in a word most people, particularly those interested in sports, can readily identify with. Especially when the person using it can't even spell it correctly. While this may seem like a very minor point (which it is), the little things, in combination, make the difference between total commitment and lukewarm support. Accordingly, the phrase *management by goalz* is substituted for *management by objectives* where appropriate in the following discussion.

Management by objectives is a well-accepted "system" for improving both organizational effectiveness and organizational efficiency. Unfortunately, many managers have embraced the concept as a thing or a magic wand that when applied will magically and mystically improve organizational performance, regardless of the operating climate. Management by objectives is not a system, nor a thing, nor a magic wand capable of overcoming everything that remains wrong within the work place. Management by objectives is an attitude or a philosophy. It is an internalized concept embraced by high-performance managers having an awareness that human needs must be fulfilled if performance is to improve.

Management by objectives as understood and practiced by most managers over the last several years has, in my opinion, been a dismal failure. Were we to poll a number of managers in different work situations many, if not most, of them would claim to practice "management by objectives." As stated, it is a well-accepted "system." In most cases, the only difference between management by objectives as practiced today and managerial practices and philosophies of a hundred years ago is the addition of goals to the system. What is most often lacking and not an integral part of the management-by-objectives approach are the key concepts that:

• People perform best when they have an overview of the total work situation and a feeling that what they are doing is important and worthwhile to the total effort.
• People will strive to achieve the organization's goals if they know what those goals are, understand them, and can derive some need satisfaction from contributing to their achievement.

Management by goalz is more than goals, or targets, or quotas. It is a philosophy that manifests itself, not in the setting of goals alone, but in managerial acceptance of all employees as being important to the achievement of those goals. Further, it recognizes employees as worthy of being provided the overview, or "big picture"; and that the big picture will better enable employees to maximize their contributions to the organization. The mushroom theory of management—keeping employees in the dark and feeding them horse manure—is not compatible with the philosophy of management by goalz. I have said that management's job is to achieve the organization's *potential*, rather than some unquantified degree of results. To achieve that worthwhile goal is dependent upon maximizing the contribution of all employees toward that end. The extent that managers plan ahead, set reasonable and worthwhile goals, and communicate with employees in terms of the big picture and the desired results determines whether they are managing by goalz.

## Management by Control vs. Management by Goalz

When a manager's operating method is to provide step-by-step instructions to an employee, the employee is dependent upon that manager's continuing inputs to know what must be done. When a job is completed, the employee must get the next assignment from the supervisor. This mode of operation, though practiced by many managers, will never result in the realization of the employee's potential contribution to the organization. When telling an employee what to do in step-by-step fashion, we are by implication telling what not to do: "Do not do anything that I specifically have not told you to do!" A consequence associated with this method of operation is a situation wherein the employee should have obviously responded to some unforeseen event but didn't, because of being conditioned to do *only* what had been ordered. This method of operation can most accurately be called *management by control.*

In contrast to management by control is the manager who provides employees with an overview of what is trying to be accomplished, allowing the employees to contribute their own common sense, experience, and good judgment to doing their assigned job well. To the extent that the employees understand the organization's goals, they can continue, to some extent, on their own. The manager's presence is not required for employees to properly respond to some unforeseen event. The employees can pursue the objectives, to some degree, without the manager being nearby. Not only has the manager been liberated from the need for providing minute-to-minute direction but the employees have been liberated as well. This method of operation is truly management by goalz.

## Management Style and Performance

Why are some managers consistently able to generate wholehearted support and best efforts from employees, while other managers tend to alienate employees and are continuously struggling with them in an attempt to achieve results? The late Douglas McGregor, noted behavioral scientist, studied a variety of work environments and related them to the various managerial styles displayed by the key managers in those organizations.[1] McGregor concluded that the differences in managerial style originated from differences in underlying managerial attitudes toward their employees as people. He believed that managers who could inspire employees to high levels of performance operated on a common set of assumptions about people, which differed greatly from the more common feelings shared by less successful managers. The more common, but less successful, set of managerial attitudes about people in the work situation was labeled *Theory X*. Theory X included the following assumptions:

People do not like work. For the most part, they find work distasteful and will avoid it whenever possible. The only reason people work is to acquire money.

Because people dislike work, they must be coerced into working. They must continuously be given direction, closely monitored, and completely controlled to ensure they properly perform assigned tasks.

People dislike responsibility and will avoid it whenever possible. "Security" is the single most important thing. The most effective means to induce employees to work toward achieving organizational objectives is to manage

[1]Douglas McGregor, *The Human Side of Enterprise*, McGraw-Hill, New York, 1961.

them in a manner which increases security stress, or makes them anxious about their continued employment.

While some managers are not hesitant to express such opinions openly, others seem to embrace them more or less unconsciously. McGregor contended that most managers act as if they hold these statements to be essentially true.

McGregor advanced an alternative set of assumptions about people at work, which he felt more accurately portrayed human behavior in terms of environmental influences. He believed that few managers operated according to this more enlightened set of assumptions. He labeled this other set of assumptions *Theory Y*. According to Theory Y:

People want and need activity. The work activity is just as natural to people as that activity we refer to as "play."

People will work effectively toward achieving organizational objectives if they are rewarded in some manner for doing so.

Likewise, if people are rewarded, they will accept responsibility for assigned work and the achievement of results.

Theory X and Theory Y lead to distinctly different patterns of managerial behavior. According to McGregor, a manager who holds Theory X to be essentially true will manage in a watchful, nontrusting, controlling style. A manager who embraces Theory Y will more empathetically manage in a creative style based on human interaction and careful attention to individual needs, including the need for recognition and other forms of reward.

For the purpose of examining management by goalz, we need a model for studying managerial behavior rather than subjective characteristics. Studying the elements of McGregor's two theories, we can identify three key categories of behavior which may be said to define the manager's individual style. They are:

**Use of autonomy.** The extent to which a manager permits and expects employees to operate under their own control in the work situation.

**Use of reward factors.** The nature and extent of the reward factors, both positive and negative (punishment), which the manager uses to influence employee behavior.

**Use of group process.** The extent to which the manager clarifies roles and responsibilities among employees, promotes teamwork, establishes and maintains communication networks, and permits group members to influence managerial thinking.

Each of these three behavioral dimensions can range from negative, destructive patterns, to positive, constructive patterns. A manager who grants employees little or no autonomy, punishes more frequently than rewards, and restricts communications to "one on one" (dealing separately with each employee and never allowing group interaction) would merit a "negative" rating for each of the above three elements.

On the other hand, a manager who grants so much autonomy and so little direction that employees seldom truly understand what is expected of them; who neither punishes nor rewards; and who merely reacts to problems as employees present them would also merit a negative rating based on the above three categories.

A manager who communicates objectives and delegates whole problems to employees capable of handling them; who establishes and maintains a work environment based on reward and recognition; and who capitalizes on group interaction to increase individual involvement and contribution to achievement of organizational objectives would merit a "positive" rating in each of the three categories, and is practicing management by goalz.

The management style of the organization's top manager, and to some extent the group of highest-level managers, will influence the style of all managers within the organization. Managers tend to manage as they are managed. This relationship between style and environment is an important key to making management by goalz work.

## Effectiveness in Delegation

A manager's primary job is to accomplish organizational goals through the efforts of others. To be most effective, managers must multiply their efforts by delegating responsibility and authority to those employees working with them. Delegation goes beyond the assignment of specific responsibilities to a subordinate. Delegation must be with regard for the employees' capabilities and must also provide whatever authority is required to fulfill the assigned responsibilities. Further, delegation entails holding the subordinate responsible for results and the wise use of that authority.

I have encountered the concept of "delegation with control," meaning delegation with limited scope, limited authority, and continual checking by the manager to ensure everything is going okay. The concept is contradictory in the sense that the control must precede the act of delegation in the form of sound judgment aimed at assessing the capabilities of whomever you plan to delegate to. When an employee is assigned a responsibility, the assigning manager must be reasonably confident the employee is capable. If you lack that confidence, you should delegate to an employee in whom you have the necessary confidence. If you don't have any employees in whom you have confidence, then I suggest you have a problem, probably of your own making.

Since you must get most work accomplished through the efforts of others, you will find both your effectiveness as a manager and your stature as a leader will increase if you understand and base your action on the following:[2]

- The best way to increase your effective authority is to delegate it. If you hoard it, you lose it.
- When delegating responsibility, be certain you delegate the necessary authority with it.
- The positive effects of delegation can be negated by after-the-fact efforts to control. If you give an employee responsibility and the required authority, you will destroy your right to hold that person accountable by unnecessarily interfering with the work.
- Delegate only when you have confidence that the employee is capable of properly handling the authority you have given.
- Delegating responsibility does not lessen your responsibility. It does provide an increased capacity for you to handle greater responsibility.
- Clearly define the responsibilities delegated to each subordinate. Communicate this information to the employees' peers.
- Once you have delegated, follow up to ensure the job is being properly done, but be careful not to "oversupervise."
- Delegate in a manner that avoids "dual supervision," an employee receiving instructions from and/or being held accountable to more than one manager.
- Avoid delegating only those responsibilities which you find personally unpleasant or distasteful.
- When you delegate authority to a subordinate, be sure to back the employee up should her or his authority be questioned.
- Let every subordinate know just what decisions she or he has authority to make. Emphasize decisions being made at the lowest-possible level in the organization.

Delegation is the foundation of effective organizations and the mark of managers wisely striving to multiply their efforts through the increased involvement and participation of others.

### Effectiveness in Providing Rewards

Building and maintaining a highly productive work group is dependent upon generating and maintaining a high level of motivation among employees. Much has been said and written about the value of monetary incentives in the work place. While such incentives can have definite value, more often than not they fail for one or more of the following reasons:

[2]J. Clifton Williams, *Dynamics of Motivation Management*, SMI International, Inc., Waco, Tex., 1969, pp. 141–142.

- Incentive programs are often poorly designed and include faulty measurements.
- Incentive programs are viewed by some managers as a viable substitute for supervision.
- The administration of incentive programs often generates the question of fairness.
- Provided incentives are generally less than the *minimum* 15 percent of total wages required to generate employee interest and impact performance in a positive manner.

In many, if not most, work situations, potential productivity improvement via a financial incentive program is offset by the skill and expertise required to design, implement, and administer such a program. Unless such expertise exists within the organization, it is prudent to shift managerial focus to more basic methods for motivating employees.

The most basic requirement is that employees be told, on a timely basis, when they have performed either very well or very poorly. A pat on the back from a respected manager goes a long way to boost self-esteem and increase employee awareness that the organization and its managers recognize and appreciate good performance. In repeated surveys of many organizations in which both the managers and employees have been asked to rank factors related to *employee* job satisfaction, "full appreciation for work done" usually is the highest-ranking factor among employees. Table 8-1 summarizes the results of such surveys.

The outcome of such surveys generally provides a remarkable mismatch between managers' perceptions and how employees actually feel. Managers—

**TABLE 8·1.** Ranking of Employee Job Satisfaction According to Employees and Managers

| Job Satisfaction Factors | Importance Ranking by Employees | Perceptions by Managers of How Employees Feel |
|---|---|---|
| Full appreciation of work | 1 | 8 |
| Feeling "in" on things | 2 | 10 |
| Sympathetic understanding of personal problems | 3 | 9 |
| Job security | 4 | 2 |
| Good wages | 5 | 1 |
| Interesting work | 6 | 5 |
| Promotion and growth | 7 | 3 |
| Management loyalty to employees | 8 | 6 |
| Good working conditions | 9 | 4 |
| Tactful disciplining | 10 | 7 |

SOURCE: Based on Karl Albrecht, *Successful Management by Objectives,* Prentice-Hall, Englewood Cliffs, N.J., 1978, pp. 60–61.

who, on one hand, consider "good wages" as being most important to employees in general and who, on the other hand, are constrained to giving periodic, general increases agreed upon by others—may be saying that they see themselves as not having much to offer in the way of satisfying their employees' needs. Employees at all levels of the organization come to work for a variety of reasons. Earning a paycheck, to satisfy other personal needs outside the organization, is an important reason around which the other reasons revolve. It is, however, becoming increasingly apparent that once the paycheck becomes routine, a person's work plays a much broader role in his or her life than just earning a paycheck. People want to have a place to go; they need to belong. They want to interact with others and to receive recognition and appreciation for putting forth their best efforts. It is generally accepted that people can satisfy these needs within their work environments. Organizations have all the possibilities for satisfying these needs within their structures and within the resources available to their managers. Managers are gradually beginning to grasp the significance of nonmonetary rewards in the work place. Because many of these rewards have no associated costs, there exists a great, and generally untapped, potential for the work environment to become more reward centered, thereby enhancing productivity.

Although they must be used judiciously, reprimand and discipline are equally important as effective motivators to be used within the organization for the purpose of maintaining, if not improving, productivity. When the need for their use is clearly indicated, they must be utilized, as is necessary, to protect the organization from a decline in productivity. In one sense of the word, authority has failed when the power behind it must be used. The respected and fully recognized power of a manager's authority enables him or her to function without using it. The manager who could have issued a direct order but makes a request and gives an explanation instead is building a reserve of goodwill and respect. If able to develop and train a subordinate who might have been fired due to substandard performance, the manager is using leadership in preference to power, and will, most likely, be respected for it. On the other hand, it must be noted that a manager who is viewed by subordinates as using persuasion and related approaches because of the lack, or fear of the lack, of the authority to use more forceful methods is not respected, and may even be disrespected for his or her actions. Any manager with a weak organizational power base will be viewed by subordinates as personally weak and not worthy of being followed. The unspoken logic seems to be that a manager worthy of power would have it; and a manager not worthy of backing by the organization is not worthy of support from subordinates. The ideal situation would be for each manager within the organization to have ample power and to use it sparingly. While the positive rewards of recognition and appreciation are preferred, it is Pollyanna thinking that dismisses the occasional need for managers to use negative rewards in the form of reprimand and discipline.

### Effectiveness in Using the Group Process

Participative management is based on the concept that no one person, or small group of persons, within the organization has all the best answers for all problems. The concept of the single thinker at the top, or brain trust—surrounded by a sea of nonthinking employees, only there to execute "orders from the top"—never had any basis in fact. In today's work place, employee resentment and hostility are sure to result where such an attitude is implied through the organization's policies or its managerial practices.

Participative management is often misconstrued as meaning a form of wishy-washy, sentimental democracy in which the manager asks the permission of subordinates before making decisions. Obviously, such a system has no use in a results-oriented business organization. The value of the "soft" and permissive approach is limited to voluntary associations where people work without monetary reward and for sometimes whimsical motives.

By definition, the manager is the leader of the work group. More accurately considered the "formal leader" of the group, the manager has been delegated certain authority and has been given certain privileges and assigned certain responsibilities by the organization. When some other person within the work group is looked to for leadership, that other person might be called an "informal leader." That person has no authority but because of an ability to help coworkers satisfy their personal needs, his or her power and influence may be great. An informal leader may be an outstanding worker with a sense of loyalty to the organization and good common sense or, alternatively, may be a troublemaker who seeks followers to satisfy a personal desire to work against the goals of the organization and thereby increase self-glory.

Just as there are formal and informal leaders, there are also formal and informal work groups. While formal work groups are defined by the organizational chart, informal work groups are formed because of common needs and desires of certain employees. Members of informal work groups choose to associate with people having common interests. During breaks or lunch periods, employees like to be with people who have similar interests, work, national background, or even common problems. The factors determining the structure of an informal work group may be highly complex, but there is always a common basis for the association. Some common needs of the members are satisfied by the association and all feel more secure and accepted as part of the group.

As long as the manager is an effective leader, both informal leaders and informal work groups can be highly constructive. Informal leaders and informal groups are neither good nor bad in themselves, but they are inevitable in any work environment. If the manager does the job well, they will be centers to promote high morale and increased job satisfaction. The key lies in the manager being able to channel potentially negative forces, and diverse interests, into a constructive work effort aimed at achieving goals which will be of benefit to all.

The means is to deal with employees in a way that generates loyalty, rather than hostility, toward the company. The objective must be to motivate in such a way that group pressure is applied to supporting, rather than subverting, the organization's policies and goals. When attitudes toward the organization are generally good, employees will do an effective job of internal control by making it an unpopular practice to waste time or materials or to turn out products of substandard quality.

The following specific managerial skills can form the basis for effective employee participation and maximum contribution toward achieving organizational goals.

**Sensitized observation.** Tuning in to the organization's interpersonal on-the-job relationships in a routine and attentive manner—detecting the apparent roles which individual employees seem to adopt toward one another; observing relationships between people and between groups in the work place; spotting adversary situations, misunderstandings, and counterproductive competition among both managers and employees.

**Listening.** Staying alert for new information and new ideas; listening attentively to what employees and other managers say; demonstrating respect for the capabilities and potential contributions of others by soliciting their ideas and inputs; using techniques such as questioning and feedback while maintaining empathy.

**Encouraging communications.** Initiating and maintaining action aimed at encouraging communications and keeping communication channels open—encouraging employees to express their ideas and opinions by maintaining an operating climate conducive to frank and open communications without fear of embarrassment, retaliation, or disapproval; using statements such as "What do you think?" "Do you have any questions?" and "Do you have any suggestions?" to get employees to open up and express their feelings; teaching effective communication techniques to employees and openly praising effective communications behavior.

**Providing "strokes."** Providing recognition and acceptance messages to employees as individuals—simple but important acts like learning the names of all employees, saying "hello" or "good morning" when you see them, and stopping to chat briefly with the employee on topics you know she or he is interested in.

**Generating enthusiasm.** Consistently demonstrating a positive attitude toward the organization and its employees—saying things to employees, and backing them up with action, which demonstrate support for company policies and goals and confidence in employees as individuals and as a group, and pro-

viding public praise and recognition for jobs well done while not being so pro-
fuse or so frequent that the effect of such compliments is cheapened.

**Developing teamwork.** Stressing cooperation and common interest among
employees in the work situation—developing a common feeling that all
employees are important as individuals but most effective when working
together to achieve common goals; providing praise and recognition to each
member of the work group when group goals are accomplished; and striving to
generate an esprit de corps or common sense of pride and capability among all
employees.

## The Key Success Factor

Successful implementation of the management by goalz philosophy is dependent upon many factors. Of all the critical success factors, one stands out as key
or most fundamental. Employee commitment is the heart of successful management by goalz. The attitude of employees in general toward the organization
as an abstract entity, toward their managers, toward the work itself, and toward
the social and physical environments in which they work exerts the single most
important influence on achievement. Without employee commitment, the best-
designed and most appropriate plans and programs will never get off the
ground. With employee commitment, marginal plans and programs can produce outstanding results.

Employee commitment cannot be assumed or taken for granted. Instead of
creating the foundation of employee commitment before initiating a manage-
ment-by-objective (MBO) program, many organizations have overlooked the
matter entirely. Not surprisingly, many MBO failures can be directly attributed
to such oversight. When employee morale and acceptance of the changes
implemented by management are viewed as relatively unimportant issues, any
MBO-related effort is doomed to failure. Managers must be capable of perceiving the organization as a human system. When a number of individuals identify
themselves as members of a common organization, they immediately begin to
build social networks. Such networks facilitate the business of living and working together. While they take direction from their designated managers, they
derive rules of behavior from the larger context of their social system.

Employees and people, in general, will behave in only those ways which are
believed will either bring them things they want or help avoid things they do
not want. If employees fail to perceive a particular type of activity within the
work place as being associated with something they want, then they will, at
best, reluctantly engage in it. The only way managers can solicit commitment
from their employees is by providing situations in which employees can get the

things they want in exchange for the desired behavior. This basic fact lies at the heart of success in managing by goalz.

## The Goal-Oriented Manager

Goal-oriented managers think and act differently than do their counterparts, the reactive managers. While the reactive managers see themselves as coping with a hostile and threatening environment, the goal-oriented managers see themselves as capitalizing on opportunities provided by the environment. Whereas the reactive mode is a defensive one, the goal-oriented mode is an offensive one. Being goal oriented means being end result or payoff oriented. It means identifying worthwhile payoffs and generating a plan of action to achieve them. It means adopting the big-picture perspective, thus providing meaningful structure to day-to-day activities. Goal orientation is more than an attitude. It is a specific pattern of behavior. The following characterizes the goal-oriented manager's behavior pattern.

**A questioning attitude.** The goal-oriented manager frequently asks questions related to the purpose of various activities, including her or his own. Such inquiries are never made in an antagonizing way, and more often than not, leave the recipient asking, "Why didn't I think of that?" This questioning but constructive attitude conditions subordinates to also think in terms of payoffs. Recognizing that valuable resources can be dissipated on activities, rather than focused on payoffs, the goal-oriented manager takes the initiative to poke, to pry, and to ask questions.

**Communicating in terms of payoffs.** In discussing problems with employees and other managers, the goal-oriented manager attempts to identify the payoffs they desire before proposing actions to provide those payoffs. If a committee or problem-solving group is believed to be straying from its objectives, the goal-oriented manager politely reminds the members of the payoff they must focus on achieving. When considering the allocation of the organization's resources, the goal-oriented manager relates resources to payoffs and attempts to maximize the cost-effectiveness of his or her proposals. Only after communicating the value of the proposed objectives, does the goal-oriented manager solicit support for the proposed actions.

**Sensitivity to payoffs for others.** The goal-oriented manager focuses on accomplishments, not failures, and searches to find accomplishments which deserve recognition and a pat on the back. In convincing others to support a course of action he or she has proposed, the goal-oriented manager attempts to understand the other persons' position by thinking, "What is in this for them? Why should they support my proposal?" and tries to help others find personal value in the proposal and to realize that his or her success will also be their success. The goal-oriented manager recognizes that new ideas are oftentimes fragile and need further development and, for that reason, resists harshly pre-judging the ideas of others, no matter how half-baked they may be. It is far better to prolong evaluation, searching for possible related payoffs.

**The right to be wrong.** The goal-oriented manager recognizes her or his own fallibility, realizing that the only person who never makes mistakes is the person who never does anything and that every person makes bad judgments from time to time. While some managers are more than willing to constantly make snap judgments for the purpose of projecting a "dynamic" image, the goal-oriented manager feels unpressured to make on-the-spot decisions when they do not have to be made. Though possessing faith in her or his own judgment, the goal-oriented manager will solicit the inputs of others that might be of value. The goal-oriented manager reserves the right to change her or his mind, and will do so gracefully when it is warranted; and reserves the right to be wrong and, if wrong, gracefully acknowledges the mistake.

**Maintains an open mind.** The goal-oriented manager recognizes that not all good ideas come from managers and, consequently, respects the ideas and suggestions of others and evaluates them in terms of potential payoffs. By actions, as well as words, the goal-oriented manager maintains an open mind and is receptive to all payoff-related ideas, no matter what the source.

## Summary

The system of management by objectives has often failed because, as a system, it focuses on "things." In contrast, management by goalz focuses on people and the work environment and is based upon the belief that employees, in general, are capable and stand prepared to contribute to the achievement of organizational goals. The responsibility for realizing the contribution potential of employees rests squarely on management. Common behavior traits of successful managers include providing the employees some degree of autonomy to operate on their own within the work environment; the use of rewards, more positive than negative; and the use of the group process to build teamwork and a sense of commitment to the organization's goals. Effectiveness in all three of these areas can be improved by following certain guidelines. Successful implementation of the management-by-goalz philosophy is dependent on many factors, the most important of which is employee commitment. If the organization's productivity potential is to be realized, employees must be committed to achieving the organization's goals. People, in all situations including the work place, will exhibit behavior appropriate to fulfilling their personal needs. Managers must recognize that employees need to derive some personal benefit in exchange for their contribution to the achievement of organizational goals. Should they see nothing in it for them, they will, at best, be reluctant to maximize their contribution.

Goal-oriented managers think and act differently than their counterparts, the reactive managers. Goal-oriented managers tend to be more self-assured. They focus on payoffs, rather than activities. They are able to maintain the big picture and derive satisfaction from day-to-day activities because they understand their relationship to payoffs. They recognize they do not have all the good ideas and maintain an open mind to the ideas and suggestions of others. Management by goalz recognizes the work place as a human system. Accordingly, its philosophy focuses on the human element and the creation of a reward-centered work environment.

# 9 Goal Setting

Setting goals, both personal and organizational, is as practical and as sensible as deciding how and where you are going before you take a trip. If you are personally embarking upon a journey you have made several times previously, you may choose to rely on habit, assuming the previous journeys went reasonably well. Unfortunately, habit, regardless of previous successes, cannot be effectively employed in organizational goal setting. In most cases, the organization is choosing to go somewhere where it has never been before—an unprecedented level of productivity, quality, and/or profitability. Even when striving to duplicate a previous level of success, the emphasis is on achieving and at least maintaining that higher level, which must be contrary to previous experience (or else you would now be there and wouldn't need to improve to again reach it). The process of setting goals is, in effect, preparing to go someplace in particular. Success has been defined as the progressive realization of personal, worthwhile goals.

## The Benefits of Setting Goals

The better the managers can visualize how goal setting works, the more likely they are to take it seriously and make it serve them. Following are some benefits both the managers and the organization can expect to derive from a goal-setting program.

• Organizational goal setting requires that managers define specifically what the organization would like to accomplish. It is not unusual that managers misunderstand specifically what the organization is trying to achieve and how

157

their work group can best contribute to the overall effort. Goal setting tends to broaden managers' perspectives and reduces tunnel vision. Managers can strive so hard to succeed in one area that they tend to undercut their own success. For example, the manager who focuses on production at the exclusion of meeting minimal quality standards thereby damages chances for long-range success.

- Goals serve as criteria to sharpen managerial decision making. One feature of a successful organizational goals program is that in establishing priorities, it enables managers to decide quickly and accurately which of two conflicting courses of action to take.
- Goals accompanied by specific plans for their achievement tend to build managerial confidence. Not only do goals build managerial confidence, but others, who lack direction, sense the difference, and the goal-directed manager tends to automatically assume a leadership role.
- Goals provide a sense of order and purpose capable of generating and sustaining a high level of interest and motivation over long periods of time. By factoring out the trivial, management's attention is focused on what really matters and is less likely to be dissipated on irrelevant activities. Goals mutually agreed upon by a boss and a subordinate define expectations clearly and channel the subordinate's efforts toward striving to accomplish them. As there is no misunderstanding as to what is expected, a higher degree of motivation and persistence results.
- As managers become goal-directed, their sense of personal respect and self-worth increases. Even high achievers often fail to reap the psychological rewards of achievement because they are sometimes unsure of the "worthwhile" nature of their accomplishments. Because success, by definition, is the progressive realization of worthwhile goals, managers who routinely practice goal setting tend more to derive psychological benefits from their achievements.

Organizational goal setting, more than any other managerial tool, can, when properly implemented, fuse together all human resources for the achievement of unprecedented levels of productivity, quality, and profitability.

## The Criteria for Setting Goals

One well-accepted criterion for a goal is that it should describe specific, desired end results. Robert F. Mager was the first to use the term *fuzzy* to describe a "goal" that is less than specific. Karl Albrecht later incorporated the term in his discussion on objectives.[1] Albrecht defines an *objective* as any desired end result,

[1] For this development of the use of "fuzzies," see Robert F. Mager, *Goal Analysis*, Fearon, Belmont, Calif., 1972; and Karl Albrecht, *Successful Management by Objectives*, Prentice-Hall, Englewood Cliffs, N.J., pp. 73–76.

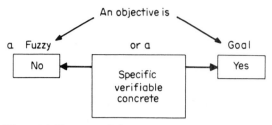

Figure 9-1. The range of objectives.

no matter how vaguely or specifically it may be stated. Using the term in this fashion opens the definition to include everything from a generally stated want to a very specifically stated performance target. Within that broad spectrum, we have fuzzies in the less-than-specific category and goals in the specific category (see Figure 9-1).

Fuzzies are preliminary statements of objectives. Many important changes are the direct result of a vague statement, such as "We need some kind of program to improve quality" or "Let's do something to reduce our order-processing time." While such statements do not direct action, they do serve the useful purpose of channeling thinking in a certain direction. They serve as a starting point for thought processes. In this sense, fuzzies can be thought of as a useful communication tool and a contributor to thinking in terms of what "could be" rather than what "is."

Goals require a much more specific statement than do fuzzies. The criteria for goals are as follows:

**Mutually agreed upon.** To be most effective in an organizational setting, goals must be mutually agreed upon, if not mutually set by boss and subordinate. Ideally, the goal would be set by the subordinate with the boss providing after-the-fact approval. Generally, such is not the case, at least in the early stages of implementing goal setting within the organization. Managers tend either to migrate to the comfortable by establishing goals which aren't sufficiently challenging or to go beyond realism in an effort to favorably impress their boss with false bravado. In either event, the boss must intervene to play a more active role in the goal-setting process.

**Realistic.** Goals must be realistic; that is, difficult but achievable. A common mistake in this regard is managers setting goals in terms of absolute "should bes" rather than in terms of "improvement"—going from where they are to where they should be in a quantum leap. The motivational factor of goal achievement plays an important part in any goals program. It is both frustrating and demoralizing to always fall short and to never achieve a goal. For that reason, near-term operational goals must be achievable if manager and employees put forth a reasonable amount of effort. As goal setting is the process of continually striving for improvement, goals—when accomplished—can be replaced by new, more ambitious goals. This is not to suggest that performance can improve ad infinitum without significant changes in conditions—methods and equipment—but rather that shorter-term goals, the achievement of which is more realistic, can serve as the springboard to achieving, in time, more ambitious goals.

**Specific.** Goals must state, in specific terms and with a specific timetable for accomplishment, what you plan to achieve. "To improve quality" is not a goal statement. Goal statements focus on desired end results and identify specific qualitative and/or quantitative conditions which ensure there will be no question as to whether or not they have been achieved. "To reduce customer complaints within a period of six months from the present rate of 2 percent of items sold to a rate of 1.5 percent of items sold" is a valid goal statement. The incorporation of target dates in goal statements tends to generate a sense of managerial urgency, which might not otherwise exist. Until you are ready to say *when* you are going to achieve a goal, you probably have not decided *that* you are going to achieve it.

**Comprehensive.** Goals must cover every area of the organization's activities where achievement or improvement is important. Goal setting in some organizations has included only manufacturing or order-processing activities and perhaps selling activities. Even then, sometimes goals relate only to quantities of output and do not include such important factors as cost, service, quality, and contribution to profit. Goals can be generated for all important elements of all activities within the organization, both line and staff. In so doing, and assuming coordination of goals between departments, departmental barriers are removed and effectiveness increases.

**Worthwhile.** Organizational goals must be worthwhile in the sense that they are compatible with, and contribute toward, fulfillment of the organization's primary purpose or reason for existence. Goals that are either incompatible with the organization's primary purpose or make no contribution toward fulfilling that purpose are not only meaningless but also disruptive and wasteful. Furthermore, the person or group of persons, who will work toward the achievement of any organizational goal, must deem that goal worthwhile in the sense that its achievement is perceived as having the potential for individual reward. The individual must believe that some desired reward (i.e., recognition, a personal sense of accomplishment, or a material reward) will automatically be forthcoming when the goal is achieved.

**Written.** Writing crystallizes thought and thought motivates action. When goals are written, they generate dedication to their achievement. You tend to put yourself on the hook to make certain they will be accomplished. Written goals help you keep track of exactly what it is you want to achieve, as well as provide a standard against which progress can be readily measured. Written goals help managers overcome distractions in the work situation that are constantly bombarding them from every direction. They provide a checkpoint enabling you to reorient your efforts, should you be sidetracked or moved off your intended course.

The closer organizational goals meet the above criteria, the greater will be their value in achieving the desired end results.

## Focus on Key End Result Areas

When setting organizational goals, it is essential to focus all available resources on a few key end result areas. By selecting a handful of really important areas on which to concentrate managerial action and attention, you can both simplify the mission and improve the results. This is not to suggest that other possible areas of payoff will be ignored, but that priority must be assigned to certain high-potential areas. Such concentration of attention requires a surprising level of discipline for most managers. This holds true, despite general acceptance of Pareto's 80-20 rule—80 percent of the possible payoffs exist within 20 percent of the problems and opportunities—and Dickie's ABC analysis which focuses attention on the high-cost items in inventory.[2]

Key end result areas on which goal setting related to productivity improvement efforts should focus are:

Sales
Effectiveness
Quality
Efficiency
Service
Financial return

End results in each of these areas are of key interest to the typical industrial organization. Another kind of organization may define different key areas. Having a simple diagram, such as Figure 9-2, displayed in a prominent location can constantly remind managers and employees of what is deemed most important.

Within each of the key end result areas are a number of specific payoffs or elements that are measurable. These elements provide ideal subjects on which goal-setting efforts can be focused. Some of the payoffs could just as easily be listed as an element of one key area as of another. For example, the payoff of "return on assets" could just as appropriately be listed in the key area of efficiency. Such technicalities are unimportant. What is important is that goals be focused on payoffs within key end result areas.

[2]H. Ford Dickey, "Hard Nosed Inventory Management," in Donald G. Hall, Ed., *The Manufacturing Man and His Job,* America Management Association, New York, 1966, pp. 238–254.

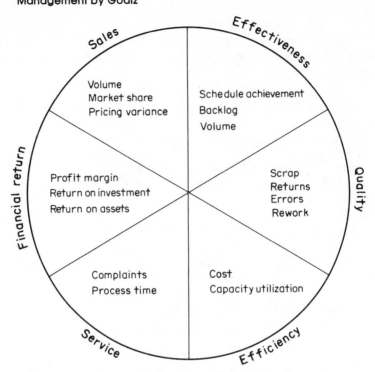

**Figure 9-2.** Sample of an office sign which highlights the key end result areas for managers and employees.

## The Process of Goal Setting and Achieving

The process of goal setting and achieving is a series of specific steps designed to assist you in everything from pinpointing productivity problems and opportunities for improvement through realizing that improvement. Figure 9-3 shows the steps of this important process. Further detail is provided as follows for the purpose of enhancing your understanding of this process.

**Step 1 Identifying opportunities for productivity improvement.** Productivity improvement begins with a systematic review of current problem conditions, coupled with a deliberate effort to perceive productivity-improving possibilities beyond the current problems. While problem situations are more readily identified because you have lived with and suffered from them, other situations that are characterized by "underachievement of potential" often offer equal, if not greater, opportunities for improving productivity. Whereas problems tend to be recognized, if not well defined, possibilities generally require more digging to identify. A good starting point for such digging is to look at areas that are labor intensive and areas wherein the majority of costs are concentrated. This initial step is critical in the sense that it defines both the potential scope and benefits of your productivity improvement efforts.

**Step 2 Quantifying long-term productivity potentials.** Problems and possibilities are both characterized by unfavorable variances between what cur-

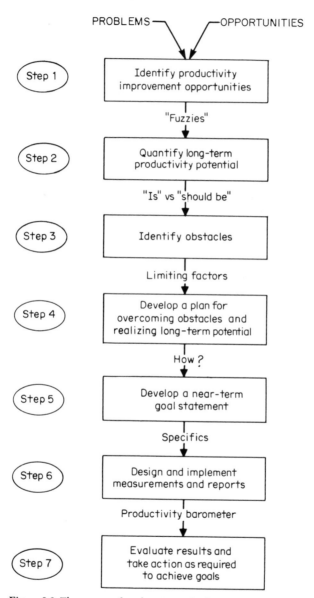

PROBLEMS ─┐            ┌─OPPORTUNITIES

Step 1 — Identify productivity improvement opportunities

"Fuzzies"

Step 2 — Quantify long-term productivity potential

"Is" vs "should be"

Step 3 — Identify obstacles

Limiting factors

Step 4 — Develop a plan for overcoming obstacles and realizing long-term potential

How ?

Step 5 — Develop a near-term goal statement

Specifics

Step 6 — Design and implement measurements and reports

Productivity barometer

Step 7 — Evaluate results and take action as required to achieve goals

**Figure 9-3.** The process of goal setting and achieving.

rently "is" and what ideally "should be." This second step of the process focuses on quantifying what should be in the sense of long-term, ultimate potential; ultimate, as used here, meaning constrained only by existing technology and long term generally defined as possible within a year or longer. It is intended to open minds as to what is *possible*, within a year, using available technology, rather than what might be considered "reasonable." It is also intended to extend the "reach" or increase near-term aspirations in Step 5.

To quantify both what is and what should be requires that a suitable productivity measure be designed and applied: to the current situation based on actual inputs and outputs and to the long-term, ultimate potential based on projected ideal inputs and outputs. This selected measurement, or productivity ratio, is deliberately reevaluated in Step 6 for the purpose of ensuring its validity.

**Step 3 Identifying obstacles.** This step consists of defining and deciding the priorities of all those factors recognized as having actually limited past productivity achievement and those factors that have a reasonably high probability of limiting future productivity achievement; both sets of factors should be related to a specific "opportunity activity." Obstacles, as used here, are anything that has, is, or could probably in the future block or limit the achievement of your goals. Obstacles can come in many forms, including equipment capability, process capability, quality of materials, availability of required resources, and resistance to change, just to mention a few. This step should result in an objective listing, in order of importance, of specific reasons for past underachievement, as well as those factors that could thwart future efforts.

**Step 4 Developing a plan to overcome both actual and anticipated obstacles, enabling you to reach the long-term productivity potential.** The premise on which this step is based is that changes in conditions are a prerequisite to achieving improved results, the specific "conditions" in this case being the previously defined obstacles. While plans, in the form of specific, intended actions to be taken for the purpose of overcoming obstacles, are important, the generation of a managerial attitude characterized by persistence is at least equally important. One of the greatest mistakes made related to overcoming obstacles is relying too heavily upon a single course of action. Realistically, the willingness to persist and to continue to develop and implement different courses of action when others have failed is of prime importance to overcoming obstacles. Both the obstacles and the plans to overcome them must be committed to writing. As many alternate courses of action as possible should be developed and listed in order of priority or anticipated effectiveness.

Occasionally, no near-term viable plans can be developed to overcome certain obstacles. In that event, the goal should be adjusted accordingly with some means established to force continued search for a solution. Every problem has a solution, but some solutions take longer to develop than others. Again, the key is persistence.

**Step 5  Developing a near-term goal statement.** Only after having completed steps 1 through 4 are you ready to develop your near-term goal statement. You are, after examining opportunities, quantifying potentials, defining obstacles, and developing plans for overcoming those obstacles, now ready to develop a near-term goal statement. The goal should be relevant to the organization's purpose and compatible with other goals. It must relate to a specific level of desired end results, which are measurable, and incorporate a time limit for achievement. The manager responsible for achievement should set the goal—or if not the one who actually sets the goal, the manager should at least agree to it as being reasonable and worthwhile. The resulting statement should be shared with top management and coordinated with other groups. Accountability for the achievement of the goal must be fully understood and agreed upon.

**Step 6  Designing and implementing measurements and reports.** In Step 2 of this seven-step process, you have defined productivity measurements related to identified opportunities for improvement. Subsequent steps of the overall goal-setting process have placed you in an improved position to reevaluate the validity of those measurements at this point. Regardless of whether or not changes in these measurements are made, the result will be increased confidence in whatever measurements you now decide upon.

Periodic reports that accurately communicate actual productivity performance as compared to goals on a timely basis are critical to achieving productivity improvement. The format for such reports should contribute to economical and timely preparation, as well as the ease with which operating performance can be readily assimilated.

**Step 7  Evaluating results and taking managerial action as is required to achieve productivity goals.** The seven-step process of goal setting and achieving comes down to this, the last and most important step—achieving results in the form of improved productivity. The results of the productivity effort are evaluated to determine the degree to which goals are being achieved and to ensure that productivity-improving managerial processes are in place and operating. Results of this evaluation determine what additional action, if any, must be taken. Accumulated data enables trends to be recognized and also serves as the basis for future planning and goal setting. It also provides the basis for objective performance appraisal.

The seven-step process of goal setting and achieving provides a framework within which you can develop your own productivity improvement program. As previously mentioned, the process is secondary to the more important work environment resulting from the philosophy of management by goalz. A genuine concern for fulfilling employee needs in the work place, including generation of a reward-centered work environment, coupled with the above process of goal setting and achieving will have a positive impact on productivity within any organization.

## Success Essentials for Goal Achievement

Successful managers, and successful people in general, exhibit a common set of qualities. While they may not be consciously aware that they conform to the common pattern, such appears to be the case. For you, as a manager, to achieve more than the average, or to realize improvement over previous performance, you must find a means to utilize more of your managerial potential than you are now using. Acquiring the following success essentials, as a managerial habit, will enhance your ability to achieve organizational goals.

**You must crystallize your thinking into goals.** If you are not satisfied with the work-related progress you are making and are aware that you should be doing better, the seeds of healthy discontent have been sown in your mind. Comparing where the organization now stands, with regard to some activity for which you are responsible, to where it should be enables you to pinpoint specific, desirable payoffs. Once those desirable payoffs have been transformed into written goals, with the roadblocks or obstacles to the achievement of those goals recognized and also committed to writing, you are ready for the second success essential.

**You must have a written plan for the achievement of goals.** When both goals and obstacles to their achievement have been committed to writing, the process of searching for solutions to those obstacles is the first step toward developing a plan for goal achievement. The plan transforms your goals from the realm of thought and conjecture into practical know-how and action. A deadline for goal achievement should be an integral part of your plan. Both the plan and the deadline must be committed to writing and in that way will better serve as a road map for achieving your goals. Referring to that road map keeps you on the proper course even when forces in the work place are acting to distract you. The written plan and deadline may be revised if required by changing circumstances.

**You must develop a strong desire to achieve your goals.** The single ingredient that often makes the difference between accomplishment and failure is desire. Without an intense desire, your organizational goals are not destined to be realized. The intensity of your desire is related to the personal benefits you anticipate deriving from the achievement of the organization's goals. Like other employees, managers must be able to personally relate to the organization's goals before a strong commitment can be made to contribute toward their achievement. As managers tend to have high achievement and self-esteem needs, the personal benefits derived can be internal and intangible in nature. Though a manager doesn't think in terms of such satisfaction consciously, the benefit remains. Perhaps more tangible personal benefits can be associated with achievement of organizational goals. In any event, anticipated rewards intensify desire, and desire contributes greatly to the achievement of organizational goals.

**You must develop confidence in yourself and your abilities.** Hard work alone will not bring success. It must be accompanied by creative thinking and a firm belief in your ability to execute your ideas and achieve your goals. As strange as it may sound, managers usually get what they expect. If you expect to achieve your goals, you have an invisible friend, in the form of self-confidence, that is working day and night to ensure your success. Pragmatic managers do not wait for time and circumstances to come along and transform their goals into reality. They work progressively toward them, and most important, they have confidence in themselves and their abilities.

**You must exhibit persistence.** As Murphy's law, which states, "Whatever can go wrong, will go wrong," impacts their best-laid plans, some managers become frustrated and simply give up. Exhibiting persistence does not mean the same as being dogmatic or having a blind devotion to the organization's goals. Persistence or determination is the result of knowing *why* you are pursuing organizational goals and of having a deep personal commitment to those goals. By demonstrating persistence or determination, you can more than compensate for whatever shortcomings you may have or problems you may encounter. Grover Cleveland said it best:

Nothing in the world can take the place of persistence. Talent will not; nothing is more common than unsuccessful men with talent. Genius will not; unrewarded genius is almost a proverb. Education will not; the world is full of educated derelicts. Persistence and determination alone are omnipotent.

The above-mentioned success essentials are common to every achiever. While some are undoubtedly now a part of your managerial personality, others may not be. As you develop all these essentials into constructive habits, you will progressively improve your ability to achieve organizational objectives.

## Appraising Performance

Performance appraisal, at all levels of the organization, must be an integral part of any plan of action designed to improve productivity. While performance appraisal is a common activity in most organizations, it plays a more meaningful role in a work environment characterized by the philosophy of management by goalz. In such an environment, it is easier for such appraisals to be both more objective and more constructive. Whether consciously or subconsciously, regular day-to-day appraisals are being made in every manager's mind. The philosophy of management by goalz, coupled with the process of goal setting and achieving, provides the basis for the systematic and objective appraisal of each employee's work performance. Performance appraisals are most meaningful when there is a positive focus on goals and their accomplishment. Appraisal systems can, in fact, become motivators, rather than "threats," when they relate directly to goal achievement.

While goals and progress toward achieving those goals serve as the basis for appraising the performance of any individual, the approach to the appraisal process can be any one or combination of three possible approaches: the achievement approach, the progress approach, or the comparative approach. The *achievement approach* compares actual performance to the goal. The underlying philosophy is that "a miss is as good as a mile"; the goal is either achieved or it is not achieved. The *progress approach* focuses on improvement, or the progress made from where the employee started toward achievement of the goal. The *comparative approach* gauges relative performance as compared to others who perform the same or similar tasks. The approach you use will vary, depending upon the situation and the individual whose performance you are appraising. The goal-achieving employee must be given recognition for performance. Generally, providing lesser recognition to those who have not achieved their goals but who have made progress has a positive impact on individual motivation. The top-notch worker and the worker making top-notch progress should both be rewarded with recognition for their accomplishments.

Fear and anxiety are normal employee responses to the performance appraisal process—particularly (1) when such reviews are months apart with no interim performance feedback being provided by the employee's direct supervisor and (2) in the absence of an organizational goal-setting program that includes the employee being appraised. As incentive programs are not a substitute for supervision, neither are goal-setting programs nor periodic performance reports a substitute for frequent comments on performance from the employee's direct supervisor. Objective verbal feedback relating to performance is very important to both improving productivity and minimizing security stress. Even when that feedback communicates awareness of substandard performance on the part of the employee, it serves a useful purpose. First, it reinforces expectations; second, it places all the cards on the table. The greatest single threat to employees is to be ignored by their supervisor. The supervisor's unspoken thoughts and hidden feelings—the unknown—generate more security stress than does unfavorable verbal feedback. High-performance organizations are characterized by managers who provide constant verbal feedback relating to performance, based on mutually agreed upon goals, to their subordinates.

The performance appraisal process should be viewed as a means for counseling employees and motivating them toward improvement. Ideally, the appraisal climate will be not only supportive of employees but also one in which the employee actively participates in the process. Unfortunately, most appraisals can be likened to the employee going before the "judge" and a "verdict" being handed down. Providing recognition and encouragement, as well as actively soliciting the employee's participation aimed at developing a plan to improve performance, should be part of the performance appraisal process.

# Summary

The process of setting goals provides direction to the efforts of all the organization's members. Goal setting takes us from vague generalities, or nonspecific wants, which may or may not contribute to the organization's central purpose, to the pursuit of specifics, which are in line with the organization's purpose. Organizational goal setting is an invaluable tool that, when properly implemented, directs diverse activities and employees toward a common purpose. Goals provide a sense of order and purpose capable of generating and maintaining a high level of interest and motivation over long periods of time. As managers and employees become goal-directed, their self-worth tends to increase.

To be effective, goals must meet certain criteria. They must be mutually agreed upon between the manager and subordinate; realistic in the sense their achievement is difficult but attainable; specific in that expectations are quantified and a deadline for their accomplishment is set; comprehensive in that they are applied to all areas of activity within the organization; worthwhile in the sense that they contribute to the organization's reason for existence; written; and focused on payoffs rather than activities.

The process of goal setting and achieving starts with the identification of productivity problems and opportunities for improvement. The productivity as it "is" is then compared to what it "should be," or the long-range potential of the present process. Obstacles or roadblocks to the achievement of that long-range potential are recognized, and a plan is developed to overcome them. A near-term goal is set, and measurements to track progress toward achievement are designed and implemented. Reports to communicate progress are designed and implemented with managerial action being taken, as required, to keep all efforts on track toward achieving the goal.

There are five managerial success essentials related to achieving organizational goals: (1) You must crystallize your random thoughts and wants into specific goals. (2) You must then develop a written plan for their achievement. (3) By relating organizational goals to personal goals, you must develop a strong desire for goal achievement. (4) You must develop confidence in yourself and in your abilities. (5) You must exhibit persistence as you strive to reach your goals.

Performance feedback in the form of individual appraisals is an integral part of the program to improve productivity. The goal-setting process provides everything required to objectively evaluate individual contribution to the achievement of organizational goals on a timely basis.

# 10 Including All Activities

The philosophy of management by goalz and the process of goal setting and achieving can and should be applied to all areas of activity within the organization. It is not uncommon within organizations that the goal-setting effort be confined to manufacturing and related activities. Whether the result of oversight or of managers who do not know how to apply the effort to other areas, the result is the same: opportunities for productivity improvement are ignored. As the makeup of our work force shifts at an increasing pace from blue-collar to white-collar employees, the productivity of the white-collar work force becomes increasingly important to the organization's success. The following is intended to broaden your managerial scope and to improve your understanding of how to apply the goal-setting process to all activities.

## Responsibilities, Indicators, and Objectives

To provide a base, on which the process of goal setting and achieving can be applied, it is helpful to think in terms of responsibilities, indicators, and objectives.

**Responsibilities.** Define the scope of employee accountability. Focus is upon pinpointing those duties, tasks, and activities for which the employee is responsible.

**Indicators.** Signal progress toward the achievement of objectives. Productivity measurements are indicators that communicate such progress.

**Objectives (or goals).** Are mutually agreed upon payoffs which contribute to the accomplishment of the organization's stated purpose. Objectives must be

170

both measurable and specific to generate the motivation required for achievement.

Before getting into the area of objectives or specific payoffs, it is essential that the manager and subordinate have a mutual understanding as to exactly what the subordinate's responsibilities are. Even in organizations having job descriptions, there is often some degree of misunderstanding between manager and subordinate in this regard. This step provides the opportunity to correct any such misunderstanding, should it exist. Focusing on the key end result areas of effectiveness, quality, efficiency, service, financial return, and sales can be helpful in generating a related listing of individual responsibilities. A single meeting between manager and subordinate can usually resolve the question of responsibilities—providing that a few days prior to that meeting, the manager requests from the subordinate a written list of responsibilities as the employee sees them. The following meeting can serve as the opportunity to discuss, if necessary, revise, and agree upon the set of responsibilities for that employee. Ideally, the process of defining and agreeing upon individual responsibilities would start at the top and work down through the organization—the top manager working with immediate subordinates, they in turn working with their immediate subordinates, and so forth.

Indicators, or productivity measurements, have been discussed in detail in previous chapters. The key points to remember are that those measurements are ratios of output to input and that to be effective, those measurements must be:

1. *Valid:* Accurately reflect changes in productivity.
2. *Complete:* Take into consideration all components of both inputs and outputs.
3. *Comparable:* Enable accurate measuring between periods.
4. *Inclusive:* Take into account and measure all activities.
5. *Timely:* Minimize the time delay between measuring and reporting.
6. *Cost-effective:* The value of the measurements exceeds the cost of their taking and reporting.

Measurable goals or objectives are required to focus all resources upon specific payoffs, the realization of which will contribute to the achievement of overall organizational goals.

## Eleven Examples of Goal Setting and Achievement

The following examples illustrate how the process of goal setting and achieving can be applied to all areas of the organization for the purpose of improving productivity:

## Example Number One

**Position.** Salesperson

**Responsibility.** To sell products in a manner which contributes to the profitability of the organization.

**Productivity improvement opportunity.** Increase sales at a rate higher than the corresponding rate of increase for selling related expenses.

**Long-term potential**

$$Productivity\ indicator\ =\ \frac{net\ sales\ volume\ generated}{total\ selling\ expenses}$$

$$Base\ period\ =\ ``is"\ =\ \frac{\$870,000}{\$45,000}$$

$$=\ \$19.33\ net\ sales\ generated\ per\ dollar\ of\ selling\ expense$$

$$Long\text{-}term\ potential\ =\ ``should\ be"\ =\ 15\%\ improvement$$
$$=\ \$19.33\ \times\ 1.15\ =\ \$22.23$$

### Obstacles

1. Competition.
   a. Is increasing; more competitors now than before.
   b. Competitors prices are generally lower.
2. Costs are increasing.
   a. Entertainment expenses are up due to increased competition.
   b. Advertising costs are increasing at a rate of 20% annually.

### Plan

1. Eliminate advertising expenses—a study shows marginal benefit, at best.
2. Evaluate and possibly revise client entertainment expenditures.
   a. Eliminate less popular expenditures.
   b. Better tailor expenditures to individual client.
      (1) Possibly increase theater, sporting, and other events that clients' families could attend.
      (2) Acknowledge clients' special interests.
3. Revise sales presentation to focus on quality and service rather than price.
4. Lay the groundwork for customers' acceptance of pricing which incorporates cost increases.

**Near-term goal.** To achieve a 21.5 to 1 average rate, net sales to selling expenses for this year.

**Evaluation and corrective action.** Productivity index is 1.4% off target; specific expenditures will be reviewed for the purpose of better controlling sales-related costs while striving for a greater volume of sales bookings.

Productivity Report Highlights

| Measure | Near-Term Goal | Actual | Productivity Index |
|---|---|---|---|
| Net sales | $1,000,000 | $950,000 | |
| Total selling expenses | $46,510 | $44,811 | |
| Productivity ratio | $21.5 | $21.2 | 98.6 |

## Example Number Two

**Position.** Design engineer

**Responsibilities.** To determine methods for improving, or at least maintaining, the reliability and user acceptance of product A while reducing the related manufacturing costs.

**Productivity improvement opportunity.** Reduce the weight of the product so as to reduce its cost while improving performance.

**Long-term potential**

$$Productivity\ indicator\ 1\ =\ \frac{weight\ reduction\ per\ unit}{starting\ weight\ per\ unit}$$

$$Base\ period\ =\ ``is"\ =\ \frac{0\ (no\ reduction\ as\ yet)}{800\ lb\ starting\ weight\ per\ unit}$$

$$Long\text{-}term\ potential\ =\ ``should\ be"\ =\ 10\%\ weight\ reduction$$

$$=\ \frac{800\ -\ (800\ \times\ 0.9)}{800}$$

$$=\ \frac{80\ lb\ per\ unit\ weight\ reduction}{800\ lb\ starting\ weight}$$

$$Productivity\ indicator\ 2\ =\ \frac{actual\ cost\ reduction\ per\ unit}{starting\ cost\ per\ unit}$$

$$Base\ period\ =\ ``is"\ =\ \frac{0\ (no\ reduction\ as\ yet)}{\$1600\ starting\ cost\ per\ unit}$$

$$Long\text{-}term\ potential\ =\ ``should\ be"\ =\ 10\%\ cost\ reduction$$

$$=\ \frac{1600\ -\ (1600\ \times\ 0.9)}{1600}$$

$$=\ \frac{\$160\ per\ unit\ cost\ reduction}{\$1600\ per\ unit\ starting\ cost}$$

$$Productivity\ indicator\ 3\ =\ \frac{miles\ per\ gallon\ (mpg)\ improvement}{starting\ mpg}$$

$$\text{Base period} = \text{``is''} = \frac{0 \text{ (no improvement as yet)}}{18.5 \text{ starting mpg}}$$

Long-term potential = "should be" = 15% mpg improvement

$$= \frac{18.5 \times 1.15}{18.5}$$

$$= \frac{2.775 \text{ mpg improvement}}{18.5 \text{ starting mpg}}$$

### Obstacles

1. Removal of metal could adversely affect structural strength of product.
2. Both material and labor inputs are increasing at an annual rate of 10%.
3. Government-mandated standards of air pollution adversely affect fuel efficiency.

### Plan

1. Replace metal components with engineered plastics; plastics are lighter, less expensive, and meet strength requirements.
2. Reduce the number of labor hours required to assemble the product via redesign of components and assemblies.

**Near-term goals.** To reduce the weight by 50 pounds per unit, the manufacturing cost by 5%, and to increase average miles driven per gallon of gasoline by 10%, all during the upcoming year.

### Productivity Report Highlights

| Measure | Near-Term Goal | Actual | Productivity Index |
|---|---|---|---|
| Weight reduction / Starting weight | 50 / 800 | 60 / 800 | |
| Productivity ratio | 0.0625 | 0.0750 | 120.0 |
| Cost reduction / Starting cost | $80 / $1600 | $78 / $1600 | |
| Productivity ratio | 0.050 | 0.04875 | 97.5 |
| mpg improvement / Starting mpg | 1.85 / 18.5 | 1.93 / 18.5 | |
| Productivity ratio | 0.10 | 0.1043 | 104.3 |

**Evaluation and corrective action.** Weight reduction productivity index exceeds goal by 20%; miles driven per gallon of gasoline productivity index exceeds goal by 4.3%; and manufacturing cost per unit productivity index is 2.5% above goal—focus will be on further redesigning the product in an effort to further reduce the amount of labor required for assembly.

## Example Number Three

**Position.** Purchasing agent

**Responsibilities.** To purchase materials and services to be provided when needed, and at the best possible cost, without compromising company standards.

**Productivity improvement opportunity.** Reduce the purchased materials and services expense rate while eliminating stockouts and reducing purchasing responsible scrap and warranty expenses.

**Long-term potential**

$$Productivity\ indicator\ 1\ =\ \frac{purchased\ materials\ and\ services}{net\ sales}$$

$$Base\ period\ =\ ``is"\ =\ \frac{\$1,800,000}{\$6,000,000}\ =\ 0.30\ expense\ rate$$

$$Long\text{-}term\ potential\ =\ ``should\ be"\ =\ \frac{\$2,200,000}{\$8,000,000}\ =\ 0.275\ expense\ rate$$

$$Productivity\ indicator\ 2\ =\ \frac{net\ sales}{number\ of\ stockouts}$$

$$Base\ period\ =\ ``is"\ =\ \frac{\$6,000,000}{60\ stockouts}\ =\ \frac{\$100,000\ sales}{stockout}$$

$$Long\text{-}term\ potential\ =\ ``should\ be"\ =\ \frac{\$8,000,000}{60}\ =\ \frac{\$133,333\ sales}{stockout}$$

$$Productivity\ indicator\ 3$$
$$=\ \frac{purchasing\ responsible\ scrap\ and\ warranty\ expenses}{net\ sales}$$

$$Base\ period\ =\ ``is"\ =\ \frac{\$40,000}{\$6,000,000}\ =\ 0.0067\ expense\ rate$$

$$Long\text{-}term\ potential\ =\ ``should\ be"\ =\ \frac{\$45,000}{\$8,000,000}$$
$$=\ 0.005625\ expense\ rate$$

### Obstacles

1. Prices of purchased materials are increasing at an average rate of 10% annually.
2. Vendor lead times are increasing; some materials are being allocated.
3. An increasing number of defective and short (less than the quantity invoiced) shipments are being received from vendors.

### Plan

1. Investigate the costs and resulting benefits of buying in larger quantities.
2. Develop alternate reliable suppliers.
3. Increase surveillance related to vendor lead times and consumption; improve inventory control procedures.
4. Increase receiving inspection activities and follow up to ensure all defective products are returned and credits are provided for both defective and "short-shipped" receipts.

**Near-term goals.** Based on $7,500,000 in annual net sales: to reduce the purchased materials and services expense rate to 29%; stockouts to 1 per $125,000 net sales; and the purchasing responsible scrap and warranty expense rate to 0.0061, all averages for the next year.

### Productivity Report Highlights

| Measure | Near-Term Goal | Actual | Productivity Index |
|---|---|---|---|
| Purchased materials and services | $2,175,000 | $2,250,000 | |
| Net sales | $7,500,000 | $7,610,000 | |
| Productivity ratio | 0.29 | 0.2957 | 102.0 |
| Net sales | $7,500,000 | $7,610,000 | |
| Number of stockouts | 60 | 70 | |
| Productivity ratio | $125,000 | $108,714 | 87.0 |
| Purchasing responsible scrap and warranty expense | 45,750 | 44,800 | |
| Net sales | 7,500,000 | 7,610,000 | |
| Productivity ratio | 0.0061 | 0.005887 | 96.5 |

**Evaluation and corrective action.** Purchased materials and services expense rate exceeds goal by 2%; stockouts exceeded goal by 13%; the only favorable variance was purchasing responsible scrap and warranty expense rate which was 3.5% below goal—efforts to focus on quantities purchased as a possible means of reducing costs and on marginally increasing safety stock in an attempt to offset increasing unreliable lead times; a new, more difficult goal related to scrap and warranty expense to be evaluated.

## Example Number Four

**Position.** Records storage and retrieval clerk

**Responsibility.** To establish and implement a system for storing, locating, and retrieving written records and documents.

**Productivity Improvement opportunity.** To reduce the per-document cost of storage and retrieval while improving the locator system so that the average time to retrieve any document is reduced.

**Long-term potential**

$$Productivity\ indicator\ 1 = \frac{\text{total storage and retrieval expenses}}{\text{total documents processed}}$$

$$Base\ period = \text{"is"} = \frac{\$17,500}{39,000\ \text{documents}}$$
$$= \$0.4487\ \text{per document processed}$$

Long-term potential = "should be" = 10% cost reduction
$$= 0.4487 \times 0.9 = \$0.4038$$

$$Productivity\ indicator\ 2 = \frac{\text{total elapsed-time request to retrieval}}{\text{total documents retrieved}}$$

$$Base\ period = \text{"is"} = \frac{67,000\ \text{min}}{5,200\ \text{retrievals}}$$

$$= 12.88\ \text{min average elapsed time}$$

Long-term potential = "should be" = 30% reduction elapsed time
$$= 12.88 \times 0.7 = 9.02\ \text{min}$$

**Obstacles**

1. Clerical wages are increasing at an annual rate of 10%.
2. Some persons retrieve and relocate their own records but sometimes fail to return them to the proper location.
3. The storage area is very congested, hindering both storage and retrieval efforts.

**Plan**

1. Limit access to the storage area to only authorized personnel.
2. Allocate a certain amount of time each week to verifying the location of all stored documents on a rotational basis—correct the location and/or the location file as is necessary.

3. Initiate a program to discard old documents after specified periods of time.
4. Install storage shelves from floor to ceiling to enable more documents to be stored in the available space.

**Near-term goals.** Based on 50,000 documents being processed annually, including 7500 retrievals, reduce per-unit processing cost to $0.42 and average elapsed time for retrieval to 10 minutes, all averages for the upcoming year.

### Productivity Report Highlights

| Measure | Near-Term Goal | Actual | Productivity Index |
|---|---|---|---|
| $\dfrac{\text{Total storage and retrieval expenses}}{\text{Total documents processed}}$ | $21,000 / 50,000 | $22,000 / 50,700 | |
| Productivity ratio | $0.42 | $0.433 | 103.3 |
| $\dfrac{\text{Total elapsed-time request to retrieval}}{\text{Total retrievals}}$ | 75,000 / 7500 | 78,000 / 8000 | |
| Productivity ratio | 10.0 min | 9.75 min | 97.5 |

**Evaluation and corrective action.** The processing cost per unit exceeds goal by 3.3%; the average time for retrieval is 2.5% better than the targeted elapsed time; a cost-benefit study will be made related to microfilming all stored documents—a new, more difficult goal related to retrieval time to be evaluated.

### Example Number Five

**Position.** Personnel director
**Responsibility.** To hire qualified candidates while controlling recruiting expenses.
**Productivity improvement opportunity.** To reduce the average cost associated with hiring new employees.
**Long-term potential**

$$Productivity\ indicator\ 1 = \frac{\text{total nonmanagerial recruiting costs}}{\text{number of nonmanagerial persons hired}}$$

$$\text{Base period} = \text{``is''} = \frac{\$24,650}{21\ \text{new hires}}$$
$$= \$1173.81 \text{ average recruiting cost per nonmanagerial hire}$$

$$\text{Long-term potential} = \text{``should be''} = 10\% \text{ cost reduction}$$
$$= \$1173.81 \times 0.9 = \$1056.43 \text{ average cost}$$

$$Productivity\ indicator\ 2 = \frac{\text{total managerial recruiting costs}}{\text{number of managers hired}}$$

$$\text{Base period} = \text{``is''} = \frac{\$48,900}{10 \text{ new hires}}$$

$$= \$4890 \text{ average recruiting cost per managerial hire}$$

$$\text{Long-term potential} = \text{``should be''} = 15\% \text{ cost reduction}$$

$$= \$4890 \times 0.85 = \$4156.50 \text{ average cost}$$

### Obstacles

1. Advertising costs are increasing.
2. Employment agencies and management recruiters are both raising their fees.

### Plan

1. Use state employment agency in lieu of private firms.
2. Seek referrals from present employees.
3. Have a company representative visit college placement services for referrals.
4. Reduce, if not eliminate, advertising.

**Near-term goals.** Based on an estimated 25 nonmanagerial and 15 managerial new hires in the upcoming year, to reduce average per-person recruiting costs to $1000 and $4300, respectively.

### Productivity Report Highlights

| Measure | Near-Term Goal | Actual | Productivity Index |
|---|---|---|---|
| Total nonmanagerial recruiting costs | $25,000 | $24,500 | |
| Number of nonmanagers hired | 25 | 23 | |
| Productivity ratio | $1000 | $1065.22 | 106.5 |
| Total managerial recruiting costs | $64,500 | $68,456 | |
| Number of managers hired | 15 | 16 | |
| Productivity ratio | $4300 | $4278.50 | 99.5 |

**Evaluation and corrective action.** The average cost of recruiting a nonmanagerial employee is 6.5% higher than goal, whereas the average cost of recruiting a managerial employee is 0.5% below goal; related to nonmanagerial positions, civic and fraternal organizations will be added as a source for referrals and a study made to evaluate effectiveness of current advertising expenditures—with regard to managerial recruiting costs a new, more difficult goal to be evaluated.

## Example Number Six

**Position.** Credit and collections manager
**Responsibilities.** To authorize credit, collect receivables on a timely basis, and

reduce bad debt write-offs—all without adversely affecting the company's profitability.

**Productivity improvement opportunity.** To reduce bad debt write-offs as a percentage of total sales, and to reduce the percentage of receivables more than 45 days old to total outstanding receivables.

**Long-term potential**

$$Productivity\ indicator\ 1\ =\ \frac{total\ bad\ debt\ write\text{-}offs}{total\ sales}$$

$$Base\ period\ =\ "is"\ =\ \frac{\$462,000}{\$50,000,000}\ =\ 0.924\%$$

Long-term potential = "should be" = 40% reduction
$$=\ 0.924\%\ \times\ 0.6\ =\ 0.5544\%$$

$$Productivity\ indicator\ 2\ =\ \frac{receivables\ more\ than\ 45\ days\ old}{total\ receivables}$$

$$Base\ period\ =\ "is"\ =\ \frac{\$4,500,000}{\$10,000,000}\ =\ 45\%$$

Long-term potential = "should be" = 20% reduction
$$=\ 45\%\ \times\ 0.8\ =\ 36\%$$

**Obstacles**

1. High interest rates result in customers delaying payment.
2. Some customers habitually delay payment, and to date, no real effort has been made to speed up their payments.

**Plan**

1. Analyze, on an individual account basis, the cost-benefit relationship related to slow-paying accounts.
2. Respond to those accounts individually and in accordance with the above analysis.
3. Increase the volume of outgoing calls made for the purpose of collection.
4. Develop an improved screening criteria for potential new accounts.

**Near-term goals.** Based on projected annual sales of $60,000,000 and average outstanding receivables of $12,000,000, reduce next year's bad debt write-offs to 0.6% of total sales and reduce the monthly average percentage of receivables more than 45 days old to total outstanding receivables to 40%.

Productivity Report Highlights

| Measure | Near-Term Goals | Actual | Productivity Index |
|---|---|---|---|
| Total bad debt write-offs / Total sales | $360,000 / $60,000,000 | $372,000 / $62,500,000 | |
| Productivity ratio | 0.6 | 0.5952 | 99.2 |
| Receivables more than 45 days old / Total receivables | $4,800,000 / $12,000,000 | $4,700,000 / $11,750,000 | |
| Productivity ratio | 0.4 | 0.4 | 100.0 |

**Evaluation and corrective action.** The bad debt write-offs were 0.8% lower than permitted by the goal, and the percentage of total receivables more than 45 days old was right on target—existing program and emphasis to continue, and a new, more difficult goal to be evaluated and set.

## Example Number Seven

**Position.** Controller

**Responsibility.** To prepare and distribute on a timely basis reports that communicate financial performance to annual plan.

**Productivity improvement opportunity.** To implement a reporting system which accurately communicates, within 7 working days from the last work day of the month, actual results vs. budgeted performance.

**Long-term potential**

$$Productivity\ indicator\ 1 = \frac{\text{total period expenses which did not match period sales as reported}}{\text{total annual expenses}}$$

$$Base\ period = \text{"is"} = \frac{\$1,000,000}{\$10,000,000}$$
$$= 10\% \text{ of period expenses did not match period sales as reported}$$

Long-term potential = "should be" = $0.10 \times 0.2 = 2\%$

$$Productivity\ indicator\ 2 = \frac{\text{number elapsed days actual}}{\text{number elapsed days allowed}}$$

$$Base\ period = \text{"is"} = \frac{10 \text{ work days}}{7 \text{ work days}} = 1.43 \text{ as much time as allowed}$$

Long-term potential = "should be" = 7 days = 1.0

### Obstacles

1. Limited resources are available to prepare the report.
2. Expenses aren't booked until related invoice is approved; approval is sometimes delayed.

### Plan

1. To reset priorities so that report preparation will be given a higher priority.
2. If necessary, but as a last resort, work overtime to ensure report is out on time.
3. Log all invoices out for approval, and follow up near month's end to ensure all have been reviewed and returned by the last work day of the month.

**Near-term goals.** Based on projected annual expenses of $12,000,000, to reduce average time required to prepare and distribute the monthly financial report to 8 days maximum and to reduce the volume of expenses not matched to period sales to 5% maximum, both in the upcoming year.

### Productivity Report Highlights

| Measure | Near-Term Goal | Actual | Productivity Index |
|---|---|---|---|
| Total period expenses which did not match period sales as reported | $600,000 | $525,000 | |
| Total expenses | $12,000,000 | $11,800,000 | |
| Productivity ratio | 0.05 | 0.04449 | 89.0 |
| Number elapsed days actual | 8 | 7 | |
| Number elapsed days allowed | 7 | 7 | |
| Productivity ratio | 1.143 | 1.0 | 87.5 |

**Evaluation and corrective action.** Actual performance resulted in a favorable variance to goal related to both indicators: the dollar volume of expenses not matching period sales was 11% lower than goal and the average elapsed time to prepare the report was 12.5% less than goal—the "mismatched" expenses goal will be evaluated as to the possibility of making further near-term improvement.

### Example Number Eight

**Position.** Public relations person
**Responsibility.** To enhance the company's reputation within the community.
**Productivity improvement opportunity.** To enlarge the scope of contacts

within the community without reducing the frequency of personal contacts with key people.

**Long-term potential**

$$Productivity\ indicator\ 1 = \frac{\text{total actual contacts}}{\text{total planned contacts}}$$

$$Base\ period = \text{"is"} = \frac{2100 \text{ total actual contacts}}{2500 \text{ total planned contacts}}$$

$$Long\text{-}term\ potential = \text{"should be"} = \frac{4000}{4000}$$

$$Productivity\ indicator\ 2 = \frac{\text{total key people contacts made}}{\text{total key people contacts planned}}$$

$$Base\ period = \text{"is"} = \frac{950 \text{ total actual key people contacts}}{1000 \text{ total planned key people contacts}}$$

$$Long\text{-}term\ potential = \text{"should be"} = \frac{1500}{1500}$$

**Obstacles**

1. Limited amount of time available for personal contacts.
2. Tendency is to keep contacting the same people over and over again.
3. Difficulty in locating new people to talk to.

**Plan**

1. Convert some of the time now being used for one-on-one contacts to group contacts (i.e., speeches before groups of people).
2. Apply the time savings to more frequent personal contacts with key people.
3. To weight repeat contacts as follows for the purpose of enlarging the scope of contacts:
   a. *Key people.* Any and all contacts with a single key person after three in a single quarter will be credited as 0.5 (rather than 1.0) per additional contact.
   b. *Other people.* Any and all contacts with a single other person beyond two per year will be credited as 0.5 per additional contact, also.

**Near-term goals.** To personally contact each of 100 key people 3 times each quarter, and to increase total annual contacts to 3000, both in the upcoming year.

Productivity Report Highlights

| Measure | Near-Term Goal | Actual | Productivity Index |
|---|---|---|---|
| Total actual contacts | 3000 | 3050 | |
| Total planned contacts | 3000 | 3000 | |
| Productivity ratio | 1.0 | 1.017 | 101.7 |
| Total key people contacts | 1200 | 1250 | |
| Total planned key people contacts | 1200 | 1200 | |
| Productivity ratio | 1.0 | 1.042 | 104.2 |

**Evaluation and corrective action.** Total contacts exceeded goal by 1.7%, and total key people contacts exceeded goal by 4.2%—a new, more challenging goal will be evaluated for next year.

### Example Number Nine

**Position.** Assembly supervisor

**Responsibilities.** To meet assembly schedule using no more resources than allowed by standard, and to maintain a high quality level of outputs.

**Productivity improvement opportunity.** To meet the assembly schedule while improving both efficiency and quality.

**Long-term potential**

$$Productivity\ indicator\ 1\ =\ \frac{actual\ output\ in\ units}{scheduled\ output\ in\ units}$$

$$Base\ period\ =\ \text{``is''}\ =\ \frac{460\ average\ outputs\ per\ day\ actual}{480\ scheduled\ outputs\ per\ day}$$

$$Long\text{-}term\ potential\ =\ \text{``should be''}\ =\ \frac{480}{480}$$

$$Productivity\ indicator\ 2\ =\ \frac{actual\ direct\ labor\ hours\ per\ unit}{standard\ direct\ labor\ hours\ per\ unit}$$

$$Base\ period\ =\ \text{``is''}\ =\ \frac{11.2\ actual\ direct\ labor\ hours\ per\ unit}{10.0\ standard\ direct\ labor\ hours\ per\ unit}$$

$$Long\text{-}term\ potential\ =\ \text{``should be''}\ =\ \frac{9.6}{10.0}$$

$$Productivity\ indicator\ 3\ =\ \frac{total\ number\ of\ defects}{total\ units\ produced}$$

$$\text{Base period} = \text{``is''} = \frac{54 \text{ average total daily defects}}{460 \text{ average units produced daily}}$$

$$\text{Long-term potential} = \text{``should be''} = \frac{0}{460}$$

### Obstacles

1. Excessive downtime.
2. High turnover resulting in many new employees—new employees, on the average, make twice as many errors as do employees who have been on the job for longer than 60 days.

### Plan

1. Communicate consequences of downtime to all employees; record all downtime, both duration and responsibility, for feedback and corrective action.
2. Initiate a training program for new employees to include a basic assembly manual; follow up with new employees more often; assign new employees to work adjacent to a qualified longer-term employee capable of providing assistance when necessary.

**Near-term goals.** To meet assembly schedule on a daily basis with present people resources and not working overtime; to reduce assembly defects to a maximum of 8 for every 100 units assembled, all within 60 days.

### Productivity Report Highlights

| Measure | Near-Term Goal | Actual | Productivity Index |
|---|---|---|---|
| Actual daily output | 480 | 476 | |
| Scheduled daily output | 480 | 480 | |
| Productivity ratio | 1.0 | 0.992 | 99.2 |
| Actual average direct labor hours per unit | 10.0 | 10.6 | |
| Standard direct labor hours per unit | 10.0 | 10.0 | |
| Productivity ratio | 1.0 | 1.06 | 106.0 |
| Total defects | 38.08 | 40 | |
| Total units produced | 476 | 476 | |
| Productivity ratio | 0.08 | 0.084 | 105 |

**Evaluation and corrective action.** Average total units produced daily fell 0.8% short of schedule; average direct labor hours per unit assembled exceeded standard by 6%; average defects exceeded goal by 5%—progress will be communicated to all employees, and their continued best efforts aimed at making further progress will be solicited; individuals responsible for more than the average number of errors will be retrained; persons responsible for downtime will be counseled—a buzzer will be installed to signal when an assembly conveyor is not running.

### Example Number Ten

**Position.** Data processing project leader
**Responsibility.** To maximize benefits resulting from application of computerized systems.
**Productivity improvement opportunity.** To develop and install computer programs so as to meet targeted implementation dates, and to increase the value of all efforts based on a cost-benefit analysis.
**Long-term potential**

$$Productivity\ indicator\ 1 = \frac{\text{actual elapsed time in employee work days to complete assigned projects}}{\text{targeted time in employee work days to complete those same projects}}$$

$$\text{Base period} = \text{"is"} = \frac{\text{4400 employee work days actual}}{\text{3800 employee work days goal}}$$

$$\text{Long-term potential} = \text{"should be"} = \frac{3800}{3800}$$

$$Productivity\ indicator\ 2 = \frac{\text{first-year savings}}{\text{cost of development and implementation}}$$

$$\text{Base period} = \text{"is"} = \frac{\$200,000}{\$385,000}$$

$$\text{Long-term potential} = \text{"should be"} = \frac{\$600,000}{\$400,000}$$

### Obstacles

1. Project priorities are often changed.
2. All significant opportunities for potential savings may not have been identified.

### Plan

1. Make a concentrated effort to identify areas of greatest potential savings via improved interface with "users."

2. Include users as members of the project team.
3. Compile data necessary to crystallize priorities in the minds of all managers, set priorities accordingly, and get top-management approval.

**Near-term goals.** To meet targeted implementation dates on assigned projects, and to get a first-year payback exceeding development and implementation costs by 25% minimum, both in the upcoming year.

Productivity Report Highlights

| Measure | Near-Term Goal | Actual | Productivity Index |
|---|---|---|---|
| Actual elapsed development time in employee work days for completed projects | 4200 | 4350 | |
| Targeted elapsed time in employee work days for those same projects | 4200 | 4200 | |
| Productivity ratio | 1.0 | 1.036 | 103.6 |
| First-year savings | $500,000 | $575,000 | |
| Development and implementation cost | $400,000 | $416,667 | |
| Productivity ratio | 1.25 | 1.38 | 110.4 |

**Evaluation and corrective action.** Actual time in employee days required to complete projects exceeded the goal by 3.6%; actual ratio of first-year savings to the cost of development and implementation exceeded goal by 10.4%—to evaluate the impact of working overtime on a controlled basis upon both cost and benefit derived from meeting targeted implementation dates.

## Example Number Eleven

**Position.** Rental car manager
**Responsibilities.** To rent cars to customers at a profit and with a minimum number of complaints.
**Productivity improvement opportunity.** To increase profit margin while reducing the rate of complaints.
**Long-term potential**

$$Productivity\ indicator\ 1 = \frac{average\ number\ of\ cars\ rented}{average\ number\ of\ cars\ available}$$

$$Base\ period = \text{``is''} = \frac{164\ average\ number\ rented}{200\ cars\ available}$$

$$\text{Long-term potential} = \text{"should be"} = \frac{200}{200}$$

$$Productivity\ indicator\ 2 = \frac{\text{net profit}}{\text{total revenues}}$$

$$\text{Base period} = \text{"is"} = \frac{\$45,000 \text{ net profit}}{\$400,000 \text{ total revenues}}$$

$$\text{Long-term potential} = \text{"should be"} = \frac{\$78,000}{\$487,800}$$

$$Productivity\ indicator\ 3 = \frac{\text{total complaints received}}{\text{total car days in operation}}$$

$$\text{Base period} = \text{"is"} = \frac{6,800 \text{ total complaints}}{59,860 \text{ total car days in operation}}$$

$$\text{Long-term potential} = \text{"should be"} = \frac{4,000}{73,000}$$

### Obstacles

1. Heated pricing competition.
2. Too few cars during the week, too many available on the weekend.
3. Towing and on-the-road repair expenses increasing.

### Plan

1. Provide rental incentive, such as trading stamps.
2. Provide free delivery and pickup for local customers.
3. Develop and implement a preventive maintenance program.

**Near-term goals.** To increase average number of rented units to 180 without increasing the size of the rental fleet; to improve net profit by 20% minimum; to reduce customer complaints to 7 per 100 rental days maximum—all for the next year of operation.

### Productivity Report Highlights

| Measure | Near-Term Goal | Actual | Productivity Index |
|---|---|---|---|
| Average number of cars rented | 180 | 184 | |
| Average number of cars available | 200 | 200 | |
| Productivity ratio | 0.90 | 0.92 | 102.2 |

Productivity Report Highlights ( *continued* )

| Measure | Near-Term Goal | Actual | Productivity Index |
|---|---|---|---|
| Net profit | $59,268 | $60,842 | |
| Total revenues | $439,025 | $444,100 | |
| Productivity ratio | 0.135 | 0.137 | 101.5 |
| Total number of complaints received | 4,599 | 4,480 | |
| Total car days in operation | 65,700 | 67,160 | |
| Productivity ratio | 0.07 | 0.0667 | 95.3 |

**Evaluation and corrective action.** The number of cars rented exceeded goal by 2.2%; net profit exceeded goal by 1.5%; and the number of complaints received was below goal by 4.7%—the existing plan will continue to be emphasized, new goals evaluated and set.

Note that in the previous examples, the quantifying of "long-range potential" is a best guess based on the experience and subjective feelings of the manager who is responsible and, if need be, the supervisor. In all the previous examples, the "near-term goal" was set at somewhat less than the agreed upon long-range potential. While this need not be the case, experience has shown that setting goals at a difficult-but-achievable level generally results in a more positively motivated manager than does a higher-level goal with a greatly reduced probability for achievement.

## Summary

The philosophy of management by goalz coupled with the process of goal setting and achieving can be applied to any position within any area of the organization. The pinpointing of individual responsibilities helps in identifying productivity improvement opportunities. Likewise, productivity indicators, or ratios, are the natural result of understanding specific responsibilities. Objectives, or near-term specific goals, are generated only after gaining an awareness of where you are now with regard to fulfilling a certain responsibility and estimating the longer-term potential. Obstacles, or roadblocks limiting progress, must be identified, and a plan must be designed and implemented to overcome them. Based upon actual performance to your near-term goal, you may choose to modify your plan and/or revise your goal.

# 5
# Increasing
# Contribution

# 11

# Employee Participation

Effectiveness in using the group process was briefly covered in Chapter 8. This chapter provides additional detail related to furthering the involvement of all employees and thereby increasing their contribution to the achievement of organizational objectives.

Leadership may be defined as the ability of a single person to influence the behavior of others. Four factors influence leadership within the organizational setting: the leader's behavior, the followers, the goals of both the organization and of its employees, and the operating climate within the organization. Leadership is situational. Different operating environments, different goals, different groups, and differences within the same group all influence what style leadership will be most effective in any given situation. No single leadership style can be considered best for all work situations. On the other hand, when the factors influencing leadership can be controlled, a single style would be most effective because the situations would be essentially the same. Leadership acts may be viewed in either one of two ways. Some leadership acts are favorable, as they tend to motivate followers toward achieving the organization's objectives. Other leadership acts are unfavorable for the reason that they tend to demotivate followers; that is, they interfere with the followers' natural desires to work together to accomplish something.

A leader uses three different skills: technical skills which relate to things; human skills which relate to people; and conceptual skills which relate to ideas. Technical skills relate to the leader's proficiency in dealing with any process or technique, such as those related to accounting, marketing, or engineering. Generally, these skills are used more by managers at lower levels than by managers at higher levels. The higher the managerial level, the more dependent the leader on the technical skills of subordinates.

Human skills relate to the leader's ability to interact effectively with others. The leader who possesses such skills is better able to motivate followers and peers and to generate a spirit of cooperation and teamwork. Human skills are equally important at all managerial leadership levels.

Conceptual skills relate to the leader's ability to be creative, make plans, and generate projections. Conceptual skill enables the leader to deal effectively with abstractions. Generally, higher-level managers are required to possess greater conceptual skills than lower-level managers. The nature of their responsibilities is such that more time is devoted to planning and other more abstract activities. Different types of functions and different leadership levels require different mixes of skills.

## Motivational Styles of Leadership

Leadership is applied in different ways dependent upon the manager's style. For example, there can be a distinct difference in the manner in which managers approach subordinates in an attempt to motivate them to take certain desired actions. If that approach emphasizes rewards, the leader is using "positive leadership." If, on the other hand, the approach emphasizes penalties or punishment, the manager is using "negative leadership." The greater the reward, monetary or nonmonetary, the more positive the leadership. Likewise, the greater the penalty, the more negative the leadership. The manager's style is related to his or her theory of organizational behavior. Those that embrace *Theory X*—people are basically lazy and do not want to work—will usually exhibit a negative leadership style. Managers that embrace *Theory Y*—people have a psychological need to work and to achieve results—will usually exhibit a positive style of leadership. The word *usually* is used in both cases because leaders generally exhibit a mixture of both positive and negative styles with one style dominating the leader's behavior. In certain situations, even the most competent and positive leader must revert to a negative style in an effort to shock a subordinate out of complacency. The factors of better-educated employees, a higher degree of employee independence, and widespread unionism, just to mention a few, all require today's manager to be more positive in leadership style.

## Power Styles of Leadership

The manner in which managers use the power delegated to them also establishes a style of leadership. There are three basic power styles of leadership with many "shades" between each distinct style: autocratic, free reign, and participative. As with motivational styles, managers exhibit a mixture of all three styles with one style dominating the manager's leadership behavior.

## Autocratic Managers

Autocratic managers centralize power and decision making in themselves. They structure the entire work situation, providing employees little opportunity to express individual initiative. Employees do what they are told and only what they are told. The autocratic manager takes full authority and assumes total responsibility within the assigned area. Employees are generally uninformed, insecure, and suffer security stress because of the leader's behavior. In that sense, the leadership provided is generally negative. On the other hand, the leader may dispense rewards to the group. In that event, the leadership is positive. When exhibiting a positive style of leadership, the autocratic manager is called a *benevolent autocrat*. The benevolent autocrat can be effective in improving productivity and can develop meaningful relationships with subordinates. Some managers, because of an "authoritarian set" based on experience, may not be as ready for the participative power style as are other managers. The autocratic manager can achieve short-term results but usually falters in the long run because negative style erodes employee morale and dampens their enthusiasm. The benevolent autocrat is capable of achieving both short- and long-range results but is incapable of realizing the organization's productivity potential because that power style limits employee contribution. There can be no synergistic, or multiplying-of-results, effect within the work group because the benevolent manager chooses to be the "brain"or sole source of ideas—everything is dependent upon his or her personal talents and abilities.

## Free-Reign Managers

While the autocratic manager relishes power, the free-reign manager does everything possible to avoid the use of personal power. Subordinates perform their work independent of influence from the manager. They set their own standards of performance and work out their own problems. The free-reign manager serves primarily as a contact person between the work group and resources outside the work group. If they need something, such as instructions or materials, the free-reign manager obtains from others what is needed and provides it to his or her subordinates. Whereas the autocratic power style ignores the subordinate's contribution, the free-reign power style ignores the leader's contribution. The free-reign power style is not a viable predominant style. It can, however, be employed in isolated situations where a manager can leave choices entirely to the work group.

## Participative Managers

Unlike either the autocratic manager who makes all the decisions or the free-reign manager who makes no decisions, the participative manager makes decisions but seldom makes unilateral ones. Managers who employ the participative

**TABLE 11·1.** Productivity Potential as a Function of Managerial Power and Motivational Styles—Short Term and Long Term

| Power Style | Motivational Style | Productivity Potential | |
|---|---|---|---|
| | | Short Term | Long Term |
| Autocratic | Positive (autocratic benevolent) | High | High |
| | Negative | High | Low |
| Free reign | Positive | High | Low |
| | Negative | High | Low |
| Participative | Positive | Highest | Highest |

power style recognize they can multiply their efforts through subordinates and that they can be most effective by generating a work climate which increases employee involvement and is reward-centered. Participative managers keep their subordinates well informed of what is happening both within and without the immediate work area by (1) involving subordinates in problems to the extent of their experience and abilities and (2) soliciting ideas and suggestions related to ongoing situations. The participative manager willingly delegates responsibility and the corresponding authority on a selective basis. Whereas the autocratic manager controls through personal power and authority, the participative manager exercises control through the work group. He or she generates an esprit de corps, or spirit of teamwork, that motivates achievement as a means of fulfilling individual self-esteem needs. While the free-reign power style is dependent upon the attitude and motivation of subordinates and provides generally unpredictable results, the autocratic power style is capable of producing short-term results; the autocratic benevolent power style can produce long-term results; and the participative power style is capable of maximizing those results, due to the increased involvement in and contribution by subordinates. Only the participative power style has the potential for realizing the organization's productivity potential. Table 11-1 illustrates the productivity-improving potential of various managerial power and motivational styles.

## The Nature of Employee Participation

Employee participation may be defined as the involvement of the employee in the processes of the organization. This involvement is of both a mental and an emotional nature and encourages the employee to contribute to organizational goals and share responsibility for their achievement. The definition incorporates three important aspects of the participative process.

**Mental and emotional involvement.** In most organizations, employee involvement focuses on the physical aspects of the job. While a person working on an assembly line may be the stereotype of a work situation that limits the employee to task involvement, similar limitation, in varying degrees, is prevalent in most work situations. In a work situation characterized by employee participation, the whole person is involved rather than just the skill in performing assigned tasks. This total involvement in the work situation is a product of mind, emotions, and skills. Instead of being restricted to physical or task involvement, an employee who participates is psychologically or egotistically involved, as well. Some managers hold meetings with their employees and ask them job-related questions while communicating via their attitude and actions that they are really not interested in employee-generated ideas. This is *not* participation for the reason the employees fail to become ego involved.

**Contributative involvement.** The participative power style motivates employees to contribute to the achievement of organizational goals. It draws upon their mental and emotional resources, as well as their physical capabilities. Employees are provided the opportunity to exercise their initiative and creative abilities toward achievement of the organization's goals. Some managers mistakenly think they are practicing participative management by presenting their own plans and ideas to subordinates for their consent. Employees who give their consent are not contributing; they are simply approving. Participation is a two-way process. It is not imposing ideas from above. Its value lies in tapping the creative potential of employees, the persons who should have the clearest perspective related to their own work situation and know what it will take to reach the organization's goals.

**Increasing responsibility through involvement.** Participation encourages employees to accept responsibility for their work group's assigned activities. As their involvement in the work situation increases, employees become more willing to accept responsibility and more interested in the achievement of organizational goals. Improved teamwork is another natural result when employee participation is increased. Teamwork and cooperation are viewed in a more positive light by employees in a work situation characterized by participation. Such employees feel responsible for, and are interested in, achieving results and recognize improved teamwork and cooperation to be of value toward that end.

Management's focus over the last 50 years on oversimplifying the job and oversupervising the employee has contributed to the improvement of efficiency, but at the cost of employee creative potential and the resulting benefits of such potential not being realized. If we are to improve productivity and realize organizational goals in the future, we must better utilize all available resources, including the potential of all employees to contribute toward that end.

## Situational Prerequisites
## for Effective Participation

As previously discussed, the work situation influences which managerial power style will be most effective. With the participative style offering the greatest potential for productivity improvement, it is worthwhile to review the set of conditions, or the situation, most conducive to the application of participative management. The principal conditions are as follows:

- Adequate time to participate must be provided before action is taken. Emergency situations are, obviously, not conducive to participation.
- The cost of participation should not exceed the value of benefits it provides. Whereas some benefits may be difficult to calculate in terms of dollars, it is suggested you attempt to do so. Should employees spend too much time in participation, their assigned work will not get done.
- The employees, as individuals, must be interested in participation. If they show no interest, you should respect their right to not be involved and exclude them from the process. It is suggested that you periodically offer the involvement opportunity to employees who have previously refused. After the process becomes more of a "known" than an "unknown," the employee may welcome the second chance. In no way should employees who do not want to participate be forced or intimidated into doing so.
- The employee should possess the ability to participate. This required condition restricts employees from being involved in problems not related to their own work area or in matters beyond their knowledge and experience. It would be inappropriate, for example, to involve a personnel employee in an engineering design problem.
- The participants must be able to communicate with one another in order to exchange ideas.
- Neither the employee nor the manager should feel threatened by participation. If the manager views participation as a reduction of authority, participation cannot work effectively. If the employee feels a loss of status due to participating, she or he should not participate.
- Participation by employees who are also union representatives should be viewed as "individual" rather than "union" participation.
- Focus of the participatory effort must remain on results in the form of achieving organizational goals. The constraints of company policy, contractual labor agreements, legal requirements, and other similar requirements must be communicated to all participants as guidelines for achieving those results.
- The most critical factor in the total work situation on which effective participation is dependent is the manager's philosophy for dealing with people. The proper philosophy manifests itself in the form of a positive leadership style and a belief that the fulfilling of both managerial achievement needs and the organization's goals is dependent upon increasing employee contribution.

The work situation must generally meet the above criteria before employee participation can be effective. If those conditions cannot now be substantially met, focus must be on gradually changing the conditions to best complement the building of participation. As a plant cannot grow and flourish unless conditions are right, so it is with employee participation.

## Programs to Build Participation

When conditions supportive to participation are in place within the organization, the next step is to design and implement programs which will build that participation. Defining a *program* as a set of prescribed practices focusing on activities of limited scope within the organization, a number of coordinated programs will be required to produce the best results. The introduction of programs designed to build productivity should be scheduled so that one program has been assimilated before introducing another. Following is a group of programs, each capable of building participation. The order of listing is the suggested order in which they are to be implemented.

### Communications Meetings

Communications meetings are intended to keep employees well informed on the basis of what is happening, or is being planned, in the work place. The information must be communicated in a manner which tends to dispel rumor and speculation while enhancing the credibility of the area manager. Requirements for such meetings are as follows:

- Each manager should conduct the communications meetings with his or her subordinates. The purpose of these meetings is as much to build up the status of the area manager as a person "in the know" as it is to keep employees informed.
- Communications meetings should be held periodically (i.e., once each week), at the same time and place, in an environment conducive to communication, and be brief in duration. Preferably, communications meetings will last about 15 minutes, be held in the work area, and be scheduled just prior to a break period or the lunch period. Preparation on the part of the manager is key to making such meetings successful.
- Topics discussed in communications meetings should be limited to work-related topics that directly or indirectly relate to the group. Suggested topics are schedule; introduction of new employees assigned to work in the area; introduction of new managers assigned to work in other areas; sales; products; plans; anticipated changes; and quality.
- The tone of the meeting should remain positive and supportive. If problems

are being experienced, they should be mentioned, but in a manner that communicates confidence that they will be resolved.

- Whatever is communicated, it must be presented in a truthful, frank, and sincere manner. Avoid unwarranted speculation. You will be viewed as the authority, and whatever you say must be backed with facts.
- Whenever possible, use diagrams or charts to communicate problems, trends, and progress.
- Limit questions by requesting that all questions be held until you have finished talking, and schedule what you have to say so that questions are limited to five minutes at the most. At the conclusion of the meeting, which must end at the scheduled time, offer to later answer any and all remaining questions on a one-to-one basis. Do your best to answer all remaining questions that same day.

## Consultative Supervision

The essence of consultative supervision can be summarized in four words: "*What do you think?*" Consultative supervision, as the name implies, means that a manager consults with employees in an effort to get the benefit of their ideas and suggestions before she or he makes a decision. Although not consulting with employees on every issue, the manager does generate a climate conducive to employees offering their ideas and suggestions. To be successful, consultative supervision requires that the manager be genuinely interested in and receptive to the ideas offered by subordinates. Only in this manner will employees perceive their inputs as being worthwhile and useful. A manager applying consultative supervision must have the humility to admit to not having all the good ideas and that members of the work group are capable of occasionally generating superior ideas.

The practice of consultative supervision should strengthen, rather than weaken, a manager's authority. The manager retains the right to decide, and responding to the ideas of subordinates helps make the manager the representative of the employees, as well as the representative of the employer. As a by-product of consultative management, understanding between manager and employees is normally improved. Better communication often results in fewer grievances because both parties better understand each other's problems. Two major advantages of consultative supervision are that a manager can consult with employees at any time on an informal basis and can choose when to consult with any or all of the group.

## Key People Committees

Key people, as used here, are defined as those employees who, either because of the nature of their assigned duties or because of talents, abilities, experience, and a positive attitude, are best able to contribute to the achievement of organizational goals. The contribution potential of such employees must be nurtured if it is to be realized. One means is to select a limited number of such persons as representatives of their peers to participate in regularly scheduled meetings to be held in an office, cafeteria, or conference room for the purpose of addressing specific problems. These meetings are to be conducted by the group's manager with managers from support groups also attending. Detail relevant to specific problems is presented in the format of "is" vs. "should be," the *should be* representing the organization's related goal. The manager directs the discussion. Minutes are taken and later posted on the bulletin board or in some other way communicated to all employees. The duration of these meetings is to be limited to a set time, usually one hour maximum. For key people committees to be most effective, less than one half of the total time available should be consumed by the attending managers. At *least* half the available time, preferably more, should be provided for the attending employees to express their ideas and to ask questions. Common sense governs key people meetings—a representative from each work group should be on the committee. Care must be exercised to maintain open lines of communication. It is not necessary that all, or even any, of the ideas presented be implemented. Obviously, all ideas and suggestions deserve a complete hearing, and those that are worthwhile should be implemented on a timely basis.

## Democratic Supervision

The practice of democratic supervision goes beyond consultative supervision in that some decision-making power is released to employees. While it is not uncommon for organizations to form joint manager-employee committees related to employee recreation, safety, the credit union, and perhaps the Christmas party, few organizations permit employees to make significant decisions related to the work process itself. In every work situation, there are certain jobs that provide a realistic opportunity for employees to be given latitude in deciding how it should be done. Such opportunities can range from deciding whether required overtime should be added to the daily work schedule or should be worked on a Saturday to deciding which of two pieces of equipment, both of which meet management's criteria, should be purchased for a certain activity.

The effective use of democratic supervision is dependent upon two major considerations. Employees provided the opportunity to make a decision must possess knowledge, skill, and common sense required to make a good decision; and the manager must focus attention on the related organizational goals and be sensitive to the possibility of conflicting personal goals.

## Employee Goal Setting

Some organizations have experimented with letting employees set their own work-related goals. In situations where the previously mentioned programs to build participation have been successfully implemented, or when working with a group of superior performers, allowing employees to set their own work goals can be a viable option. In work situations in which an incentive program is in effect, an employee-initiated goal revision that is not accompanied by a management-initiated methods change should not penalize the employee via an "incentive adjustment." Also important in making an employee goal-setting program work effectively is ensuring compatibility with the organization's goals.

## Quality Circles

A Quality Circle is a group of from eight to ten people doing similar work, under the direction of the same supervisor, who meet for about an hour each week for the purpose of identifying, analyzing, and solving problems, including but not limited to quality problems, related to either the product or service they produce. Quality Circles embody the practical application of industrial-humanist ideas first presented by Douglas McGregor, Abraham Maslow, Frederic Herzberg, and David McClelland. While few American managers were quick to recognize the benefits to the balance sheet of Theory Y styles of management, Japanese managers were generally better able to recognize the potential payoffs. As a result, 600,000 Quality Circles involving about 6 million workers, or about 1 in every 8 employees, are established today within Japanese companies. This compares to an estimated 3000 to 4000 Circles in existence today within the United States.

Quality Circles are based upon a participative problem-solving technique. The concept goes beyond asking employees for suggestions which will be evaluated and perhaps implemented by others. By asking employees to both contribute ideas and implement solutions, Quality Circles serve to reestablish the dignity of employees and the importance of their jobs. The solutions reached by group consensus may or may not be the most effective. Accordingly, Circles incorporate a people-building philosophy for the purpose of increasing the effectiveness of solutions generated by the group's members. Training in basic quality control techniques, such as Pareto diagrams, cause-and-effect diagrams, and histograms, is an integral part of the Quality Circle concept and is provided for the group's leader as well as its members. The solutions reached by consensus will undoubtedly enjoy increased and broader-based support than would solutions generated by an individual.

Table 11-2 illustrates the problem-solving process employed within Quality Circles. There are nine distinct steps which are used to effectively investigate and solve problems in an orderly fashion.

Specific techniques employed by Quality Circles include brainstorming and cause-and-effect diagraming.

**TABLE 11-2.** The Quality Circle Method of Problem Solving

1. Determine the problem you are going to attack and the benefits to be derived by solving it.
2. If the stated problem is of a general nature, select a specific part of that problem for detailed investigation and analysis.
3. Gather and then analyze data related to the problem for the purpose of sorting out actual causes from possible causes.
4. Determine a specific course of corrective action aimed at solving the problem.
5. Develop a plan and timetable for initiating those actions.
6. Implement the plan.
7. Follow up to determine the effectiveness of the solution.
8. Communicate to top management, via a presentation, the group's accomplishments.

*Brainstorming* is based on six rules:

**Generate a large number of ideas.** Ideas build on and result from other ideas. They are often the combination or extension of other ideas. The greater the number of ideas generated as possible solutions, the broader the base for effective problem solving.

**Encourage freewheeling.** While an idea may be unsuitable in itself, it serves as a stimulus for thought on the part of other members of the group. Even half-baked or undeveloped ideas have thought-provoking value.

**There is to be no criticism of ideas presented.** Critical judgments are to be deferred until a later time in the idea-development process.

**All members of the Circle must have an equal opportunity to participate.** Each member of the group must be provided the opportunity to speak and contribute. When a member has nothing to offer, provide the person another opportunity to contribute after other members have presented their ideas. An employee not interested in participating or one who chooses to withdraw from the Quality Circle must be allowed to do so without fear of reprisal.

**Record all ideas.** Only by committing all ideas to writing as they are presented can the group and its members achieve the required overview of what has been said.

**Let ideas incubate.** Give your subconscious the opportunity to contribute by extending the time period for presentation of ideas to at least the following week's meeting.

*Cause-and-effect diagrams* (sometimes called *fishbone diagrams* because of their shape) contribute to the problem-solving process by pictorially summarizing, via a systematic approach, all possible causes of the problem quality characteristic, or effect. Figure 11-1 illustrates the basic components of such a diagram.

Figure 11-2 illustrates the specifics of a cause-and-effect diagram based upon the common, broad-based, possible causes of methods, work force, machinery, and materials as they relate to a problem of "defective units."

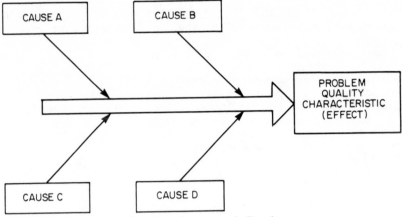

**Figure 11-1.** The general configuration of a cause-and-effect diagram.

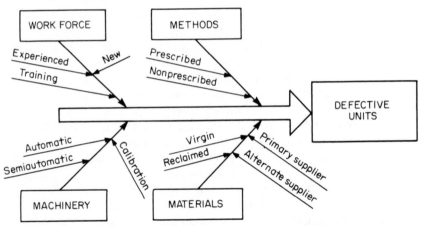

**Figure 11-2.** A specific cause-and-effect diagram related to a problem of "defective units."

## Summary

Realizing the productivity potential of the organization is dependent in large part upon maximizing the contribution of employees. The greater the opportunity for the employees to participate in the processes of the organization, the greater will be their contribution toward the achievement of the organization's goals. The effectiveness of employee participation is dependent upon the characteristics of the work situation. Effective participation depends on open communication within the work group and a high degree of interpersonal trust. When low trust is coupled with an autocratic managerial style, it is difficult to practice participation.

The substance of participation is not in its programs and procedures but is in its philosophy. Programs and procedures do make for effective participation, but only when used at the right time and in the right setting do they make it possible for participation to be viewed constructively by those involved. Participation is the mental and emotional involvement of a person within a group situation which encourages the person to contribute toward organizational goals and to their achievement. Some of the programs that can be implemented to improve participation are communications meetings, consultative supervision, key people committees, democratic supervision, employee goal setting, and Quality Circles.

# 12 The "Going Places" Attitude

The difference between the professional golfer who makes $510,000 a year and the one who makes $190,000 a year is less than an average of one stroke per eighteen holes played.[1] While the more successful golfer's score is only 1.3 percent lower, his earnings are more than 2.5 times greater. The concept of the slight edge, which provides a disproportionately greater reward for a slight advantage, is applicable to most, if not all, areas of human endeavor. Generally, those that are the best in their field command financial and nonfinancial rewards much greater than those received by persons who produce results that are only slightly less.

As it is with individuals, so it is with organizations. Two organizations may both be characterized by a generally high level of motivation among employees and an operating climate conducive to growth and productivity improvement; however, whereas one organization does well, the other does *exceptionally* well. The difference, or the slight edge, is usually the result of a *going places* attitude that seems to permeate the atmosphere and electrify the employees of the more successful organization. When a going places attitude exists in a reward-centered work environment where meaningful productivity measurements, goals, performance feedback, and employee participation are all well established, all systems are "go" and the sky is the limit. It is essential that the prerequisites of high-level employee motivation and an operating climate conducive to produc-

---

[1]Through September 11, 1980, Tom Watson, the year's leading money winner, had won $510,258 with an average score of 69.93, as compared to $191,659 in winnings for the eighth leading money winner, Mike Reed, whose average score was 70.83.

tivity growth be well established before a going places attitude can be developed. Until these prerequisites are satisfied, managerial action taken to develop such an attitude could be interpreted as attempts at manipulation. Employees must first be motivated and goal-directed before they will view attempts to develop a going places attitude as a means of helping them accomplish their personal and organizational goals. There are many things a manager can do to generate a going places attitude. This chapter covers the four areas in which you should concentrate your related efforts:

1. Sharing the "grand design"
2. Striving for excellence
3. Accentuating the positive
4. Generating a competitive spirit

## Sharing the "Grand Design"

It is important that all employees be aware of where the company is going. This does not mean divulging sensitive information. It does mean being open and candid with employees concerning top management's aspirations regarding the company and its general plan for realizing those aspirations. Many organizations are extremely reluctant to share any information with their employees concerning their plans until long after the die has been cast, and perhaps even after a public announcement in the media. The result is that employees do not feel "in the know" or cannot generate a sense of belonging to a group if the first word they get regarding the group's plans is received from an outside source.

While I have seen top managers become paranoid—in the sense they greatly feared the consequences should a competitor gain insight into their operations and their plans—I would guess that, in the long run, more harm has been done by employees not knowing, than by competitors knowing, such information. By sharing plans with employees, they become emotionally involved in their fulfillment. If every employee is aware of the "grand design," they can better accept the company's plans as their personal plans and will more willingly contribute to their success.

No matter the level that employees work within an organization, they derive prestige from knowing what the company plans to do. That knowledge provides the employees with something to talk about with family and friends. Because they know what is going on and what is planned, they are looked upon as "worthy," if not "favored," particularly when family and friends may work in an environment in which the mushroom theory prevails. As the employees' awareness of the company's plans increases, they are more likely to project a favorable public image for both themselves and the company.

Sharing the grand design with employees has a compound positive effect

upon the organization. Not only is the employee's sense of belonging and motivation to achieve organizational goals increased, but negative rumors are not
provided the informational void they require to flourish and generate security
stress throughout the organization. Rumors are less rampant in organizations
when the number of unknowns is reduced. I am reminded of the story wherein
prisoners of war were supposedly given a choice of entering one of two doors.
Before being forced to make the decision, each prisoner was allowed to look
through a peephole in one of the doors. Through that peephole, they could see
a high-walled room with no windows, or means of escape, in which there was
a ferocious lion. What was behind the second door remained an unknown.
When forced to enter one of the two doors, the prisoners, without exception,
chose to become the lion's lunch rather than to take a chance on the unknown.
As the story goes, the second door opened into the street and would enable the
prisoner to walk to freedom. Whether the story is fact or fancy is unimportant.
It does emphasize what most managers learn over an extended period of time:
nothing is as feared by most people as is the unknown. Whatever was behind
the second door had to be more dreadful than the lion; or at least that was what
all the prisoners thought. Rumors tend to be negative in nature. They are supposed facts, usually from an unknown source. They generate security stress
among employees which grows in the absence of facts provided by a person of
authority in the organization. As security stress increases, more and more productive energy is dissipated by the individual employee. Sharing the grand
design with employees increases their motivation and commitment to achieving
organizational goals while dispelling rumors and the waste of energy associated
with security stress.

## Striving for Excellence

When we speak of a going places attitude within an organization, we are talking
about a prevailing positive anticipation: a feeling that tomorrow will be better
than today for all persons associated with the organization. For the anticipated
benefits to be realized, there must exist a persistent striving for excellence
among the organization's leadership. Implicit is a feeling of being unsatisfied.
Notice I do not say *dis*satisfied. Being dissatisfied means being unhappy with
what has transpired to date. Being unsatisfied, in contrast, means that you look
favorably on what has happened to date; but, on the other hand, you fully
expect more of the same, or continued progress. Whereas dissatisfaction has a
negative connotation, being unsatisfied has a positive connotation. A good anal-
ogy related to being unsatisfied is when you have just eaten a delicious meal—
so good, in fact, that your appetite has been whetted and you would like another
serving of the same. For an organization, however, to realize continued prog-

ress, something must change. Striving for excellence requires an open-minded attitude concerning creativity and change within the organization. For results to continue to improve, conditions must continue to change. Employee flexibility and open-mindedness regarding change are functions of the climate generated by the manager. Following are suggestions related to creating a work climate conducive to tapping the creative potential of employees and reducing their resistance to change.

## Tapping the Creative Potential of Employees

**Place a high value on ideas.** Start by creating a feeling of excitement and personal involvement among your employees related to making further progress. Stress the value of creativity and the generation of new ideas as being of prime importance to achieving that progress. Elaborate on the benefits that can be derived from the successful implementation of such ideas: resolution of problems now consuming much time and effort, cost reduction, increased market share, and greater job security, just to mention a few.

**Make open-mindedness your policy.** If flexibility and change are not the well-accepted norm within your company, as in most companies, employees are apt to feel threatened when change is promoted. If, personally, you maintain a flexible attitude and a willingness to accept new ideas, you not only dispel their fears but also encourage them to be creative, to explore new possibilities, and to devise new and better ways of getting the job done.

**Highlight the most challenging areas.** The ideas that are of greatest value are those which eliminate key problems or increase capability in vital areas. While all ideas have importance, focus your employees' creativity on those areas where the potential payoff is the greatest. Whether talking with your employees individually or as a group, avoid the abstract. Show them what you are talking about. Demonstrate the operation; let them observe the condition for which you need ideas.

**Demonstrate your willingness to help develop ideas.** Seldom do ideas spring full blown from anyone's mind. What usually emerges is a wisp of the solution, something that requires further coddling and development. Communicate your interest in all employee ideas, no matter what stage they may be in. Undoubtedly, many valuable ideas are never developed to fruition, particularly in environments where interest is reserved for neat, tidy, and complete solutions to problems. When you are presented with an undeveloped idea, express the same interest as you would with a fully developed one. Sometimes you hold knowledge or information that can contribute to that development.

The manager with an outstanding record of getting good ideas from employees is the one who wins their confidence in one major respect—that manager never reacts negatively to an idea, no matter how undeveloped, stale, or inappropriate it may seem.

**Reward employees who submit successful ideas while encouraging those who are less successful.** Employees who come up with good ideas must, in some way, be rewarded for that contribution. That reward can range from a cash bonus to a pat on the back. While financial rewards are generally viewed as providing a greater incentive, the issue of fairness comes more into play when the rewards are financial. A sincere public expression of appreciation provides recognition and satisfies self-esteem needs. Rewards of nominal value, such as the ball-point pens given to Toyota's employees in Japan for patentable ideas, take on special significance when they are not available to anyone or everyone that may want one.

While providing special recognition to employees who have submitted a successful idea, also make public your gratitude for the efforts of those who have worked hard to develop an idea that never quite panned out. Let everyone know that you appreciate the effort even though no benefits were derived.

**Emphasize benefits.** When an idea is implemented, generally, there are specific benefits which result. The organization has gained, the department has gained, and the employee who generated the idea has gained by being rewarded, either tangibly or intangibly. You can motivate your employees simply by pointing out the specific benefits resulting from each idea that is implemented.

Imagination is the spark that lights the fire of enthusiasm, which is the prime characteristic of the going places attitude.

### Reducing Resistance to Change

The informal work group tends to be bound by convention, custom, and culture. There is a tendency to perpetuate the status quo and to stand like a rock in the face of change. If restriction of output was necessary in the past with autocratic management, it remains necessary now, even though management is becoming participative. Each person has needs which can be categorized as economic, psychological, or social. We can summarize an employee's reasons for resisting change by those same categories.

*Economic Reasons*
Fears unemployment
Fears a reduction in available work hours
Fears demotion and reduced wages
Fears a speedup and reduced incentives

*Psychological Reasons*
Dislikes others disrupting "her" or "his" work area
Resents implied criticism
Dislikes having to go through a relearning process
Fears that personal skills will be less valuable
Fears the unknown

*Social Reasons*
Dislikes making new social adjustments
Resents lack of participation in making the change
Visualizes the change as benefiting the company at the group's expense
Dislikes persons outside the work group being involved
Fears reduced social satisfaction

The foregoing list strongly suggests that resistance to change focuses more on human relations problems, rather than on the technological aspects of change. People resist the way that change affects their social relationships, upsets their status, and threatens their security. The technical requirements associated with change are a minor factor. Typically, in contrast to the human reasons for resistance, managerial attention within the organization focuses on the technical problems related to change. Too little time and attention is provided the social question of how to implement the change. Though management is the primary change agent within the organization, the employees control the decision to accept or reject changes. Rejection manifests itself in the form of either a slowdown or a showdown. While it is Pollyannaish thinking to believe all employees will willingly accept every change, the following managerial behaviors increase the probability of employee support.

**Eliminate surprises.** No one appreciates someone coming in and making changes in areas they consider as "theirs." This holds true for even the most seemingly minor changes. Accordingly, absolutely *no* changes should be made without advising *all* people involved prior to implementing the change.

**Restrict changes to the necessary and the useful.** Change for the sake of change is as disruptive as it is wasteful. If specific benefits cannot be derived from a change, do not implement that change. On the other hand, it is a requirement that the projected benefits of useful and necessary changes be communicated to all involved, prior to those changes being implemented. What is obvious to you, as the manager, may not be as obvious to your employees.

**Let employees play an active role.** Solicit the ideas and suggestions of employees related to making necessary changes. Let your employees make decisions related to change in their own areas of competence and responsibility, whenever possible.

**Change by evolution, not revolution.** When the organization's reach, or its ability to define needed changes, exceeds its grasp, or its ability to implement and assimilate those changes, the result is not only frustrating but is also devastating. One change must be fully assimilated before another is introduced.

**Develop a sensitivity to how employees will be affected.** Change within the organization should not disrupt the informal social system any more than is absolutely necessary. As the social system is the core of opposition to change, it is essential that managers consider the social relations of the work group when considering change. Each employee must feel that she or he will definitely not suffer, and could perhaps benefit, from proposed changes.

**Follow up.** It is essential that all changes be closely followed up to ensure a smooth and successful implementation. The difference between success and failure is often managerial awareness. When recognized in the early stages of implementation, problems can be more easily corrected. If not recognized and corrected, the consequence is greater than if a single change failed. It is the erosion of confidence and support which impacts attitudes and makes future changes more difficult.

Continued progress implies the need for change. Whether that change is supported or opposed by the organization's employees is critical to the development of a going places attitude.

The human need for self-esteem is a powerful motivator. That need cannot be satisfied by a management that does anything less than strive for excellence, or the realization of the organization's potential. Growth and success in all areas, including productivity improvement, is dependent upon managerial ability to tap the creative potential of its employees and to successfully implement change.

## Accentuating the Positive

The first outwardly visible sign of a going places attitude is the expression of positive expectancy. Positive expectancy is the faith or belief that the future will be better. As people usually get what they expect, positive expectancy is a self-fulfilling prophecy. Individuals and organizations that fully expect and anticipate success will usually achieve it. That firm belief in their abilities conquers the problems and setbacks which demoralize and defeat those who do not share a similar positive expectancy. While winners expect to win, losers expect to lose; both getting what they anticipate. Positive expectancy, or optimism, is not only the key to goal achievement, it is also the key to health and happiness. Medical doctors have long recognized mental attitudes as the link between the physical body and health, both physical and mental. Similarly, positive expectancy is the link between plans and results. Incurable optimism turns the going places attitude into reality.

As a manager, you have the responsibility of exhibiting a consistently positive expectancy to your employees and comanagers in all you say and do. The following outlines how to go about doing it.

**Problems are opportunities.** Problems are opportunities in disguise. The only way you can find or pinpoint those opportunities is to look for them. Whereas most people become depressed upon hearing bad news, or becoming aware of problems, and focus on the consequences, the optimistic manager focuses on identifying the related opportunity. Although sometimes those opportunities are not readily apparent, they are always there, waiting to be recognized and capitalized upon. View problems as opportunities, and your employees will do likewise. Optimism, like enthusiasm, is contagious.

**Stay relaxed and friendly.** The qualities of calmness and courage are both learned traits acquired through practice. The manager who earns the respect and confidence of employees is the one who remains relaxed and friendly no matter how great the pressures may be. The only way you can acquire this leadership trait is through practice. Initially, you may have to fake it. If deliberately practiced, it will, in time, become habit.

**Replace negative habits with positive habits.** By replacing negative personal habits with positive ones, you can further inspire confidence and the willingness of employees and fellow managers to share your going places attitude. Instead of criticizing, focus on praising when warranted. Instead of being cynical, practice being optimistic. Instead of being unhelpfully critical, develop the habit of being constructively helpful. While negative habits repel would-be followers, positive managerial habits, or a supportive leadership style, attract followers like a magnet.

**Get excited about the future.** Enthusiasm is contagious. When you, as a manager, are enthusiastic and excited about the organization's goals and the future of the organization and everyone associated with it, that enthusiasm will rub off on your employees and comanagers. Such enthusiasm must be as durable as it is sincere. It is a sad fact that some people find great pleasure in crushing the dreams of others. You can expect detractors. You can also expect to fully negate their influence by steadfastly maintaining the courage of your convictions.

## Generating a Competitive Spirit

When people from foreign lands visit the United States, they usually characterize Americans as people who work hard and play hard. After a hard day at the office or in the store or factory, we often go home and continue to exert effort in the form of work or recreational activities. We may be involved in Little League, or scouting, or the PTA; or we may work on a hobby, or work around the house, or play golf, or go bowling, or jog around the neighborhood. On the weekend, we may drive 300 miles to ski or go fishing; or we may play twenty-seven holes of golf in a single day. Our passion for activity—sometimes just to be doing something—results in a general attitude of competitiveness in our society and within our organizations. The popular concept of the organization's members working as a cohesive unit, or as a "team," implies competition. Its psychology is based as much on preventing someone or something from getting ahead of us as it is on unifying our efforts for achievement of a common goal. If, as a manager, you understand the way competition works and the benefits which can be derived from skillful fostering of competition, the results you achieve can be phenomenal. In contrast, the unsuccessful manager—the one who achieves little and who stirs up animosities and resentments—is generally ignorant of the reasons why people in organizations enjoy competition.

People compete in organizations because to do so fulfills many of their needs. Here are some of the human needs which can be met by competition in the work place.

**Social needs.** Competition can be effectively used to motivate all members of the work group to cooperate and work together as a team.

**Security needs.** Competition can be related to the necessity of at least meeting the achievements of other teams in competitive companies. Doing so is generally accepted as a requirement for the continued growth and prosperity of the organization and its members.

**Self-esteem needs.** Competition creates an aura of importance related to all tasks, no matter how dull or uninteresting they may be. The ego of the employee becomes attached to the results achieved.

**Achievement needs.** As either an individual competitor or as a member of a competitive team, the employee gains the opportunity to win the special recognition and attention which accrues to the winner in every competitive situation. The combative instinct, while not dominant, is strong in our culture. It is ingrained from childhood, and the prospect of winning makes the vigors of competition seem worthwhile.

Keeping the spirit of competition alive is best achieved through providing recognition. Recognition is an important motivational tool for all managers.

- People perform best when they are given credit for their efforts and achievements.
- Recognition provides employees with a sense of belonging.
- People grow through recognition and stagnate without it.

Despite the virtues of competition, it can be destructive. When employees or groups of employees realize their achievements at the expense of others within the organization, the manager(s) involved must recognize that unhealthy condition and intervene. Nothing has a greater power for pulling people together than does a *common enemy*. To ensure that the effect of competition on the entire organization remains positive, those persons or things designated as common enemies must be outside the organization—a competitor, for example.

Competition can have a strong influence on moving people toward the development of a going places attitude and the achievement of organizational objectives. It is effective only when it is combined with an effort to cooperate with other groups and individuals within the organization.

## Summary

The development and maintenance of a going places attitude separates the organizations which are exceptionally productive, over the long run, from those organizations which are either less productive or lacking in the consistency of their performance. Such an attitude cannot be developed without the proper operating climate being established and a high level of motivation being generated among employees.

There are four primary areas on which a manager can focus attention and efforts for the purpose of developing a going places attitude: (1) sharing the grand design, or the organization's plans and aspirations, with all its members; (2) striving for excellence, or the realization of the organization's potential, by tapping the creative potential of all employees while generating an environment which is supportive of constructive change; (3) accentuating the positive by demonstrating an unshakable belief in the organization and its members while maintaining a positive expectancy related to the achievement of organizational goals; and (4) generating a constructive competitive spirit which motivates employees to maximize their contribution to the achievement of organizational goals.

# 6
# Case Histories

For the purpose of providing further insight into how the productivity-improving ideas presented previously are applied, four case histories are presented. The four organizations, represented by the case histories, range in size of annual sales from 3 million dollars to billions of dollars. The number of people employed by these organizations ranges from 60 to 850,000. Focus of the activities covered by the case studies is limited from 60 to 400 employees who were directly involved. The case studies range from manufacturing to service organizations, and from union to nonunion. Some were viable and financially healthy at the time productivity improvement programs were initiated. Others were on the brink of bankruptcy. In all cases, significant productivity improvements were realized within six months. In all cases, the first year's progress became a foundation for continued improvement. Managers who had experienced difficulty in their previous attempts to improve productivity were generally able to continue on their own once they had been shown the proper approach.

# 13

## An Automotive Assembly Operation

## Background

Few industries are as exciting as is the automotive manufacturing industry. More than any other industry, it has contributed to the economic growth of the nation and our improved standard of living. Although America's long-standing love affair with the automobile has cooled somewhat due to rising prices and the increased cost of operation, we generally remain willfully dependent on this personal mode of transportation. The earning of a driver's license has been, is, and promises to continue to be an important event in the lives of young people. The strong desire most people have for the freedom provided by the automobile will most probably continue to offset the increasing costs of ownership and operation.

As the automobile impacts our society, the economy, and our personal lives, it has also impacted the principles of organization and management. The concept of decentralized operations and coordinated control contributed greatly to the growth and success of the first automotive manufacturers and, later, other industries. In the early 1920s, the complexity and magnitude of problems within the auto industry were far greater than those experienced by other contemporary industrial enterprises. Those problems forced automotive managers to think more in terms of organizational principles and philosophies than did other managers of that time.

I began working for an automotive manufacturer immediately after graduation from college. The division I worked for had been in business for almost 60 years at the time I started. The operation was vertically integrated with engines, rear axles, transmissions, and sheet metal being manufactured on site. I migrated to the final assembly part of the business where all 15,000 components are brought together and assembled into the finished product. Within the automotive business, no other activity can match the consistently fast pace of final assembly. Final assembly is the culmination of a long string of manufacturing operations. Because it is the last manufacturing activity before shipment of the completed product to the customer and because of the dependency on component inputs from hundreds of sources, both within and without the corporation, assembly is generally considered to be the "hot seat" of automotive manufacturing activities. Managers tend to either thrive or die in the environment, with the criteria for success being the same as that for any other manufacturing activity *plus* a greater than normal amount of personal stamina and tolerance for pressure.

## The Unique Challenge of Final Assembly

Of all the manufacturing activities within the automotive industry, final assembly is the most labor-intensive. Other activities lend themselves more to mechanization, if not automation, than do assembly operations. A primary reason for this is that due to the number of options offered and the number of combinations possible, the job of the assembly line worker is not to simply assemble an assigned number of parts, but rather to assemble the correct parts out of many possibilities. There is not one suspension spring for all models, for example. To provide the desired ride characteristics there may be dozens of different springs. Some are front springs, some are rear springs; some are for one model, others are for other models; some are to be installed only on models with the air-conditioning option, others are for models without air conditioning. Considering all models, colors, and options offered, it is possible to assemble more than 250,000 automobiles of a certain make and model year with no two being exactly identical.

A standard time is developed for each and every assembly operation. Dependent upon the options specified and the model type, the total standard time allowed to assemble each car varies. Only identical models having the same options, with differences being limited to color, will have the same standard time allowance. For an automotive assembly line to run both smoothly and efficiently, the workloads of individual operations must be "balanced" to the speed of the assembly line, the capacity of assembly equipment, and the scheduled sequence of cars calling for certain options. Ideally, if an assembly line is designed to produce sixty cars each hour, all operators would have an assigned workload plus allowances totaling exactly one minute. Were all cars the same, requiring identical assembly labor inputs, the problem would be simpler; but such is not the case. An operator may be assigned, for example, to assemble an air-conditioning system component. What does that operator do when a car enters the work zone that doesn't call for the air-conditioning option? If we assign the operator assembly responsibility for other parts, as well, what happens when a car calls for both parts assigned and the time the car is in the work area is insufficient for the parts to be correctly assembled by a single person? As what can reasonably be performed by an operator determines the assignment of specific tasks, it also determines the sequence in which specific options and models are scheduled. The scheduling sequence is also affected by the capacity of equipment used in the assembly process. The capacity, for example, of on-line equipment used to evacuate the air from the hoses and lines of the air-conditioning system, so that the system can be charged with refrigerant, limits the number of cars equipped with air conditioning that can be scheduled consecutively. To exceed that number would result in some cars not being evacuated and charged on line and those units having to be routed to off-line repair stations for the work to be completed.

Automotive assembly management's efforts are directed to being effective first and efficient second, as are the efforts of managers in nonrelated activities. Effectiveness is based upon completely and accurately performing all operations so that the assembly line can run continuously, without interruption. Efficiency is based upon achieving the desired number and quality of completely assembled units with the least possible consumption of labor, material, and other resources. Because of the complexity and interdependence of assembly operations, *coordination* is essential for achievement of the desired results—attaining the scheduled outputs, all of high quality, and with a minimum consumption of resources. This means coordination of material inputs; coordination of schedules; and coordination of the human effort.

A thousand or more people can be working on the assembly line at the same time in the same facility. At a scheduled output rate of 60 cars per hour and with 1000 people working on the assembly line, each *minute* of downtime costs the equivalent of 25 labor *hours* (1000 people $\times$ 1 minute lost each = 1000 lost minutes $\div$ 60 minutes per hour = 16.67 hours $\times$ 1.5 = 25 hours). The 1.5 factor represents the fact that lost time must generally be recovered by working overtime with assembly workers being paid 1.5 times their regular pay rate for all such hours worked. Contractual agreement prevents the assembly line from being speeded up to recover lost time. Besides possible labor problems if the line were to be speeded up, a speedup could cause those operators with a workload approaching maximum to fall behind and generate assembly defects. The required repair labor to correct such defects could more than offset the attempted "savings."

To maintain momentum and maximize outputs, the assembly line is not usually shut down to provide a break period for operators. Except during periods of high absenteeism, a "tag relief" system is in effect. Operators who have been trained to perform several different jobs are paid a higher rate to systematically provide a break for a number of assigned assembly line workers on a one-at-a-time basis. Several such relief persons, each working in an assigned "zone" or work area, enable all assembly operators to take a break each morning and each afternoon without the assembly line being shut down.

Much has been said and written about the supposed inferior quality of cars assembled on Mondays, a day when absenteeism is usually higher than on other workdays. Based on over twelve years of experience in the business, I am of the opinion that cars assembled on Mondays are at *least* equal in quality to cars built on other days of the workweek. True, we did experience a higher-than-average rate of absenteeism on Mondays, but independent evaluation by a specially trained audit group consistently reported the quality of those units to be generally at least equal to the units assembled on other workdays. The real consequence of high absenteeism on Mondays was having to sometimes shut down the line to provide operators their work breaks. When too few operators report to work, not enough people are on hand to provide the normal tag relief, so the line must be shut down for the alloted break period in the morning and/or in the afternoon.

An automotive assembly line is composed of distinct work areas, each having several zones of twenty to thirty employees and a supervisor. The larger areas consisting of several zones are the "body" area, the "chassis" area, and the "final" area. Car bodies were supplied to us by a codivision. Our body assembly area consisted of the assembly of hardware, including firewall-mounted heaters and brake-system master cylinders, the complete instrument panel, and miscellaneous hardware, such as outside mirrors, brake-pedal assembly, front carpet, etc. Instrument panels were subassembled and tested on a separate subassembly line and fed to the main assembly line via a conveyor. Chassis assembly consists of the complete chassis—frame, suspension, drive shaft, transmission, rear axle, engine, brake lines, exhaust system, etc. Engines and transmissions, like instrument panels, were assembled off the main assembly line in a separate subassembly area and fed to the main line via a conveyor. The "final" area is the area where the body is mounted to the chassis, and fenders, hoods, bumpers, the steering column and steering wheel, and other components are assembled. The air-conditioning system is evacuated and charged, gasoline is added, and the engine is started in the final area. Bumpers, steering columns, and fenders and hoods are all prepared in subassembly areas and fed via conveyor, in line schedule sequence, to the main assembly line.

A work zone in any area consists of operators who assemble components in proper sequence. Near the end of each zone is one or more repair persons. One or more inspectors are in each assembly zone and are assigned to check that the correct parts have been assembled in the proper manner. Discrepancies are written on an inspection ticket, and repair of those defects is attempted and often completed before the car leaves the responsible assembly zone. Unrepaired defects are tallied as each car leaves each work zone, providing a performance indicator. Supervisors continuously review the defects leaving their respective areas at the zone tally stations and move to those operations experiencing problems and attempt to correct them. Each hour a "quality index" for each area (chassis, body, and final) is calculated and phoned in to a control center. The quality index is simply the number of unrepaired defects leaving the area divided by the total number of units assembled. For example, if 12 unrepaired defects left the chassis assembly area and 60 chassis, in total, were assembled during that period, the chassis-line quality index would be 0.20.

Of major importance in an automotive assembly operation is the number of defect-free cars at the end of the assembly line. Those cars without any defects are essentially ready for shipment after front-end alignment, which is the last operation and is usually performed after the car leaves the assembly line. Those cars with defects must be routed to a repair area off the main assembly line. These repair areas are similar to a dealer's service area with the big difference being that within the assembly plant, conveyors route the cars through some of the repair areas. While a standard time allowance is provided for a nominal amount of off-line repair on each car, the allowance is generally not sufficient to cover any significant volume of defects. Further, the off-line repair areas are more difficult to manage and control for several reasons, including:

1. Repair work requires the additional time-consuming element of diagnosis.
2. Out-of-assembly-zone repairs generally do not have the same easy access to defective components as do on-line–in-zone repairs because of subsequent assembly operations.
3. Off-line repair work is not mechanically paced as is the assembly line.
4. The system rewards off-line repair persons for inefficiency—a slow repair pace generates overtime and overtime worked is compensated for at a premium pay rate.

During the introduction of new models, when the input of defects to the off-line repair area is the greatest, it is not unusual for persons working in that area to work 10 to 12 hours each day and 6 or 7 days each week. From the September or October date of new-model introductions to at least Thanksgiving and oftentimes longer, it is not unusual for off-line repair persons in automotive assembly to work 70-hour workweeks and, because of overtime premiums, to receive weekly paychecks for 90 hours. For obvious reasons, employees with the most seniority generally migrate to the off-line repair areas. In addition to the increased opportunity for overtime in the off-line repair areas, jobs within those areas have a higher classification than jobs on the assembly line and pay a higher hourly wage rate. Because of the repair cost consequences, plus possible order cancellations should a car get hung up in the off-line repair area, assembly management must focus on building each car correctly on the assembly line. The name of the game is to have as many defect-free cars as is possible at the end of the assembly line to avoid the off-line repair areas. The system, however, incorporated another practice that could result in managerial compromise. First-line supervisors, general-assembly supervisors, and assistant superintendents all received premium pay for all overtime hours worked. While a first-line supervisor is responsible for up to thirty people, a general supervisor is responsible for from three to ten supervisors, and an assistant superintendent is responsible for from three to seven general supervisors and could possibly have shift responsibility for an entire assembly plant. The compensation of most managers in automotive manufacturing is dependent upon level of responsibility *plus hours worked*. Possible bonus compensation was limited to full superintendents and above. You cannot help but wonder what the positive impact on efficiency and profits would be if most, if not all, managers were paid performance bonuses in lieu of overtime. But such was not the case.


## The Productivity-Improving Opportunity

In 1963, our division won a heated competition among several divisions within the corporation to produce a new personal luxury car. The assembly of that car was integrated into the assembly operation for our other larger models with some difficulty. Many of the new cars called for more options than did our other models. At that point in time, for example, the on-line evacuation and charging of air-conditioning systems was not yet routine, and many of the new cars called for that option. In addition, problems greater than usual were experienced in properly aligning the doors, hood, fenders, and bumpers. These problems coupled with the fact that the new car was viewed as an inroad to a greater market share, with appropriately stringent quality standards being applied, eventually led to the construction of a new facility. This new facility was to assemble only two models, the new personal luxury car and another distinct, low-production model. In time, the second model was dropped, leaving the entire new facility for the assembly of the personal luxury car.

Over a period of six years, the new facility provided relief, in the form of fewer problems caused by the personal luxury car, to the facility for assembly of all other models. While the operation for the assembly of all other models ran more smoothly, the new operation for the assembly of the personal luxury car continued to be plagued by problems. The larger facility was assembling cars at a rate of eighty cars per hour. The personal luxury cars were, because of a lesser demand, being produced at a rate of twenty-two cars per hour. In the larger facility, each assembly operator had a work cycle of 45 seconds. In the smaller facility, each assembly operator had a work cycle of 2 minutes and 44 seconds. For obvious reasons, it is easier to train an assembly operator for a job with a 45-second work cycle than it is to train an assembly operator for a job with a work cycle almost 4 times as long. Employees in the smaller facility, which produced the personal luxury car, were generally younger than employees working in the larger plant. Not only was the rate of absenteeism higher in the smaller plant, it was considerably more difficult to quickly train a person as a fill-in for someone who was absent. Further complicating operations within the smaller plant was the fact that car bodies were supplied by a codivision located 150 miles away. Because of the great distance and despite the good efforts of persons assigned to coordinate activities between the body supplier and the assembly plant, problems were generally not resolved on a timely basis. Consequently, because of the delays that resulted when defective car bodies were returned to the supplier, a special operation had to be maintained to inspect and repair bodies at the point of receipt. Though the associated costs were charged back to the responsible division, the activity consumed assembly management resources that should have been applied to final assembly, not body repair.

The assembly plant for the personal luxury car was a separate facility and profit center. In a six-year period, two top-notch manufacturing managers were assigned to run the plant. The manager of the plant benefited, in my opinion, in that higher-management's focus was on the larger facility and he was not subjected to outside-the-plant interference while being held accountable for the operational results. He was the undisputed boss with near-total authority and responsibility.

Due to a multitude of problems which were manifested in the form of low efficiency and unfavorable cost variances, plus other considerations which were not directly related, a decision was made to expand the small facility and to assemble another model within the new, larger facility. Assembly of the personal luxury car was to be combined with other models in another facility. By November 1972, construction of the new facility began and promised to disrupt continued assembly of the personal luxury car for the balance of the model year. As if normal operational problems within the facility were not enough, assembly would have to continue for seven months in the midst of an ongoing major construction project. In late December, the manager who ran the plant had a health-related problem, and I was asked to fill in for him for six to eight weeks, until he could recover and return to work.

Having worked in the other assembly plant for several years, I was well acquainted with assembly operations in general but lacked specific knowledge of the smaller plant and its problems. Fortunately for me, three of the four general supervisors assigned to the operation had several years of experience in that particular facility, and all four were well versed in assembly operations and, in my opinion, conscientious and capable managers. Production, downtime, efficiency, cost, and the "old car," or aging of cars built but not shipped, reports were reviewed in detail. Following are the results of that analysis:

**Production.** Scheduled at twenty-two cars per hour but consistently below that figure and averaging less than twenty cars per hour.

**Downtime.** Excessive but apparently controllable as parts shortages generally did not appear to be the problem.

**Labor efficiency.** Had averaged 71 percent from September through November but had dropped to 66 percent through the first three weeks of December, as compared to 64.4 percent for the entire previous model year and 70.3 percent for the model year before that.

## Costs

**Direct labor.** Substantial losses incurred September through December due to not achieving build schedule in eight hours and having to work overtime; assembly defects also had generated excessive repair overtime.

**Indirect labor.** Expenses for supervision and inspection were over budget, due to excessive overtime and poor quality.

**Operating supplies.** This expense category was, in total, over budget with the elements of gasoline and work gloves being the primary problem.

**Material scrap and rework expense.** Process rejects and the rework labor, applied in an attempt to reclaim such material, caused an unfavorable year-to-date variance to budget in this expense category.

**Cars assembled but not shipped aging.** The total repair float contained over 350 cars with about half that number having been built more than five workdays previously.

The overall situation was grim. All costs were over budget. While the quality of shipped cars as measured by an independent audit function was good, too many resources were being consumed to meet quality standards, especially inspection and off-line repair labor. The build schedule was being made by working overtime at a considerable cost penalty. Too many of the assembled but in some way defective cars in the repair float were more than five workdays old. Customers were threatening to cancel their orders in increasing numbers. And last, but not least, the scope of construction activities was becoming greater and causing more disruption and interference to assembly operations. One thing was for certain: no one person, and certainly not me, was capable of turning the operation around single-handedly. Whereas the whole division was very performance-oriented, based on past experience and the obvious additional problems of the construction project, the possibility of achieving operational improvements for the balance of the model year had been pretty much discounted. All that could reasonably be expected under the circumstances was to "hold on" for the next seven months and plan the new facility and rearrangement well, so that we could get off to a fast start with the new model in the fall.

What an opportunity! I sensed it then and I now know, without a doubt, that given a performance-oriented environment (license) and an operation characterized by problems with the possibility for near-term improvement having been discounted (situation), a tremendous opportunity for improvement exists. Such a situation can accurately be called a "no-lose" situation. More important than the discounting of the possibility for near-term improvement (or the no-lose factor) is the performance-oriented environment. Such a work climate conditions all employees for excellence in performance. All the responsible manager has to do is to light the fuse with the right approach, and obstacles turn into opportunities while remote possibilities become realities.

## The Plan to Improve Productivity

The planned approach was very basic: to increase the operation's effectiveness by consistently *shipping* the build schedule on a daily basis; then to enlarge managerial focus to include the same improved outputs accomplished in a more efficient manner. To achieve these improvements, it was obvious that some, as yet unspecified, conditions would have to be changed. After I spent a few days on the new assignment, it became apparent that one such change in existing conditions would have to be to increase both the awareness and degree of involvement of all managers and their employees. While I didn't have the answers to the many problems, I knew what should be happening and saw my near-term role as having five separate elements:

1. Communicate expectations or what should be happening without attempting to place the blame for it not having happened, to date, on any person or group of persons; to gain an intellectual agreement as to what "should be."
2. Establish a work climate based on greater participation, involvement, and cooperation among all persons in the organization, managers and nonmanagers; to gain a "we" or "us," rather than the prevailing "look out for yourself," attitude.
3. Work with the general supervisors and they in turn with their supervisors to mutually set performance goals related to all activities; to gain managerial commitments representing improvement over the then current level of performance for all activities.
4. Make a personal commitment to all managers to help them in any way possible but short of doing for them what they were capable of doing for themselves; to communicate an interest in achieving improved results or corrective action and a willingness to personally accept whatever risks might be associated with that action.
5. Provide continuous feedback related to "actual" performance vs. "goal"; to gain the necessary emotional involvement required to realize improvement.

Note that the goals mentioned in 3 stressed only improvement over recent performance, with no pressure being applied to achieve, at least in the near term, the should bes referred to in 1.

Also note that the initial focus on effectiveness was equivalent to an emphasis on results at any cost. Only after effectiveness had been established would the focus enlarge to include being more efficient or controlling costs better.

Initial meetings were held with all managers to discuss the planned approach, quantify the should bes related to performance, discuss specific problems contributing to the overall poor results, and set goals reflecting improvement for all activities. These meetings enabled me to gain a quick understanding of what was not happening and why, provided valuable insight into individual manager attitudes, and served the previously outlined purposes. In addition to computer-generated reports comparing actual vs. budgeted performance, supplementary reports comparing actual performance to less stringent goals were manually generated daily and summarized weekly. Brief daily meetings were held with the general supervisors to discuss performance and develop plans aimed at improving results. A similar meeting of one hour or less was held once each week with all managers in attendance. Our program to improve managerial control started with housekeeping and safety inspections of each supervisor's area once each week. A group composed of the general supervisors and myself individually inspected and rated each area at random times throughout the week. The ratings were compiled at the end of the week, and a rating from best to worst was published, provided to each supervisor, and posted on the bulletin boards. As it is virtually impossible to improve housekeeping without also improving supervisory control over any area, this program achieved its purpose.

The speed of the assembly line was frequently timed by the general supervisors and myself. As the drive was subject to slippage, resulting in a reduction of line speed, it was necessary to time the speed at least once each half-hour and to have maintenance personnel make corrective adjustments as was necessary. It would have been easier to assign the timing responsibility to a maintenance worker, but the purpose was as much to sensitize management to the importance of line speed as it was to recognize and correct the repetitive problem of underbuild.

Where previously supervisors and/or operators had shut off the line for brief periods to correct assembly problems, the importance of keeping the line running was communicated to everyone. Specific direction was given that the assembly line was not to be shut off for any reason other than an emergency which endangered the safety of an employee. Management by edict didn't work any better in that situation than it does in other situations. Every time the line was shut down for any reason, I immediately called the general supervisor of the area responsible and asked three questions: "Who shut the line off?" "Why was the line shut off?" and "When will the line be restarted?" All downtime was compiled into a daily report, and the information on the report communicated as being an indicator of supervisory performance. The emphasis on keeping the line running, along with the persistence associated with checking out and recording the duration and responsibility for all downtime, soon resulted in downtime being virtually eliminated. Rather than resulting in the generation of more defects, not shutting the assembly line down for any and every problem eventually resulted in the reduction of assembly defects. Maintaining the momentum of the moving line and the rhythm of the assembly operators improved the quality.

## Increased and Well-Communicated Expectations Yield Improved Results

Within two to three weeks the barely recognizable improvements, coupled with specific and well-communicated expectations, and the prompt feedback of actual results vs. goals had altered for the better both the attitude and interest of most managers and many employees. Ideas for operational improvements were solicited and provided by many managers and some employees. Some of the forwarded ideas that were actually implemented within the first six weeks of my assignment were:

- The number of on-line operators was increased.
- Rather than assisting the off-line repair persons after assembly hours as they had done in the past, line repair persons were assigned to inspect and repair, if necessary, every unit remaining on the line in their respective work areas at the end of the assembly shift. This resulted in more defect-free cars coming off the assembly line at the start of the following shift.
- A program was designed and implemented to force a dedicated segment of the off-line repair work group to process the oldest cars in the repair float. This resulted in fewer cars over five workdays old remaining in the repair float.
- An effort was made to establish a team spirit. A logo and motto were created. The logo with motto was printed on self-adhesive stickers and was applied to the windshield of all cars after passing final inspection and before shipment to the customer. For a nominal cost, key chains and other items incorporating the logo and motto were distributed to employees as housekeeping and performance awards.
- Off-line conveyors were converted to mechanically paced repair stations. The number of units repaired and passed each day increased significantly.
- A key hourly employee from each assembly area—chassis, body, and final— was delegated to diagnose assembly defects that remained unrepaired when the car came off the end of the assembly line and to feed information related to the specific cause(s) back to the responsible supervisor. This action aided in correcting assembly problems of a repetitive nature.

The above, plus other implemented suggestions, including the measurement and feedback of individual supervisory performance to goal information, all contributed to improved effectiveness and efficiency. After six weeks, the previous manager returned to work from sick leave and was reassigned to another position in the other assembly plant.

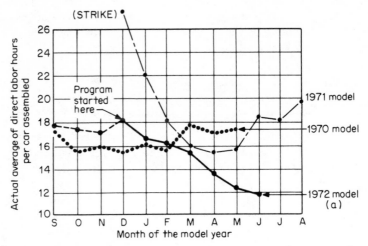

**Figure 13-1.** The actual average number of direct labor hours required per car produced. (*a*) Labor hours required to assemble a car were reduced by one-third over a six-month period.

*Despite* a significant erosion in the quality of incoming bodies from our codivision and a further drain on available resources to repair those problems on site and *despite* the increased interference caused by surrounding construction projects—which on one occasion ruptured a water main and flooded the facility, forcing a daylong shutdown for cleanup and on another occasion mistakenly tore down an outside wall, exposing chassis-line employees to the prevailing weather conditions in Michigan at midwinter—steady improvement was made until the end of the model year. Figure 13-1 illustrates the magnitude of productivity improvement achieved as compared to historical levels of productivity.

Including the month of December for which the average number of direct labor hours per car was 18.26, the average number of direct labor hours required to assemble a car from September through December was 17.68. Considering the tangible problem of the disruption caused by the construction activity and the intangible negative impact of employees facing an unknown reassignment at the conclusion of the model year, realistic expectations might have been to show no improvement for the balance of the model year. Establishing the 17.68 actual direct labor hours as the base, Table 13-1 depicts the month-by-month labor hour savings realized throughout the program. From Table 13-1, the dollar savings (assuming an average wage of $7.16 per hour) would be $7.16 times 47,957, or $343,372.

Substantial losses to budget had been experienced through December. From January through the end of the model year in June, the losses were turned into gains. The magnitude of those gains, or favorable variances, to budget steadily increased each month. Table 13-2 summarizes that improvement.

**TABLE 13-1.** Labor Hour Savings at the Assembly Plant Producing the Personal Luxury Car

| Period | Average Direct Labor Hours Required per Unit Assembled | Labor Hour Index | No. Units Produced | × | Savings in Labor Hours per Unit | = | Monthly Labor Hours Saved |
|---|---|---|---|---|---|---|---|
| Sept.–Dec. | 17.68 | 100 | | | | | |
| Jan. | 16.80 | 95.0 | 3712 | | 0.88 | | 3,267 |
| Feb. | 16.23 | 91.8 | 3700 | | 1.45 | | 5,365 |
| Mar. | 15.77 | 89.2 | 3908 | | 1.91 | | 7,464 |
| Apr. | 14.00 | 79.2 | 3553 | | 3.68 | | 13,075 |
| May | 12.91 | 73.0 | 3696 | | 4.77 | | 17,630 |
| June | 11.90 | 67.3 | 200 | | 5.78 | | 1,156 |
| Total direct labor hours saved* | | | | | | | 47,957 |

*Actual hours January through June vs. average actual hours September through December.

**TABLE 13-2.** Performance Report at the Assembly Plant Producing the Personal Luxury Car

| | Sept. | Oct. | Nov. | Dec. | Jan. | Feb. | Mar. | Apr. | May |
|---|---|---|---|---|---|---|---|---|---|
| Actual direct labor efficiency % | 71.0 | 70.6 | 71.7 | 66.2 | 77.8 | 78.7 | 81.5 | 92.8 | 93.2 |
| Direct labor $ savings to budget | (loss) | (loss) | (loss) | (loss) | 9,779 | 14,588 | 24,129 | 51,305 | 53,270 |
| Indirect labor $ savings to budget | (loss) | (loss) | (loss) | (loss) | 3,008 | (261) | 1,543 | (642) | 1,781 |
| Operating supplies $ savings to budget | (loss) | (loss) | (loss) | (loss) | 1,593 | (2,350) | 1,280 | (548) | 2,164 |
| Scrap material and rework labor savings to budget | (loss) | (loss) | (loss) | (loss) | 4,292 | 8,470 | 91 | 769 | 5,680 |
| Total $ savings to budget | (loss) | (loss) | (loss) | (loss) | 18,672 | 20,447 | 27,043 | 50,884 | 62,905 |
| **Cars Assembled but Requiring Rework/Repair as of the Last Day of the Month** | | | | | | | | | |
| Over 5 days old* | | | . . . | 104 | 75 | 54 | 48 | 63 | 21 |
| Over 2 weeks old* | | | . . . | 51 | 25 | 21 | 8 | 19 | 11 |
| Over 3 weeks old* | | | . . . | 28 | 14 | 8 | 1 | 2 | 2 |
| Total repair float* | | | . . . | 378 | 168 | 207 | 265 | 252 | 200 |
| % of total more than 5 days old* | | | . . . | 48.4 | 67.9 | 40.0 | 21.5 | 33.3 | 17.2 |
| Total repair float expressed in days of actual production | | | | 2.15 | 0.95 | 1.18 | 1.51 | 1.43 | 1.13 |

*Information not available for September, October, and November.

At the conclusion of that model year's production run in June, members of the management team were reassigned. Some were transferred with the car to the other assembly plant. Others remained in the remodeled, larger facility to assemble the new model of another car. Those that were transferred to the other assembly plant took with them the confidence borne from having contributed to making a bad situation better. Those that remained to assemble the new model of another car in the remodeled facility were able to maintain the esprit de corps established earlier. That attitude contributed greatly to the successful start-up of a new car in a new facility, which is no minor feat. Over eight years later and long after I had left the company, I was shopping for a new car in a distant city. Looking over the cars in the dealer's lot, I noticed stickers on the windshields of some models. The sticker design had been revised, but the motto, and I would bet the spirit, remains the same. When managers taste success, and if that success provides them the status and recognition they deserve, they will continue being successful. Every bad situation is just waiting to be made better, and every underachieving manager would rather be a *winner*.

# 14 A Phonograph Record Manufacturer

## Background

The record and prerecorded tape business is often compared to the newspaper business. As a demand for last week's newspaper does not generally exist, so it is with popular recordings. The name of the game for manufacturers of popular recordings is to have the records and tapes on the shelves in retail stores when a tune is "hot." Only by so doing can sales and profits be maximized. Unknown to most consumers, thousands of new songs are written, recorded, and duplicated in the form of records or tapes each year. While some are by established writers and artists, most are by persons who are pursuing a yet unfulfilled dream of becoming "stars" and achieving the fame, wealth, and recognition that accompanies that established status. "Established" is typically synonymous with success that endures for a relatively short time within the music business. While fame is fleeting when dependent upon public opinion, an artist need only ride the top of the popularity charts for a short period of time to become financially independent for life. Although the odds against success are astronomically high, so are the rewards should an artist succeed. Recording artists are usually conditioned by years of failing to be able to get "air play," or radios to broadcast their songs. If and when they do record what generates interest among program directors of radio stations, disc jockeys, and the public, pressure is applied to the manufacturing plants to produce large quantities of records and tapes within a few days. As it is unpredictable if and when a tune will become a hit, record companies tend to be conservative on the quantity of records and tapes initially produced. The manufacturing plants, likewise, have no idea of what will hap-

233

pen with new releases. Accordingly, assuming a volume of unprocessed orders is on hand, manufacturing resources are committed to those new orders via a schedule. That schedule becomes critical as the product must be available when disc jockeys start to play new tunes and advertising campaigns are launched. With all equipment normally scheduled for at least a week ahead, a problem results when a hit develops and a production rerun of that tune must be promptly made. The business is characterized by continually juggling available resources in an attempt to keep customers happy.

All music is recorded, either in a studio or at a live performance, on tape. The tape is delivered to a disc-mastering studio where the sound impressions on the tape are transcribed, via a sophisticated tracing and lathe device, to sound grooves in an acetate-coated aluminum disc. This disc is referred to as a *lacquer*. The lacquer is shipped to the record-processing plant. Proper packaging of the lacquers for shipment is critical because any scratch or blemish on the lacquer surface will be evident in the finished phonograph record in the form of distracting noises. Upon receipt of the lacquer at the pressing plant, the lacquer is sprayed with a silver solution. The silver adheres to the lacquer's surface, hardens, and is then peeled away as a perfect negative reproduction of the recorded sound grooves. The silver mold, referred to as a *master*, is not durable enough to withstand high-volume record-pressing demands, so another mold must be made of a stronger nickel alloy. This nickel mold is obtained by an electroplating process which consists of placing the silver master in an electroplating tank containing a nickel solution. During the plating process, the nickel in the solution adheres to the silver master to form a new positive mold called a *mother*. The mother is stripped from the master, cleaned, and trimmed. Because they are positive impressions, or duplicates of the lacquer, mothers can be and are played to ensure quality sound reproduction before continuing the manufacturing process. If problems exist with the mother, it is either rejected and another one made from the lacquer or, if minor, repaired using a special microscope and a stylus.

Mothers are returned to the nickel-plating tank to produce negative molds that are called *stampers* because they are later inserted into plastic-molding machines, or "presses," and used to stamp out records. Several stampers are usually made from each mother as the stampers wear out or are damaged by impurities in the vinyl material, from which records are made, during the pressing process.

Two stampers, one for each side of the record, are mounted on flat metal dies having open internal passages which are used for heating and cooling the die. The dies are mounted in a hydraulic press, and the stampers are held to the dies with retaining rings and adhesive.

Bulk vinyl compound is stored in large silos removed from the pressing area. The compound is either in the form of granules or very small pellets. Pneumatic tubes from the storage silos to the *extruder*, or vinyl "melter," are used to transport vinyl to the presses. Vinyl is blown into the extruder, and it is heated,

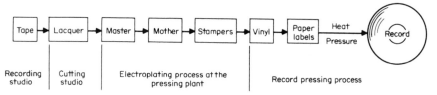

**Figure 14-1.** Production process for a phonograph record.

melted, and formed into a *biscuit,* resembling a hockey puck in appearance. Printed paper labels are placed on the top and the bottom of the biscuit before the biscuit is pressed between the two stampers to form a record. The vinyl that overflows to the edge during the pressing process is trimmed, and the record is then complete. In some plants, this process is manual, with operators placing the biscuits and labels in the press manually, removing the record from the press, and trimming it. In other plants, the entire process is automatic, with a single operator being able to run several presses and focusing only on setups, mounting stampers to the die faces, adjusting temperature and cycle-duration settings on the presses, and tending to any press malfunction. Figure 14-1 graphically represents the production processes of the phonograph record.

## The Productivity-Improving Opportunity

The record-pressing plant I became associated with is referred to as a "custom" record presser. Though part of a vertically integrated corporation consisting of record labels which had recording artists on contract; a recording studio; a lacquer-cutting studio; printing plants that produced record sleeves, labels, and album covers; and record-pressing and tape-duplicating plants, 90 percent of this plant's business was from nonrelated record companies. Custom record-pressing plants depend largely on competing for and winning business from record companies that do not have their own pressing plants and record companies that do have their own pressing plants but occasionally need excess manufacturing capacity. Success is dependent upon both effectiveness and efficiency. Pricing competition is fierce as most of the time one or more record-pressing plants are operating below capacity and will accept jobs at a lower-than-normal price in an attempt to cover their overhead. Even in those rare periods when excess capacity does not exist, pricing competition is heated, placing much emphasis on efficiency and cost control. As previously mentioned, the perishability factor related to popularity and demand for any one tune dictates that the product be manufactured and distributed on a timely basis. For all practical purposes, records are sold to retail outlets on a consignment basis. Unsold product can usually be exchanged for other product, if not a cash refund. Returned goods are the Achilles' heel of the industry. Because of the built-in "returns factor," sensitivity toward sales that are made at the retail level and lost because of poor quality is quite high. All these and other factors combined resulted in a demanding operating environment.

My joining this company makes for a good study in the transferability of managerial skills. At the time I came aboard, and without exaggeration, all I knew about records was that they were round, and black, and had a hole in the center. Within a short period of time, I had learned that they were usually round, usually black, and had a hole that was usually in the center. Fortunately for me, the person to whom I reported had considerable record-pressing experience and was, even more importantly, a good delegator capable of creating a work climate conducive to making productivity gains.

The plant had previously made the change from manual to automated record presses. Such a change can be devastating, at least in the short term, for even a well-managed operation. Unfortunately, this had not been a well-run operation prior to the conversion. Key people from other divisions of the corporation had been assigned to assist in attempting to gain operating momentum. Although managers were working very long hours and obviously putting forth a lot of effort, the results were poor. The sales force was looking good in the sense they were readily able to book more business than the plant could produce. Much of that business was being subcontracted to a competitive pressing plant. The company's cost for such externally produced pressings was significantly less than the cost of internally manufactured product. There was no question that the subcontractor was making money on a lesser selling price and we were losing money by the bucketfuls while charging a higher price.

Whereas managers were generally working hard personally, some were unable to get their assigned employees to do so. It was not unusual to walk through the plant during working hours and see a number of employees openly sitting on cardboard boxes and either smoking, or drinking a soft drink or cup of coffee, or simply chatting with another employee. The limited number of records that were being pressed were often delayed for days before they could be shipped because the corresponding record jackets could not be found within the 100,000-square-foot warehouse portion of the plant. The typical warehouser's response to a request for jackets was "We have them, but we can't find them." The entire situation was best summarized by a veteran manager who had been transferred in from another division when he said:

During my life I have had three truly traumatic experiences. The first was during the Great Depression when I thought I was going to starve to death. The second was during World War II when I was trapped behind enemy lines for nine days and was sure I would be killed. The last is being here [in our plant] right now; and do you know this, by far, is the worst of the three.

Frustration, among the managerial group, bordered on despair.

At the time I came aboard, it had been projected we had to turn around this unprofitable subsidiary within two years. Other operations within the corporation were generally considered to be in good enough condition to support this particular operation for up to two years. Though the corporation's debt was such that it could not be further increased, it was felt that the other operations could service the corporate debt, cover their own operating expenses, and supply the required operating capital for our ailing record-pressing plant, all from cash generated by those other businesses. Unfortunately, it did not work that way. Within a couple of months, one of those other, supposedly viable, operations was virtually shut down. While their inventory valuation of component parts was several million dollars, they did not have the parts needed to assemble products and complete customer orders. (At the end of that fiscal year that subsidiary wrote off inventory previously valued in excess of their net sales for the year.) Both suppliers and customers became aware of the corporation's problems, and our death knell rang throughout the industry and the business community.

Most managements would have opted for protection under Chapter 11 of the federal Bankruptcy Act. Instead, top managers within the corporation, with the help of an outside consultant, focused their attention on restructuring the corporate debt. The corporation was in default on bank loans, the total of which exceeded annual sales. Though we were able to get limited financial help from some of the other subsidiaries on an occasional basis, we were pretty much on our own. The name of the game was sink or swim.

The situation was communicated in as constructive a manner as was possible to all employees within our record-pressing plant. Generally, the information provided was viewed by members of the bargaining unit as a ploy by the "new management" to get people to work harder. Everyone knew the place had been "messed up" for years, yet they had always received a paycheck every week. Employees had been conditioned, by previous management, to being rewarded for generally poor performance; and they expected the same to continue, regardless of problems other subsidiaries or the corporation *might* now be having.

## The Plan to Improve Productivity

A plan of action was developed, the purpose of which was to make the record-pressing operation profitable within six months. The general means of accomplishing that goal was to increase the volume of outputs while improving quality and, after some momentum had been established, to improve operating efficiency. In summary, our goal was to improve profitability through increased productivity. Like all other organizations, our organization's needs in ascending order were (1) a *demand* for our product; (2) *resources* enabling us to fill that demand; (3) *direction* in the form of a plan of action consisting of specific goals and a plan for overcoming obstacles and achieving those goals; (4) *effectiveness*

in the utilization of available resources enabling us to meet our customers'
needs; and (5) *efficiency* in the utilization of those resources, enabling us to
generate a profit. The following describes what was done to satisfy each of these
organizational needs.

## Demand

The plant's recent history of marginal quality and service, coupled with our
deteriorating financial condition, had a negative impact upon our demand
potential. Prospective customers feared having their materials "lost" or "held
up" should the company fold. Were we to go out of business, their release dates
would be missed and advertising efforts wasted. We continued to press records
for most of our long-standing customers, with their apprehension about continuing to do business with us being exceeded only by their desire to avoid the
hassle of transferring their materials to a competitor's pressing plant. The apprehension among our existing customers that we might fold manifested itself in
the form of their frequently going beyond the prescribed contacts with our customer service personnel and contacting persons in the plant. Very few of our
customers were content with restricting their inquiries related to orders in process to customer service. Most would contact customer service for the current
status of their order(s) and then promptly talk directly to persons in the plant
to verify what they had been told. As there existed a time lag between what
was happening on the floor and customer service being updated on each order's
status, customers began to recognize the internal communications delay and the
fact that more current information could be had by going directly to the source.
In effect, they were rewarded with more current information by communicating directly with persons on the floor. Customer service personnel were sometimes being criticized for providing "incorrect" information, when, in fact, it
was only "not the latest" information, as they were dependent on the floor for
their inputs.

Dependent upon the anxiety level of the customer, we were receiving from
two to twenty-four individual phone contacts in the plant per customer per
order per day. I asked a shipping supervisor to tally the number of incoming
calls she personally received from customers each day for a week. She was
averaging fifty-seven such calls daily. A clerical person working with her was
averaging an equal volume of incoming calls from customers each day. At least
three or four other supervisors, in other areas, were handling a volume of calls
only somewhat lower than the volume being handled by the shipping supervisor—all in addition to the calls being handled by customer service. Scheduled
deliveries were being missed, in large part, because supervisors were spending
too much time on the phone with customers, leaving less time for them to tend
to their supervisory duties. The good news related to the situation was that previous levels of demand were being maintained. The bad news was that service
requirements had increased dramatically.

While some of our customers would order from 20,000 to 50,000 albums as the initial production run of a new release (to be possibly followed by reorders), other customers were initially ordering only 300 to 1000 albums. Even when there were reorders from the smaller customers, and with a per-unit pricing anywhere from 25 percent to 75 percent higher than we were charging our larger customers, the value of the smaller orders, at the bottom line, was questionable at best. Because the setup and service requirements for our smaller customers approached the requirements for our larger customers, a plan was developed to direct the smaller customers to nonautomated competitors. Smaller customers were advised of our intent and assisted in relocating their inventory and parts to the competitive pressing plant of their choice. Those transitions were completed within three to four months.

Realistically, we had all the demand we could, at that time, handle. Increasing that demand was dependent upon better serving the customers we had, so as to reduce their levels of anxiety and thus improve our reputation as a viable supplier. As in many business situations, it was obvious that improving demand was most dependent upon improving the organization's effectiveness, or our ability to provide our customers with what they wanted when they wanted it.

## Resources

Assigning our resource requirements to the categories of equipment, facility, materials, money, or people, the following summarizes our evaluation and the preliminary action taken to meet the organization's resource needs.

**Equipment.** Record presses had been converted from manual to automated equipment; a bulk storage system with pneumatic feed to the extruders for those presses had been installed; an additional boiler had been installed to support the new presses; and two new packaging machines were in the process of being installed. Although sufficient equipment resources were in place, that equipment was generally not operating as it should.

**Facility.** The facility totaled approximately 160,000 square feet, and was being utilized on one shift in all areas and on two shifts for record pressing as well as the collating of records into sleeves and the sleeved records into jackets. The facility was adequate.

**Materials.** Our supplier of vinyl material was very reliable. When the oil crisis hit, we continued to receive enough vinyl to process all our orders. Our problems with vinyl material were limited to contaminants, primarily of internal origin. A small amount of the total vinyl needed came from the reclaiming of internal scrap. Specifically, the *flash*—or material trimmed from the outer circumference of the records after the pressing process—was reground, fed into the bulk storage silos, and mixed with "virgin" material. When that flash came into contact with hydraulic oil from the presses or other contaminants, operating problems would result in the form of damaged stampers or defective records.

At that time, our biggest material-related problem was not receiving the sleeves and jackets for albums when needed to meet delivery schedules. Whereas records could be pressed without the sleeves and jackets, they could not be collated, packaged, and shipped. Generally, it was the customer's responsibility to supply album sleeves and jackets from printing sources outside our pressing plant. When those outside suppliers failed to provide sleeves and jackets when they were needed, collating and packaging personnel could not perform their duties, even though the records had been pressed. They had no work available. Our labor contract stipulated four hours call-in pay. When our collating personnel ran out of work before the four hours had elapsed, we would either transfer them to another area, if possible, or have them assist in cleanup operations. Should they run out of work after the four hours had elapsed, they would be sent home for the balance of the day.

Also, problems existed related to other materials supplied by our customers. For example, customers were responsible for supplying the lacquer, or master disc, from which we made stampers, and the copy for labels. At that time our reported pressing "backlog" included all orders we had received, regardless of whether the customer-supplied materials were available to permit us to process the order.

The problems with customer-supplied materials were manifested in scheduling difficulties.

**Money.** Limited working capital was a problem hindering the operation of the plant. Many of our suppliers demanded cash on delivery. At the same time, our customers were stretching out payments due us for services provided. More than one customer commented that if we were to go out of business, they might not have to pay us at all. Our people resources in credit and collections were increased. As we warehoused finished product for many of our customers and drop shipped product from their inventory upon request, we had some leverage that we used when necessary to get a customer to pay overdue invoices. If they wanted their shipping orders filled, they had to pay their overdue invoices. In most cases, we found that this was not necessary as we learned the secret to collections to be activity. The old adage that the loudest wheel gets the most grease definitely holds true. The more frequently we contacted our customers, the more willing they became to pay overdue invoices and keep their account current.

**People.** In terms of quantity, we certainly had enough human resources. In terms of quality, we did not. Employees were generally not being properly trained. The problems with the automated presses were in large part due to poorly trained operators. Turnover was very high with more than 1000 employees having worked for some period of time during the previous year to fill approximately 350 positions.

The organizational structure was a mile wide and an inch deep with virtually all managerial personnel reporting directly to me, the general manager. Prior to my coming aboard, two new managerial positions, plant engineer and materials manager, were created and filled by two well-qualified individuals from outside the organization. This had provided some needed relief, enabling me to interface with customers and hopefully reassure them that we were a viable business and were dedicated to improving the service we provided them.

## Direction

While no real goals existed, fuzzies abounded. It was apparent to most that the volume of records being pressed, collated and packaged, and shipped each day would have to increase just to better satisfy the needs of our existing customers. Also, the quality of outputs had to improve, and costs had to be reduced. While all these vague desires were not expressed in terms of specific goals, a valid means of measuring press-floor outputs existed. Three different sizes of records were being produced within the plant; 12-inch long-playing albums, 7-inch singles, and 10-inch long-playing records, the latter being used primarily for educational materials such as language courses. Someone previously had developed manufacturing cost equivalents which expressed all three products in terms of a 12-inch long-playing album.

1.0 twelve-inch long-playing albums   = 1.0 twelve-inch LP
1.25 ten-inch long-playing records   = 1.0 twelve-inch LP
3.0 seven-inch singles        = 1.0 twelve-inch LP

Using this system of product equivalents, the press-floor outputs could readily be compared between any two periods, regardless of product mix as is illustrated by Table 14-1.

The following format summarizes the goal-setting process as it was applied to the press floor. The same format was applied to all operations.

**TABLE 14-1.** Quantity of Good Records Pressed

| Press-Floor Product Outputs | Base Period | | Following Period | | |
|---|---|---|---|---|---|
| | Actual | 12-in LP Equivalents | Actual | 12-in LP Equivalents | Index |
| 12-in LPs | 25,000 ÷ 1 | = 25,000 | 30,000 ÷ 1 | = 30,000 | 120 |
| 10-in LPs | 4,000 ÷ 1.25 | = 3,200 | 5,000 ÷ 1.25 | = 4,000 | 125 |
| 7-in singles | 30,000 ÷ 3.0 | = 10,000 | 27,000 ÷ 3.0 | = 9,000 | 90 |
| Total 12-in LP equivalents | | 38,200 | | 43,000 | 112.6 |

**Position.** Press floor general supervisor, day shift

**Responsibilities.** To contribute to meeting customer requirements while controlling costs.

**Productivity Improvement opportunities.** To deliver the required number of good pressings to collating so as to provide adequate time to meet shipping schedules while reducing costs.

**Long-term potential**

*Productivity indicator 1*

$$= \frac{\text{number of defective pressings found during collation}}{\text{total number of pressings delivered to collating}}$$

$$\text{Base period} = \text{``is''} = \frac{10 \text{ collating rejects}}{100 \text{ pressings delivered}}$$

$$\text{Long-range potential} = \text{``should be''} = \frac{1}{100}$$

*Productivity indicator 2*

$$= \frac{\text{actual number of good pressings delivered to collating}}{\text{scheduled number of good pressings delivered to collating}}$$

$$\text{Base period} = \text{``is''} = \frac{20,000 \text{ twelve-inch LP equivalents daily}}{25,000 \text{ twelve-inch LP equivalents daily}}$$

$$\text{Long-range potential} = \text{``should be''} = \frac{37,679^{1}}{37,679}$$

$$\textit{Productivity indicator 3} = \frac{\text{press floor goal per good LP equivalent produced}}{\text{press floor actual cost per good LP equivalent produced}}$$

[1]The figure of 37,679 was calculated in the following manner:

1. (Thirty 12-in LP presses × 30,600 operating seconds per press each 8.5-hour day × 0.90 allowance for setup, adjustments, and 2% rejects) ÷ 30-second average machine cycle = <u>27,540</u> twelve-inch LP potential on two shifts.
2. (Two 10-in LP presses × 30,600 operating seconds per press each 8.5-hour day × 0.90 allowance for setup, adjustments, and 2% rejects) ÷ (30-second average machine cycle × 1.25 factor to convert output to 12-in LP equivalents) = <u>1469</u> ten-inch LP potential expressed in 12-in LP equivalents.
3. (Ten 7-in singles presses × 30,600 operating seconds per press each 8.5-hour day × 0.85 allowance for setup, adjustments, and 2% rejects) ÷ (10-second average machine cycle per record × 3.0 factor to convert output to 12-in LP equivalents) = <u>8670</u> seven-inch singles potential expressed in 12-in LP equivalents.

The three steps added together come to <u>37,679</u>, the daily total of potential good pressings produced in 8.5 hours running time on the day shift expressed in 12-in LP equivalents.

$$\text{Base period} = \text{"is"} = \frac{\$0.150}{\$0.185}$$

$$\text{Long-range potential} = \text{"should be"} = \frac{\$0.12}{\$0.12}$$

## Obstacles

| | Related to* | | |
|---|---|---|---|
| | Quality | Volume | Cost |
| 1. High turnover of operators | − | − | − |
| 2. Poorly trained operators | − | − | − |
| 3. Excessive downtime | 0 | − | − |
| 4. Scheduling orders when insufficient labels and/or stampers are available | 0 | − | − |
| 5. Running with a high percentage of virgin vinyl—using very little reclaimed scrap | + | + | − |
| 6. Defects generally not being recognized and corrected at the press | − | − | − |
| 7. Intershift conflict | − | − | − |

*− = negative impact in area indicated.
 + = positive impact in area indicated.
 0 = no impact in area indicated.

## Plan

| | Related to* | |
|---|---|---|
| | Effectiveness | Efficiency |
| 1. Design and implement a training program for all press operators. | + | + |
| 2. Increase press floor operations from two to three full shifts. | + | 0 |
| 3. Measure and report, on a daily basis, machine downtime by press and shift. | + | + |
| 4. Assign each supervisor a group of machines and the operators to run them. | + | 0 |
| 5. Report actual good output vs. goal for every supervisor each day. | + | + |
| 6. Assign one press-floor manager the responsibility for all operating shifts. | + | 0 |
| 7. Design and implement a report which confirms label, stamper, sleeve, and jacket availability before scheduling any order. | + | + |
| 8. Increase inspection activity at the press. | + | + |
| 9. Increase employee involvement, at all organizational levels, in defining and implementing action aimed at resolving problems. | + | + |

Plan (*continued*)

| | Related to* | |
|---|:---:|:---:|
| | **Effectiveness** | **Efficiency** |
| 10. Regrind all usable flash, biscuits, and defective records for the purpose of reducing material cost. | 0 | + |
| 11. Develop and implement a better means of drying labels so as to reduce waste. | + | + |
| 12. Develop and implement the means to rework as many defective records as is possible without lowering the quality of outputs or increasing costs. | + | + |
| 13. Improve communications throughout the organization in an effort to build a spirit of teamwork while improving coordination between departments and shifts. | + | + |

\* + = positive impact in area indicated.
   0 = no impact in area indicated.

**Near-term goals.** To increase the volume of day-shift pressings provided to collating each day to 30,000 twelve-inch LP equivalents within 8 weeks; to reduce the number of collating rejects to 6% maximum within 8 weeks; and to reduce the press floor average cost per unit produced by 15% minimum within 16 weeks.

As in the application of the goal-setting process to the press floor, obstacles were defined, a plan of action generated and implemented, and near-term goals developed and set for all other activities within the organization, including the print shop, plating, collating and packaging, inspection, maintenance, credit and collections, accounting, customer service, receiving, returned-goods processing, the vinyl-reclaiming or "regrind" operation, shipping, and billing. Whenever practical, the goals incorporated the thinking of the responsible first-line supervisor. A deliberate effort was made to communicate, in a positive fashion, our customers' requirements and where we were falling short of meeting them. The grand design, outlining what were felt to be opportunities that could be captured by better realizing our potential, was communicated in a way that focused attention on the controllables. Employee ideas and suggestions were actively encouraged while their best efforts were solicited.

Where previously most supervisors and employees had worked to "do better" or to achieve some vague type and level of operating improvement, they now had specific goals as well as prompt feedback related to their actual performance as compared to those goals.

**Effectiveness**

The improving of effectiveness, or accomplishment of our prime purpose, was necessary before management interest could be focused on efficiency. In this business, effectiveness was the volume of good pressings made available to our customers on a timely basis. Although the efficiency with which we were using resources could not be totally ignored because of the company's less-than-healthy financial condition, initial focus had to be centered on better serving our customers' needs. The addition of the third work shift on the press floor was a major step toward improving effectiveness. An increased volume of outputs without regard to the quality of those outputs would have gained us nothing. Accordingly, a training program for press operators was designed and implemented. The training program made some contribution to improved quality and an increased volume of outputs, but not near enough to satisfy our customers. We knew there had to be a way to revise our order-processing methods so as to both improve quality and increase volume. More than that, some of the managers saw the inspection and sleeving of all records at the press, immediately after they had been manufactured, as a specific means of generating more volume while improving quality. In fact, the night-shift general supervisor had unilaterally and, without adequate planning, previously attempted to do just that on his shift. Unfortunately, his attempt had failed, accomplishing nothing more than upsetting the employees involved. Figure 14-2 illustrates what was then the existing method, as compared to what some supervisors thought was the preferred method.

Some advantages of the proposed method are obvious:

- As pressing would not begin until sleeves and jackets were physically brought to the press floor, the delays of waiting for sleeves and jackets would be eliminated. The average process time would be significantly reduced.
- The inspection would be made within a few minutes after the record was pressed, enabling early recognition and correction of problems. The existing method sometimes resulted in thousands of records being pressed before it was recognized that they were all defective.
- The size of the audio inspection sample would increase by a multiple of 6, providing greater confidence in the outgoing sound quality.

Other advantages are less obvious:

- It was virtually impossible to keep pressed records free of dirt and other contamination when they were stored for long periods while waiting for sleeves.
- Many records warped because of variations in temperature and/or because of

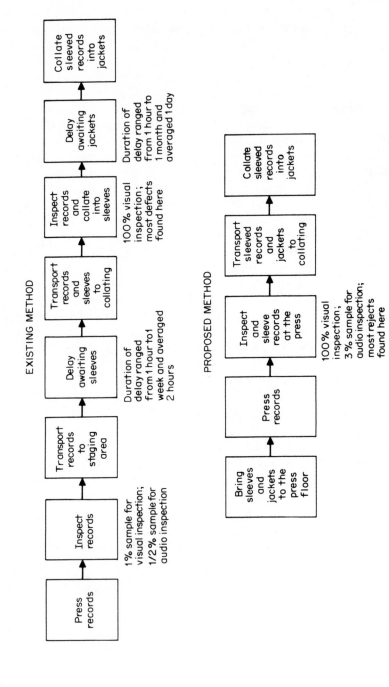

EXISTING METHOD

| Press records | Inspect records | Transport records to staging area | Delay awaiting sleeves | Transport records and sleeves to collating | Inspect records and collate into sleeves | Delay awaiting jackets | Collate sleeved records into jackets |

1% sample for visual inspection; 1/2% sample for audio inspection

Duration of delay ranged from 1 hour to 1 week and averaged 2 hours

100% visual inspection; most defects found here

Duration of delay ranged from 1 hour to 1 month and averaged 1 day

PROPOSED METHOD

| Bring sleeves and jackets to the press floor | Press records | Inspect and sleeve records at the press | Transport sleeved records and jackets to collating | Collate sleeved records into jackets |

100% visual inspection; 3% sample for audio inspection; most rejects found here

**Figure 14-2.** The existing and proposed methods of manufacturing records.

the way they were stored while waiting for sleeves or jackets. Some of these warped records could be reworked; most had to be discarded.

We had a pretty good idea of what we wanted to do, but really didn't know how to go about it. On the premise that the person who knows the most about any job is the one who performs it every day, we selected key employees from quality control, the press floor, and collating to participate with the involved managers for the purpose of generating and implementing a viable plan. It was communicated to all employees that the employees selected were to serve as representatives of their respective work groups. Though only seven employees participated directly, they were requested to solicit the inputs of all members of their individual work group. The first two meetings were characterized by obvious but unstated skepticism on the part of the employee participants. Their active participation was allowed to grow gradually, rather than anyone's active participation being forced. After the third or fourth such meeting, all of which were limited to one hour, things started to happen. An employee offered the comment that she had at first suspected management was trying to manipulate her and the other employee participants in some way. She later became convinced we were sincere and really did value her inputs.

In summary, our employees contributed greatly to the development and implementation of a specific plan. Of even greater significance was their commitment to making the plan work. Specifically, a team concept was developed wherein half the total collating work force, which was all women, volunteered to transfer from the relatively clean and comfortable collating area to the noisy and dirty press floor. Those persons from collating combined with the existing press-floor inspectors to form a work group that inspected and sleeved records within minutes after they had been pressed. A team consisted of two inspector-sleevers and one press operator for every six automated record presses. Each team of three people functioned as a unit responsible for producing a volume of quality sleeved pressings. The sleeved records and the corresponding jackets were transported hourly to the employees remaining in collating, who collated the sleeved records into the jackets.

The inspector-sleevers and the press operators were provided pastel-colored smocks. Within a short period of time, the usually dirty press floor was maintained immaculately. After attaining a never-before-experienced level of cleanliness on the press floor, the employees began requesting paint and brushes. Each team voluntarily assumed the responsibility for periodically painting the presses and the floor in their area. The inspector-sleevers were provided wheeled carts which they used as portable workbenches as they moved from press to press inspecting and sleeving records. They were allowed to select colorful contact paper to decorate their carts. What before was a dirty, noisy press floor remained noisy but became a model of cleanliness with the decorated portable workbenches providing a splash of color to an otherwise dreary work environment.

### Efficiency

After we had gained momentum related to increasing volume and improving quality, our attention shifted more toward improving efficiency. Our financial problems, which continued to be a drain on management resources, could only be alleviated by making the operation profitable. Increased volume was contributing toward that end as our substantial fixed costs were being spread over more units. Likewise, improved quality resulted in fewer rejects and a significant reduction in scrap expense.

Material cost is a substantial portion of the total cost of goods sold in any record-pressing operation. The major elements of material cost are vinyl, record labels, plating materials, poly film to wrap the jacketed album, and shipping cartons plus tape to seal those cartons. A program was designed and implemented to reduce the per-unit cost of each material element as follows:

**Vinyl.** Previously, only some flash from the record-pressing operation was being reground and mixed with virgin vinyl material. For all practical purposes, all records we produced were made from virtually 100 percent virgin vinyl. While most record-pressing operations use vinyl pellets, extruded from powder, we were using the less expensive powder. We paid for that cost advantage because the powder is so fine it can permeate most seals, resulting in material loss, not to mention the related housekeeping problem. Our finished product was made from "first-generation" material which had only been extruded once, just prior to the record being pressed. In a real sense, our reground scrap material was equivalent to the pellets used by other record pressers. Both were second-generation extrusions.

We developed and implemented a program to regrind *all* scrap materials mixing that regrind with virgin powder. The program was opposed by most of our press-floor personnel because the use of regrind caused operating problems. Contaminants in the vinyl, such as oil, paper, and metal, increased as did the percentage of regrind being used. The result was stamper damage, which caused downtime for the removal and replacement of damaged stampers. Screens were designed and installed to greatly reduce the problem of contamination. Goals specifying a targeted amount of regrind to be fed into the bulk storage system each shift were set and implemented. Feedback on the actual vs. targeted amounts of regrind introduced into the system on each shift was provided daily.

Where previously we had been paying someone to haul away our scrap, we began regrinding and using most of it. We even went a step further and began purchasing scrap from our competitors and regrinding it. When the oil crisis hit and vinyl was in short supply, we made a tidy profit by selling the excess reground vinyl that had been purchased from outside sources. Our internal vinyl cost per unit was substantially reduced while we made money by processing into usable form materials no one else had wanted.

**Record labels.** Most of the record labels we used were printed in our own print shop. The two components of our label cost were labor and material. The labor component was reduced by changing the layout and methods, thus improving our print-shop efficiency. The material component of label cost was reduced by revising our method of drying and storing finished labels. "Wet" labels, which either became scorched during the compression-molding cycle or resulted in smeared ink and illegible copy, were the specific cause of 90 percent of all rejected labels. The change in drying and storage procedures significantly reduced the number of label rejects.

**Plating materials.** Previously, the silver solution, with which lacquers were sprayed as the first step in the plating process, was discarded in a sink after use. A special trap was installed in the sink, and the silver solids were reclaimed and sold to a metal dealer. Our first such sale was 30 pounds of silver.

**Poly film.** Poly film cost per unit was reduced by improved care and handling of the heavy rolls of poly film within the plant and by shopping around for the best price.

**Shipping supplies.** We supplied corrugated cartons for the shipment of the customers' product to their distributors. Printed customer logos on cartons were discouraged as such cartons could only be used for that customer. We worked with carton suppliers to develop lower-cost cartons which were "flexible" in that they could be folded in various fashions to provide different capacities. Carton labels were replaced by ink-stamped information, and carton tape was changed to the nonreinforced variety—both resulting in considerable cost savings.

**People.** Our efforts to improve efficiency included people cost, as well. Note the focus was not restricted to direct labor, but included the wages or salaries of all employees, company-provided benefits, and any temporary help we might use. Standards related to hourly employees were developed, using the work-sampling technique, and implemented. The efficiency of other employees was measured as group expense rates, or the total cost of those groups expressed as a percentage of net sales. In all cases, specific goals were set for each activity, usually by the group's supervisor. The actual performance of all nonmanagerial work groups, as compared to their respective standard, was compiled and fed back to the group's manager in the form of a daily efficiency report. This manually prepared report was distributed by 9:00 A.M. the following morning.

| Supervisor | Area | S h i f t | Month _November_ Efficiency % | | | Actual % goal achievement each day | | | | |
|---|---|---|---|---|---|---|---|---|---|---|
| | | | Best previous | Last month | This months goal | 1 | 2 | 3 | 4 | 5 |
| B.'ll Brown | 12" LP Presses | 1 | 99.7 | 98.2 | 100.0 | 96.1 | ☺ | 99.2 | ☺ | |
| Joe Cooper | Collating | 2 | 92.1 | 87.0 | 93.0 | 92.1 | 92.7 | 87.6 | ☺ | |
| Mary Derek | Shipping | 1 | 90.6 | 90.6 | 94.0 | ☺ | 93.2 | ☺ | ☺ | |

**Figure 14-3.** The format of the progress chart.

In addition to the daily efficiency report, a large progress chart was posted in a conspicuous place in my office. That progress chart consisted of a large piece of posterboard using the format shown by Figure 14-3.

The specific monthly goal for each area was usually set by the area supervisor. Initially, a number of supervisors were reluctant to stretch when setting their goal. By sharing the overall requirements for the company in total and by appealing to them to maximize their area's contribution, supervisors began to increase their commitment in the form of their setting more difficult goals for their areas. Each day of the month that an area achieved the targeted efficiency for that month, the progress chart depicted a "smiley" sticker rather than the actual efficiency. Both employees and their managers took an interest in their work groups' efficiency.

When a work group either set a daily efficiency or quality record or achieved a monthly goal, each member of the work group was given a free record album. Our cost per album was about 40 cents. A traveling "trophy" of dubious distinction in the form of a framed picture of a donkey was given each week to the work group that failed, by the widest margin, to achieve their quality and efficiency goals. The "trophy" was displayed in a prominent position within that group's work area. At the end of each week, it was given to that week's lowest-performing work group. Never did a work group keep the donkey for two weeks in a row. In time, all groups were either achieving their goal or consistently close to achieving it, so the donkey award was discontinued.

The single-incentive system within the organization had been in effect within the collating department for years. The incentive consisted of a monetary reward beyond the base hourly wage for every 100 records beyond standard collated per person each day. The system was based on each collator turning in a count of the number of records they had collated at the end of each shift. Approximately 20 percent of all collators were earning a bonus on a consistent basis. The average amount of that bonus was about 15 percent of their hourly wage. There was much dissatisfaction among the collators about the incentive system. This dissatisfaction was usually expressed as a complaint that certain collators "always received the easier jobs" enabling them to earn a bonus while putting forth no more effort than were others who weren't earning a bonus. Compiling the counts turned in daily by the collators, we found that many more records were being supposedly collated than were actually available to be collated. This information was communicated to the collators as "errors" with a request that they double-check their counts before turning them in each day. This request precipitated allegations among some persons earning a bonus that other bonus earners were padding their counts. The matter was resolved, without consequence, by discontinuing the incentive system.

At a time when the company was in obvious, at least to the managers, trouble, a managerial bonus plan, based on profitability, was designed and communicated. Previously, managers had been told the company was unprofitable but had not been provided any specifics. Based on the personal feeling that managers have the right to know exactly how the company is doing, be it good or bad, I provided all the specific financial information related to the operation to all the managers. As grim as it was, it turned "unknowns" into "knowns" in the minds of the managers. Response to the bonus plan was less than enthusiastic, simply because it was based on profitability, and the company had not been profitable for some time.

With the company's financial situation communicated in terms of specifics, a general plan was presented to the managers for the purpose of making them aware of what must be done to turn around the situation. Attention was focused on those things that could be internally controlled. Questions were asked each manager, aimed at having them think about and define how their work group could best contribute to the overall job that had to be done. Those vague fuzzies evolved into specific goals with a managerial commitment being made to achieve them.

Daily meetings of 15 to 20 minutes were held on the shop floor and weekly meetings of one hour were held in the office area for the purpose of both coordinating activities and communicating progress. Monthly detailed financial results were communicated to all managers during one of those weekly meetings. As the operation became profitable, the bonus pool accumulated money, a portion of which was credited each month to each manager in proportion to their individual contribution. The established measurements served as the basis for assessing individual contribution. At the end of the year and based upon responsibility and performance, managers were awarded from $1000 to $10,000 in cash.

## Results

The summarized first-year results for this operation as compared to the previous year are shown in Table 14-2. Note that there was no increase in equipment

**TABLE 14-2.** First- and Second-Year Results of the Record-Pressing Operation

| | 1973 Dollars* | 1973 % of Sales* | 1974 Dollars | 1974 % of Sales | Index† |
|---|---|---|---|---|---|
| Net sales | 4,622,513 | | 6,307,930 | | 136.5 |
| Cost of goods sold | 5,298,955 | 114.6 | 5,246,419 | 83.2 | 99.0 |
| Gross profit | (676,422) | (14.6) | 1,061,511 | 16.8 | 356.9 |
| Selling, general, and administrative expenses | 559,742 | 12.1 | 396,935 | 6.3 | 70.9 |
| Other income | 22,572 | 0.49 | 201,170 | 3.2 | 891.2 |
| Preinterest income | (1,213,612) | (26.3) | 865,746 | 13.7 | 271.3 |

*Parentheses indicate a loss.

†The development of an index when the base is a negative number was achieved via the following logic. For example, let's compare the preinterest net income of $865,746 (1974) with the $1,213,612 loss in 1973:

1. If the 1974 preinterest income, expressed in dollars, were an index of 100 as compared to 1973, the 1974 income would be the same as that in 1973, negative $1,213,612.
2. If the 1974 preinterest income were an index of 200 as compared to the 1973 income, it would be negative $1,213,612 plus $1,213,612, or zero.
3. If the 1974 preinterest income were an index of 300 as compared to the 1973 income, it would be negative $1,213,612 plus $1,213,612 plus $1,213,612, or $1,213,612. In reality, the 1974 preinterest income index fell short of 300 because results, in dollars, were $865,746 rather than $1,213,612, a "shortfall" of 100 − ($865,746 − $1,213,612), or 100 − 71.3, or 28.7.
4. The 1974 index was 300 − 28.7, or 271.3.

resources, and that rising costs could not be fully offset by increasing selling prices.

The turnaround of this operation was pivotal for the corporation. A big cash drain became the biggest cash contributor. Of the corporation's other subsidiaries, two were sold within the next year. Only one other subsidiary, in addition to the two that were sold, remained unprofitable in May 1975. A decision was reached to sell that other subsidiary, and I was asked to assume the additional responsibility for managing that facility until its sale could be consummated.

# 15 A Capital Equipment Manufacturer

## Background

This company is a subsidiary of the same parent corporation as is the record-pressing plant and is engaged in the design, manufacture, and sales of sophisticated electromechanical capital equipment. It is acknowledged as the world-wide leader in the sales and distribution of high-speed, professional tape-duplicating equipment. Producers of prerecorded magnetic tape, either cassettes or 8-track cartridges, use the equipment to duplicate the original, or master tape, in large quantities for sales through retail outlets. This subsidiary also produces theater sound systems and professional recorders of the variety that are used in commercial broadcasting stations. In the area of theater sound systems, the company has received, among many technical awards, an Academy Award citation for the system it had designed and installed at the Radio City Music Hall in New York City. The company had been purchased by the parent corporation from its founder about five years previously. The founder continued to run the company for a few years, then left to pursue other business interests. He was replaced by a professional manager from the corporation's financial staff. Operating problems and a downturn in the economy, coupled with other factors, resulted in the operation becoming unprofitable and a serious cash drain on the parent corporation. Top corporate management decided to sell the company because it was unprofitable and because, unlike the remaining subsidiaries, "it was not in the mainstream of the music business." The president of only a year left the company, and I was asked to manage the operation until a sale to one of many prospective buyers could be consummated. In summary, my assignment was to "tread water" until the sale would be finalized, probably within 60 days.

Unlike operations with which I had been previously associated, this was a nonunion shop. The total number of employees was about sixty, with forty of that total working in the shop as assemblers, machinists, and material handlers. The twenty salaried employees were divided among accounting, engineering, customer service, inventory control and purchasing, administration, and sales. All foreign sales were handled through an exclusive overseas distributor. An organization of fifty-seven dealers sold the professional recorders throughout the United States. Manufacturers' representatives supplemented the internal sales force by selling duplicator systems and theater sound systems domestically.

My knowledge of the company, its operation, its products, its problems, and its people was limited to what I had gained in a briefing session with the executive vice president of the parent corporation. Since my tenure would be limited by a soon-to-be-consummated sale, my introduction to the operation was possibly more abbreviated or sketchy than it might otherwise have been.

The company had been formed less than 10 years previous, yet many of the employees had been with the company for five or more years. The 1975 recession had impacted the "Silicon Valley" area of northern California, in which the company was located. Those living and working in the area had been conditioned, during the previous years, to an economic boom which had resulted in an abundance of available jobs. Our employees were sensitive to the changing economy, and the unknown effect the sale of the company would have upon their jobs. Though the issue of the company being sold had never been directly addressed to them, they were aware that efforts were being made to sell the company, and they were understandably upset. Such was the work climate as I began my "temporary assignment."

## The Plan to Improve Productivity

My first act after coming aboard was to meet with the department managers, introduce myself, and advise them of the corporation's plans related to the company. As the companies who were considering acquiring the operation were well-known blue-chip corporations, their takeover could be expressed in "probably positive" terms—the probable being an unspoken yet generally understood qualifier related to the unknown factor of what the acquiring company would do with the existing staff. Everything I knew about the pending sale was presented. I answered related questions to the best of my ability. I also pointed out the sale was still being negotiated, and may or may not actually take place. My comment about the uncertainty of the sale, or for that matter anything that had not been fully negotiated and agreed upon, was a personal opinion based only on common sense. I further commented that because of that uncertainty, coupled with the fact that it would be a waste of time to sit around waiting for someone else to do something, I intended to approach my job as if I were going to be working there forever. I solicited their best efforts aimed at making the operation profitable while leaving the noncontrollable possible sale of the business to corporate personnel. They agreed, and we were on our way. I asked that they brief their managers on our discussion immediately after they left our meeting and to schedule a meeting of all employees in the cafeteria in 30 minutes. I discussed the same things with all the company's employees in the cafeteria as I had previously discussed with the department managers and they in turn with their managers. The only difference in the total group meeting and the previous meeting was that some questions were asked and answered that had not been asked in the earlier meeting. I stated my intent and solicited the best efforts of all employees aimed at making the company profitable, just as I had done in the previous meeting. By communicating specifics, most of the unknowns were eliminated. By communicating my intent, or how I personally was going to approach the situation, a near-term direction was provided for the company and its employees. Only after having done these things could we get on with what had to be done.

The company had three basic problems, all of which were interrelated:

1. A negative cash flow.
2. The company was losing money each month.
3. Parts needed to complete orders were not in inventory, yet the inventory was building.

These problems were impacting the company's vendors because they were not being paid for goods and services which they had delivered. Consequently, many vendors would only sell to the company on a cash-on-delivery basis. The company's customers were affected in that they were aware of the company's cash problems and were concerned that the processing of their orders might be delayed indefinitely. The parent corporation was affected because the subsidiary was a constant drain on cash. And last, but not least, the company's employees couldn't help but be aware of the problems, causing them some security stress.

Due to the previously mentioned factors, plus the fact that material expense (at nearly 40 percent of net sales) was the largest single element of cost, materials management was judged to be the most critical activity within the company at that time. A closer look into that area of the business revealed some obvious problems. Following is a summary outlining the materials-related obstacles and what action was taken to overcome them.

**Schedule.** The build schedule was generally based on an internally generated sales forecast. As each piece of equipment sold was "custom" in the sense that a wide variety of models and options were available, equipment sold from finished goods inventory, more often than not, had to be reworked to meet the customer's specifications. Because of a recessionary economy, lead times, related to most suppliers' products and services, had been dramatically reduced. Based upon a generally good availability of parts (providing we could convince the vendor to let us have them on credit), our internal order-processing time, our customers' delivery expectations, and the custom nature of our products, we quit building to a forecast. By building only to order, we could satisfy our customers' delivery requirements and eliminate costly rework and the buildup of finished goods inventory.

**Inventory valuation.** The result of the previous policy of building to sales forecast, coupled with the material value of all work in process and finished goods being increased by 53 percent (as the standard labor and overhead associated with the assembly of that material), a steady buildup of work in process inventory valuation had been experienced. Over the years, more and more items in inventory had been put together with other items to form subassemblies. The number of such subassemblies in work in process was increasing. The cost of the related overhead was applied, per standard, to increase the valuation of work in process inventory. Subassemblies in process were often being torn down, and the component parts were used in another subassembly. The result was that labor and overhead associated with certain parts had been added to inventory valuation twice but could only be relieved from inventory once, when the part was shipped. Thus the inventory was overvalued and previously reported losses should have been even greater. To ensure that this situation was not perpetuated, all labor and overhead was expensed during the period in which it was incurred and items shipped from previously accumulated work in process was expensed at 153 percent of the component valuation upon shipment.

**Parts substitutions.** While we were experiencing problems with our suppliers who were hesitant to ship us parts on credit, virtually nothing had been done in the way of attempting to use excess available parts in inventory as substitutes for what was needed. Accordingly, an engineer was assigned on a continuous basis to review both the parts needed to process on-hand orders and the parts in inventory. Based upon her knowledge and experience, many possible substitutions were recognized and implemented. The prevailing substitution-related rule was that the product could in no way be downgraded by using other than specified parts. This resulted in more reliable components being substituted in most cases. Although the parts used were sometimes more expensive than the specified parts, they were available and could generate needed cash via shipments and billings.

**Purchasing.** As the build schedule was limited to processing on-hand orders, the purchasing activity was similarly limited to buying only those parts related to an on-hand order and then only after the possibility of substituting on-hand components for what was needed had been exhausted. The persons in the buyer capacity had worked hard to develop reliable and competitively priced suppliers over a period of many years. However, they had gotten into a rut and were not checking the prices of alternate suppliers as a matter of routine. Also, they remained sensitive to price breaks for certain quantities and tended to buy more than what was needed for the purpose of saving money we didn't have. When our situation was explained to them and they were reminded that, due to the prevailing economy, suppliers were generally more flexible in their pricing, they willingly agreed to contact three different suppliers for each item purchased and not to buy parts beyond the quantity needed if they would not be used within 45 days of receipt.

**Management.** The management of all materials-related activities was the responsibility of the manufacturing manager. For the purposes of allowing him to focus on the processing of orders and to provide more time and attention to the materials-related portion of the business, the position of materials manager was created. It was filled by a technically knowledgeable person from our engineering staff who had managerial experience. In addition to the duties normally associated with the position, she was given the charter to review all on-hand inventory, identify what was either obsolete or excess, and dispose those materials in a manner which would provide the greatest immediate benefits to the company.

**Bills of material.** Part of our materials-related problems was traceable to the fact that our bills of material had not been kept updated. A tape-duplicating system, for example, consists of more than 2000 component parts. When the bills of material specifying the parts needed to build the subassemblies and the manner in which they were combined was outdated, some needed parts were not recognized and ordered, while other parts that were not needed were being ordered. In addition, the cost of material related to goods sold could not be accurately quantified. The engineering manager was requested to update the bills of material and to make some provision for keeping them updated on a continuous basis, both of which he did.

**Interface with suppliers.** Suppliers to the company were generally upset because they were not being paid promptly, and then when they did receive a check, it often bounced because of a lack of funds in our account. In addition, they could not get a straight answer from anyone within the company, even in those rare instances when they could get someone to talk with them. I made it a personal point to contact each supplier that we were overdue in paying. At the same time, the controller was instructed to ensure adequate funds were available before writing any check. When possible, I met personally with those suppliers whom we owed large amounts of money. The purpose of these actions was obviously to reassure our creditors that they would be paid, as well as to keep the lines of communication open so that they could talk with someone whenever they wanted and get a straight answer. When payment commitments could not be met, I took the initiative to call the supplier, prior to the due date, and so inform the person. A revised commitment would be made at that time. Our suppliers, for the most part, were very patient and reasonable. While I didn't dislike talking with an average of fourteen suppliers each workday, the solution to our dilemma was to generate cash so they could be paid.

**Generating cash.** Many unnecessary expenses were being incurred within the company contributing to our poor cash position. Other necessary expenses were being incurred without a corresponding return in the form of outputs. For example:

- The company participated in many trade shows in a "first-class" manner, yet was booking very little business as a result of this participation.
- Internal salespersons were generally ineffective and were not held accountable for their expenses.
- Travel and entertainment expenses were extravagant, including attendance at the Cannes Film Festival in France.
- The organizational structure was not in balance with the company's needs; human resources were not being applied where they were needed but were available in abundance where they were not needed.
- The company was paying too much for a substandard medical plan which it provided for all employees.
- WATS telephone service had been installed and the postinstallation billing for long-distance calls was twice the monthly expense of the preinstallation billing for the same service.

Within the first month, changes were implemented related to these and other categories of expense. A net annual cost reduction of more than $125,000 was realized while improving the employee medical insurance plan, adding key people in critical areas, and doing nothing that would adversely affect the organization's effectiveness, either short term or long range.

Compounding the company's cash problem was the fact that billings were not being generated for weeks after shipments had been made; an agressive collections effort aimed at bringing in overdue receivables was not being made; and the payment of overdue monies on the part of customers was not being made a prerequisite to our processing subsequent orders for them. All these situations were presented to the persons responsible as obstacles to the genera-tion of monies required to satisfy our suppliers and put the company in a viable operating position. They contributed to the generation of a plan to overcome those obstacles and committed themselves to doing everything they could to make the implementation of the plan produce the desired result. It did. Within

**DAILY REPORT**          Activity thru _____

**CASH FLOW**

Opening bank balance on 1st of month  $ _____

Opening bank balance this date      _____      MTD
  + Daily receipts                   _____      receipts  $ _____
  = Total available funds            _____      MTD
  − Daily disbursements              _____      disburse _____
  = Bank balance carried forward     _____      MTD ± _____

**ACCOUNTS PAYABLE AND RECEIVABLE**                          Aging

| | Total | 1 – 30 | 31 –60 | 61 – 90 | 91 + |
|---|---|---|---|---|---|
| Receivables | $ _____ | $ _____ | $ _____ | $ _____ | $ _____ |
| Payables | _____ | _____ | _____ | _____ | _____ |

**SALES**

| | Day actual | vs | Day goal | Daily variance | MTD actual | vs | MTD goal | MTD variance |
|---|---|---|---|---|---|---|---|---|
| Net selling price of shipments | $ _____ | | $ _____ | $ _____ | $ _____ | | $ _____ | $ _____ |

Total order backlog  $ _____

On hold− credit $ _____    On hold− other $ _____    Shipable $ _____

**MANUFACTURING**

Sales value of completed orders

| | Day actual | vs | Day goal | Daily variance | MTD actual | vs | MTD goal | MTD variance |
|---|---|---|---|---|---|---|---|---|
| Electronic assembly | $ _____ | | $ _____ | $ _____ | $ _____ | | $ _____ | $ _____ |
| Head assembly | _____ | | _____ | _____ | _____ | | _____ | _____ |
| Mechanical assembly | _____ | | _____ | _____ | _____ | | _____ | _____ |
| Total completed assemblies | _____ | | _____ | _____ | _____ | | _____ | _____ |

**Q. C. ACTIVITY**

Sales value of goods

| Awaiting inspection @ start of day | Added to be inspected | Inspection completed accepted | rejected | Awaiting inspection @ end of day |
|---|---|---|---|---|
| $ _____ | $ _____ | $ _____ | $ _____ | $ _____ |

**PURCHASES**

Commitments @ costs

| Daily actual | vs | Daily goal | Daily variance | MTD actual | vs | MTD goal | MTD variance |
|---|---|---|---|---|---|---|---|
| $ _____ | | $ _____ | $ _____ | $ _____ | | $ _____ | $ _____ |

**INVENTORY**                    Inventory valuation @ 1st of month $ _____

Beginning value this date  $ _____  +  Receipts @ cost $ _____  −  Material cost of goods shipped $ _____  =  Ending inventory value  $ _____

| | Actual | Goal | Variance |
|---|---|---|---|
| Value of substitutions (Day) $ _____ approved and made (MTD) _____ | MTD mat'l. cost of shipments  $ _____ | $ _____ | $ _____ |
| $ Received  (Day) $ _____ from sale of obsolete or excess (MTD) parts _____ | −MTD mat'l receipts _____ = MTD inventory reduction _____ X 153% = Total reduction _____ | _____ _____ _____ | _____ _____ _____ |

**Figure 15-1.** The format of the daily report.

**TABLE 15-1.** Operating Results of the Manufacturer of Electromechanical Capital Equipment

| Line | Item | Previous 7-Month Period | | Following 7-Month Period | | Index |
| | | Dollars | % of Net Sales | Dollars | % of Net Sales | |
|---|---|---|---|---|---|---|
| 1. | Net sales | 1,886,300 | | 1,634,920 | | 86.7 |
| | *Less:* | | | | | |
| 2. | Materials | 742,800 | 0.3937 | 643,602 | 0.3937 | 86.7 |
| 3. | Direct labor | 247,400 | 0.1312 | 123,581 | 0.0756 | 50.0 |
| 4. | Controllable overhead | 320,200 | 0.1698 | 207,215 | 0.1267 | 64.7 |
| 5. | Noncontrollable overhead | 133,200 | 0.0706 | 84,341 | 0.0516 | 63.4 |
| 6. | Total cost of goods sold | 1,443,600 | 0.7653 | 1,058,739 | 0.6476 | 73.3 |
| 7. | Gross profit | 442,700 | 0.2347 | 576,181 | 0.3524 | 130.2 |
| | *Less:* | | | | | |
| 8. | Engineering expense | 203,300 | 0.1078 | 44,356 | 0.0271 | 21.8 |
| 9. | Selling expense | 256,600 | 0.1360 | 126,080 | 0.0771 | 49.1 |
| 10. | Administrative expense | 242,900 | 0.1288 | 164,595 | 0.1007 | 67.8 |
| 11. | Total operating expenses | 702,800 | 0.3726 | 335,031 | 0.2049 | 47.8 |
| 12. | *Add (less):* Other income (expense) | (1,800) | (0.0009) | 8,824 | 0.0054 | |
| 13. | Net income (loss) precorporate charges | (261,900) | (0.1388) | 249,974 | 0.1529 | 295.4 |

*See the footnote (†) to Table 14-2 on page 252 for an explanation of the method of calculating an index when the base is a negative number.

30 days, and consistently thereafter, adequate cash was generated, enabling our suppliers to be paid on a more timely basis.

The process of goal setting and achieving was implemented with goals relating to each of the following specific key end results being set:

Cash flow
Accounts receivable aging
Accounts payable aging
Sales backlog
Shipments
Manufacturing outputs
Quality control contribution
Purchasing commitments made
Inventory valuation

We selected dollars as the unit of measurement for each of these indicators. Where practical, both daily and month-to-date actual performances were reported as compared to their respective goals. The format of the report is illustrated in Figure 15-1. The report was manually prepared each morning and was the principal topic of discussion at a meeting held with department managers on the assembly floor at 8:30 A.M. each morning.

On the first workday of each month, a one-hour meeting with all employees was held in the lunchroom. The previous month's results, in the form of actual performance as compared to goal, was presented first. After any questions relating to those results were answered, each department manager presented the department's goals, for the upcoming month, to all employees. In addition, special projects, both planned and in process, were presented by the manager responsible in summarized form. While specific financial data was not presented, anything and everything else that directly pertained to the group was openly discussed. Generally, employees were not only aware of changes related to them before they were implemented but they also were frequently provided the opportunity to contribute their knowledge, feelings, and experience to the development of plans related to those changes.

## Results

Within a few weeks, the entire work group was functioning as a team sharing a common purpose. The previous lack of direction had been replaced by worthwhile goals related to each area of activity within the organization. The previous widespread apathy was replaced by a general spirit of enthusiasm. The focus of employee attention had shifted from an overwhelming concern about the status of the company and their jobs to the achievement of organizational goals. Operating results improved dramatically as is illustrated by Table 15-1.

Though sales decreased by 13.3 percent over the previous period, due primarily to the economy, net profit increased from a $261,900 *loss* in the prior period to a $249,974 gain in the following period. Table 15-2 summarizes the changes related to each category of cost and provides comments related to those changes.

**TABLE 15-2.** Magnitude of and Reasons for Change in Expense Rates Summarized

| Line | Category | Change in Expense Rate, in %* | Comments |
|------|----------|-------------------------------|----------|
| 2. | Materials | none | |
| 3. | Direct labor | −42.4 | Improved productivity resulted from increased employee participation and the implementation of the process of goal setting and achieving. |

**TABLE 15-2.** Magnitude of and Reasons for Change in Expense Rates Summarized  *(continued)*

| Line | Category | Change in Expense Rate, in %* | Comments |
|---|---|---|---|
| 4. | Controllable overhead | −25.4 | Expense review resulted in the elimination of unnecessary expenses and the reduction of other expenses, all without adversely impacting effectiveness. |
| 5. | Noncontrollable overhead | −26.9 | Operations were consolidated into one of the two buildings previously used, resulting in a significant reduction in rent. |
| 8. | Engineering | −74.9 | One new project, a sound system for smaller multiscreen theaters, was initiated and brought to market, and the long-abandoned project of an automatic cartridge tape loader was reinitiated and soon after brought to market, both while reducing people resources. |
| 9. | Selling | −43.3 | Sales force was reduced, and commission was changed to a "contribution to profit" basis. |
| 10. | Administrative | −21.8 | Travel and entertainment expenses were reduced. |

*(Following period expense rate − previous period expense rate) ÷ previous period expense rate.

Whereas my charter was to tread water until the business could be sold, it was never sold. The operation became consistently profitable. Its contribution and importance in the eyes of corporate management increased to the point that the name of the parent corporation was changed to the name of the subsidiary. All because employee needs were better aligned with organizational needs, resulting in an improved contribution in the form of increased productivity from all employees.

# 16 An Electronics Distributor

## Background

Unlike the previously mentioned companies, this company does not manufacture anything but rather distributes products manufactured by other companies. As a division of a $300 million firm listed with the New York Stock Exchange, this company distributes over 100,000 different items supplied by 190 manufacturers. Those items range from semiconductors and integrated circuits to tools and shop supplies. The company primarily serves the maintenance and repair, instead of the original equipment, market. Accordingly, the emphasis is on availability and service, with price being of secondary importance to most customers. In the five-year period prior to my joining the organization, sales had increased at a compound annual rate of 12 percent. During the same period, operating profit had increased by 1000 percent. The company is marketing-oriented, its emphasis being placed on continually expanding the number of sales branches located throughout the country.

Many of the problems within the organization were the challenges presented by rapid growth. Much time and effort was spent recruiting and training additions to staff in all areas, but particularly in marketing. More salespersons generated more orders, and the increased volume of orders, with the help of exceptionally good controls on pricing deviations, generated more profit. Whereas the volume of incoming orders grew rapidly, the resources to fill those orders were subject to several constraints, most of which were internally induced.

1. Order-processing expenses were a relatively small portion of total expenses. Accordingly, management, while interested in effectiveness in the form of

263

volume of orders processed, assigned little importance to order-processing efficiency. Additional volume was thought to more than compensate for order-processing inefficiencies.

2. Top management, though sincerely people-oriented, manifested that attitude in the form of sensitivity toward employees' lower-order needs: a paycheck and security. The higher-order ego or self-esteem and achievement needs, except for salespersons, were ignored. Performance was deemphasized to the extent that management policy forbid the communicating of expectations by managers to other than sales-related employees, let alone the implementation of work standards. The sales division was the single exception to the rule, with performance being emphasized via an exceptional goal-setting program and top salespersons being provided rewards, both tangible and intangible.

3. The willingness to compromise the efficiency with which orders were filled contributed to a high rate of order-processing errors. The permissive attitude toward the quantity of employee outputs resulted in deteriorating accuracy of order fills. This consequence was predictable, as management either has control of all elements in a given situation or it has no control at all. Although the forfeiting of efficiency was by choice, the resulting deterioration in quality was not. Compounding the negative impact of order-processing errors were order-entry errors being made by an increasing number of new salespersons in the field.

4. Most orders were filled by a large, centrally located distribution center. While limited inventories were maintained in selected larger sales branches throughout the country, those inventories were generally not being used. It was easier for salespersons in stocking branches to enter their orders via the computerized system of order entry, to be shipped from the larger, remote distribution center, than it was for them to manually write the order and have it filled locally. Besides, with daily consolidated shipments being sent air freight from the large remote center to those stocking branches, customers could receive their orders almost as quickly as if they had been filled locally.

This almost total dependence on the large, centrally located distribution center made management hypersensitive to the possibility, no matter how remote, of a work interruption at that facility. That hypersensitivity reinforced the previously mentioned attitude about efficiency. It also resulted in the creation of a very active employee relations function, the purpose of which was to closely monitor employees for any signs of dissatisfaction with the company or its representatives. As employees were encouraged to go around their supervisor and bring their problems to an employee relations person, supervisory effectiveness was undermined.

5. As the business grew, more and more inventory and people were added to the primary distribution center. The facility could not be expanded, on the one hand, and, on the other, top management, though generally top notch in the area of marketing, had difficulty in relating to necessary operational

changes. The situation was paradoxical with the feeling being openly expressed that "operations and planning do not mix" while nonoperating personnel lacked the skill and experience required to plan effectively in the area of operations.

6. As a result of minimal interest in the efficiency with which other than sales-related outputs were being generated, measurements related to order processing were inadequate. Focus was on measuring sales inputs and outputs, with little interest in measuring what resources were being consumed in the processing of orders, or in identifying order-processing problems.

7. Systems development resources could barely keep abreast of the order-entry requirements. Systems related to order processing were manual. Support systems were generally not available, and virtually no resources were allocated to their development.

8. As vendors raised their prices, a concentrated effort was made to buy more inventory so as to avoid those price increases. This additional inventory plugged the access aisles in an already congested distribution center. Order fillers frequently had to climb over stacks of boxes to access materials needed to fill orders.

9. Despite an abundance of stock on hand, the service level, or percentage of ordered items that could be filled from inventory, was falling. Order fillers were wasting progressively more time going to empty bins. Part of this problem was the result of certain high-demand items being in scarce supply while the balance was caused by internal inventory control problems.

This division accounted for approximately 40 percent of both total corporate revenues and profits. Further, it was well positioned in a dynamic market and could be expected to increase its contribution to the corporation's success, providing order-processing effectiveness could be maintained. As it became apparent that order processing was an increasingly limiting factor to the realization of the division's potential, I became associated with the company. My charter was to increase the capacity of order processing within the primary distribution center, thus enabling sales growth to continue.

As previously mentioned, many of the company's customers worked in the areas of repair and maintenance. Although cost is generally of secondary importance to such customers, the timeliness and accuracy of order fill is critical. A customer, for example, may have an expensive piece of equipment down because of a component failure. Such customers expect to receive that needed component on a timely basis. They want what they need as soon as they can get it. Whereas occasional problems related to the timeliness of order fills were encountered, many problems with accuracy existed. Too frequently, either the wrong parts or an incorrect number of parts were shipped to the customer. At the same time, neither a quality control program nor internal quality measurements existed. For all practical purposes, the only quality indicator was the frequency and severity of customer complaints. Whereas those persons who packed orders for shipment were assigned to verify the correct parts in the correct quantity prior to sealing each package, they discretely corrected noted errors, generally without bringing those errors to their supervisor's attention. Obviously, order pickers were making too many errors, and a number of those errors were not being caught and corrected by the persons assigned to inspect and package the orders.

## The Plan to Improve Productivity

Initial efforts focused on retraining the order fillers in an attempt to reduce the number of errors while quantifying the problem. A practical hands-on-type training program was designed and implemented for the order fillers. The program evolved to include a practical test of each order filler's understanding. The test consisted of filling certain types of orders ranging from the most basic to the complex. A lack of understanding, just as in real life, was manifested in the form of order-filling errors. The only difference was that in the controlled training setting, employees needing help could be more readily recognized and given assistance.

Third-party salaried personnel were assigned to randomly sample sealed outgoing packages just prior to shipment. They recorded who filled and who packed each order, as well as the specific nature and frequency of all noted errors. As such inspections could only compare what was prepared for shipment with what was ordered, the element of salespersons possibly ordering the wrong item was eliminated. After a number of internal random samples were made over a few days, it was confirmed that we had a problem with the accuracy of order fill. A few in-process auditors were placed in strategic locations for the purpose of monitoring and recording the accuracy of outputs closer to their source. A single, full-time person was assigned to audit and record randomly selected orders just prior to shipment. A quality performance record, based on in-house inspections and specific customer complaints, was implemented for each individual employee. Employees who were the source of an abnormally high number of errors could be identified and assisted in correcting their problem; at the same time, those who seldom made an error could likewise be identified, but congratulated on their performance. Each and every employee's quality performance for the previous week, be it good or bad, was communicated to the employee by her or his supervisor, on a one-to-one basis, at least once each week. As orders were audited prior to shipment, the order-entry time was noted, and the time it took to fill those orders was calculated and recorded. Where management could previously neither quantify the accuracy nor the timeliness of order fills, thereafter both were readily available. The accuracy and timeliness of daily and month-to-date order fills were communicated daily,

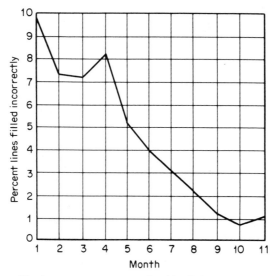

**Figure 16-1.** The positive impact on outgoing quality (the declining error rate) of the new productivity plan.

by way of a manually prepared report, to all supervisors. Quality and timeliness goals were generated for each area of activity by the responsible manager. Actual performance as compared to those goals, both daily and month to date, was an integral part of the daily report. Quality discrepancies were categorized, compiled, and reported by type and by source.

The resulting increased managerial awareness, and prompt feedback to individuals related to the quality of outputs they had generated, had a positive impact on outgoing quality as is illustrated by Figure 16-1.

The frequency of customer complaints related to order processing has confirmed this internal indicator of improved accuracy of order filling. An increased level of managerial exceptions, coupled with a measurement and reporting system which focuses on individual employee quality performance, reduced the order-processing error rate and the related frequency of customer complaints and returns. To realize the cost-savings benefit of that improvement, which was conservatively estimated at $900,000 annually, it was necessary to similarly reduce the rising and offsetting error rates from other, non-order-processing sources, such as salesperson-responsible mistakes, for example. Toward that end, a revised report, compiling customer-returns data by frequency and function responsible, was designed and implemented.

To prepare for a projected, near-term, large increase in sales, it became necessary to implement a second shift of order-processing activity. This change improved the effectiveness by increasing the volume of orders processed daily but had a negative impact on efficiency. Predictably, as increased quality expectations were communicated to order-processing personnel by their supervisors, a few employees chose to rationalize the relatively low volume of their outputs as the necessary consequence of improved quality. The addition of a second shift of order-processing activity to handle anticipated future increases in sales was widely misinterpreted among employees as a willingness on the part of management to accept lower efficiency for the purpose of maintaining a high level of quality. While the urgency attached to reducing customer complaints provided managers some latitude to express quality expectations to their employees, that latitude did not extend to productivity expectations. The company's sales and profits were both growing at an annual rate exceeding 30 percent. As specific work standards had never been installed, their implementation was viewed as possibly disruptive. Although there was no financially based sense of urgency related to improving productivity, order-processing resource limitations, including the facility and the diminishing work space due to increasing inventory, dictated that productivity be increased to keep pace with sales demands. A means to improve productivity without the use of work standards would have to be devised and implemented.

The value of work standards is that they communicate management's expectations to employees in specific terms. Standards establish what an average employee working at a normal pace within a given work situation should produce. Consistent achievement of a well-communicated, fair, and accepted standard provides the employee with an inner satisfaction gained from the knowledge that management's requirements have been satisfactorily met. Without management communicating specific expectations, employees usually have no reference point against which they can compare their own performance. Either increased employee anxiety or decreased efficiency is the result, dependent upon the individual employee and the prevailing work climate. Based on the feeling that the critical factor in improving productivity is the ability of managers to motivate their employees to perform in accordance with their individual potential, we proceeded to go about improving productivity without the benefit of standards. In summary, our approach was based on making employees feel better, about their individual job and themselves, by doing better. Most employees are not only able to understand the company's needs but, provided positive encouragement and prompt feedback on their performance by their supervisor, are also able to relate the satisfaction of those needs to their own.

Output measurements and a related daily report existed within the distribution center. Although results in terms of total orders and total lines processed were communicated, there existed no basis for comparison of actual performance with either a goal or a standard. What you saw was not only what you got but also what you could anticipate continuing to get. The first step toward improving productivity was to ensure the integrity of the measurements and then to embark on the process of goal setting and achieving as it related to order-processing productivity. Goals for output per hour were set by supervisors for their respective work groups. Those goals were not communicated to the employees. The daily report of order-processing activity was revised from communicating only daily "actual" performance data to reporting information on both daily and month-to-date "actual" vs. "goal" performance. A supervisory plan of action aimed at improving employee productivity and quality was designed and implemented.

### Plan of Action Aimed at Improving Productivity

| Supervisory Action | Purpose |
|---|---|
| Make "howdy rounds," personally contacting each and every employee in the work group at least twice daily.<br>1. Immediately after the start of the work shift<br>2. After lunch<br>3. At other times if required | • To recognize each employee as an individual<br>• To provide every employee an opportunity to ask questions and to receive the correct answer<br>• To ensure all jobs are properly covered<br>• To verify progress and the use of proper methods and procedures |
| Monitor and respond to established indicators each and every hour.<br>1. Accuracy of order fills<br>2. Timeliness of order fills<br>3. Volume of order fills<br>4. Efficiency of order fills | Early recognition and resolution of problems |
| Assume the responsibility for making all your employees successful.<br>1. The proper training and indoctrination of new and recently transferred employees<br>2. The retraining of employees who are experiencing problems | • To minimize turnover<br>• To improve operating results |
| Maintenance and weekly updating of written records of individual job performance.<br>1. Accuracy of outputs<br>2. Volume of outputs<br>3. Efficiency with which outputs are achieved<br>4. Attendance | • Recognition of individual contribution<br>   As compared to individual potential<br>   As compared to others in the same work group<br>• To provide objective data on which performance appraisals can be based |
| Brief individual performance meetings with each employee each week. | • To communicate the supervisor's opinion of the employee's performance<br>• To improve performance by providing timely feedback of<br>   Individual strengths<br>   Individual areas requiring improvement |

Plan of Action Aimed at Improving Productivity *(continued)*

| Supervisory Action | Purpose |
|---|---|
| | • To provide each employee an opportunity to discuss work-related problems |
| A 15- to 20-minute meeting to be held by each supervisor with employees as a group once each week. Meetings to be held on the floor. | • To provide an opportunity for the supervisor to accentuate the positive<br>• To develop a spirit of teamwork<br>• To communicate opportunities for improvement while soliciting employees' suggestions and best efforts<br>• To dispel rumors by communicating accurate and timely work-related information |
| A one-hour meeting with a small group of key employees at least once each month to focus upon specific opportunities for improvement. | • To increase the level of employee participation for the purposes of<br>Gaining the benefit of employee perspective<br>Soliciting employee ideas and suggestions<br>Increasing employee commitment to the achievement of organizational goals<br>• To make employees aware of what is happening in the work place<br>• To share management's grand design and thereby promote better understanding and teamwork |

## Results

This plan of action, coupled with the compiling of measurement information, consumed five hours a day of each supervisor's time at work. Most of that total time was invested in supervisory interface, in one form or another, with employees. The focus was on people and prevention, rather than on things and crisis management. Despite many obstacles—including a severely congested work place, a low service level which resulted in much time being wasted by order fillers going to empty stock bins, and interference by well-intended but counterproductive employee relations personnel—considerable progress was realized in improving order-processing productivity as gauged by a measure of output per hour. Figure 16-2 summarizes that progress.

The average number of lines processed per hour worked in fiscal year 1980 was 19.59 as compared to 17.25 in fiscal year 1979, an increase of 13.5 percent.

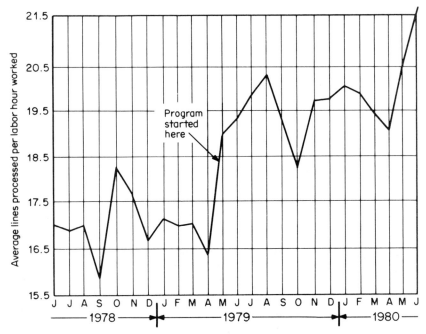

**Figure 16-2.** Order-processing productivity; average lines processed per hour worked.

While the improvement is "significant" by anyone's standard, the end result was not what would be expected. Looking at productivity as the ratio of "what you get" to "what you give," the gains failed to equal the cost of wage increases. Table 16-1 provides the details related to the situation.

An approximate 50 percent reduction in overtime hours worked in fiscal 1980 and the 13.5 percent improvement in output per hour were more than offset by a 25.8 percent increase in the average cost per labor hour worked during the year. However, had neither the overtime reduction nor the improvement in output per hour been realized, the average labor cost per line processed would have increased by 25.8 percent, fiscal 1980 over fiscal 1979, rather than the actual 9.5 percent increase.

As in many companies today, wage increases within this company were not related to performance. This case history points out the consequences of an insensitivity to the relationship between what is "given" and what is "gotten." When the improvement in outputs produced lags behind the increase in wages, prices are increased to make up the difference. Customers have to pay more for the same item or, in some cases, even more for a lesser item. Because their costs have increased, the customers must, in turn, increase their selling prices, and the inflationary beat goes on. Had the wage increases in this situation been lim-

**TABLE 16-1.** Order-Processing Activity of the Electronics Distributor

| Line | Item | Fiscal 1979 | Fiscal 1980 | Fiscal 1980 Index |
|------|------|-------------|-------------|-------------------|
| 1. | Total net sales | $90,257,000 | $128,368,200 | 142.2 |
| 2. | Total lines processed | 5,095,354 | 6,363,061 | 124.9 |
| 3. | Total hours worked | 295,342 | 324,878 | 110.0 |
| 4. | Average number of lines processed per hour worked | 17.25 | 19.59 | 113.5 |
| 5 | Order-processing wages | $ 1,309,000 | $ 2,044,200 | 156.2 |
| 6. | Order-processing overtime expense | $ 303,900 | $ 186,800 | 61.5 |
| 7. | Total employee order-processing expense | $ 1,612,900 | $ 2,231,000 | 138.3 |
| 8. | Average employee hourly wage per hour worked | $ 5.46 | $ 6.87 | 125.8 |
| 9 | Temporary help expense | $ 71,300 | $ 75,100 | 105.3 |
| 10. | Total order-processing labor expense, actual | $ 1,684,200 | $ 2,306,100 | 136.9 |
| 11. | Average labor cost per line processed, actual | $ 0.3305364 | $ 0.3624199 | 109.6 |
| 12. | Total order-processing labor expense, adjusted* | $ 1,684,200 | $ 1,848,934 | 109.8 |
| 13. | Average labor cost per line processed, adjusted* | $ 0.3305364 | $ 0.2880846 | 87.2 |

*The wage increases for fiscal 1980 have been factored out.

ited to something less than 13.5 percent, instead of the actual 25.8 percent increase granted, the company would have at least matched wage increases with increased outputs. While, on one hand, a very generous increase was provided to order-processing employees, artificial barriers were created to limit productivity improvement efforts. Both were the result of fear and a lack of understanding related to the employee needs for belonging, self-esteem, and achievement. By focusing on those needs, output per hour was increased significantly despite numerous obstacles.

Productivity improvement efforts within the operation's function of this organization were expanded to include all resources and all personnel in the various areas of activity. Fortunately, wage increases in the other, nonunion, areas of the business were closer to national averages, thus presenting less of an obstacle to the achievement of the desired results—likewise with the cost increases related to the other than labor resources consumed, which seldom exceeded 10 percent as compared to the prior year. Table 16-2 provides the total factor productivity comparison for each activity, fiscal 1980 vs. fiscal 1979, and summarizes the group's achievements.

Despite a work climate less than conducive to improving productivity, including unusually high wage increases being given without regard for per-

**TABLE 16·2.** Total Factor Productivity Comparison of the Electronics Distributor Based on Net Sales, Fiscal 1979 ($90,257,000) vs. Fiscal 1980 ($128,368,300)

| Operations-Related Activity | Expense Rates* | | 1980 Expense Rate Index | Fiscal 1980 Savings,† in $ |
| --- | --- | --- | --- | --- |
| | Fiscal 1979 (1) | Fiscal 1980 (2) | | |
| Administrative | 0.0044133 | 0.0019913 | 45.1 | 310,908 |
| Communications | 0.0230034 | 0.0195033 | 84.8 | 449,302 |
| Real estate and support services | 0.0059567 | 0.0048535 | 81.5 | 141,616 |
| Order processing | 0.0263873 | 0.0254095 | 96.3 | 125,516 |
| Maintenance and janitorial services | 0.0054221 | 0.0041405 | 76.4 | 164,517 |
| Expediting and order entry | 0.0018525 | 0.0017996 | 97.1 | 6,791 |
| Total operations | 0.0670353 | 0.0576977 | 86.1 | 1,198,650 |

*Expenses ÷ net sales.
†(Column 1 − column 2) × fiscal 1980 net sales.

formance, operations-related activities, in total, realized an actual net savings of $1,198,650 in fiscal 1980, as compared to applying fiscal 1979 expense rates to fiscal 1980 net sales. This improvement was realized by designing and implementing productivity measurements, setting results-related goals, increasing employee involvement, and providing prompt and accurate feedback on actual performance vs. goal. The key factors in realizing this improvement were managerial dedication, including a general unwillingness to succumb to the prevailing forces calling for mediocrity and satisfaction with second best, and the cooperation and contribution of employees. Paralysis and fear on the part of managers evolved into goal-directed action and the courage to direct the efforts of their employees in a positive manner. Indifference and mistrust on the part of too many employees evolved into improved awareness and a genuine concern for the needs of customers, plus an increased willingness to contribute to the achievement of the organization's goals. By doing better, most people involved felt better—about themselves, about their jobs, and about the company.

# Additional
# Perspectives

# 17

# The Behavioral Insight

*Excellence* as applied to an organization means that the organization is so well managed that it approaches realizing its potential. It has evolved beyond being consistently *good,* toward becoming all it is capable of being. Organizational excellence manifests itself in the form of members who not only identify with the organization's goals but who also enthusiastically apply, in the form of their best efforts, their talents and abilities toward the achievement of those goals. Such excellence is the result of uncompromising and enlightened management: (1) uncompromising in the sense that it is generally understood among the organization's members that its leadership will never be satisfied with second-rate efforts or second-best results and (2) enlightened in the sense that managerial behavior is based upon the premise that employee and organizational needs are, to a large extent, interdependent. To stimulate employees putting forth their best efforts and maximizing their contribution to the achievement of the organization's goals, enlightened managers recognize that employee needs must be satisfied in the process. In summary, organizational excellence can only be achieved when managers in general consistently demonstrate, via their actions, a genuine concern for both the people with whom they work and for the results achieved.

## The Managerial Grid

In their book *The Managerial Grid,* Robert Blake and Jane Mouton present the concept of assessing any given manager's job-related behavior by quantifying concerns for two important factors in the work place: coworkers and "production," or the generation of outputs. The managerial grid is a framework for

277

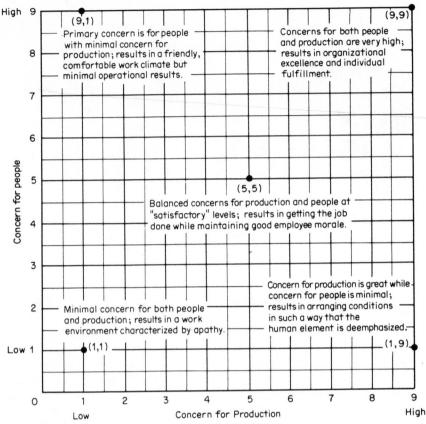

**Figure 17-1.** The managerial grid. (Based on Robert Blake and Jane Mouton, *The Managerial Grid*, Gulf, Houston, 1964.)

identifying, analyzing, and solving production-people problems. It provides the means by which any manager can analyze his or her actions and the motivation behind those actions. The managerial grid creates a useful "code" or "shorthand" for discussing production-people problems in the endless variety of ways that arise within any organization. It provides managers an abbreviated means for describing managerial actions. Two managers, both of whom are familiar with the concept, can effectively communicate managerial concerns and resulting actions by stating two numbers, which are actually coordinates on the grid. For example, one such manager may describe an action as being (9, 1), and the other manager understands the exact degrees of underlying concerns for both production and people. The managerial grid communicates those concerns graphically as is shown in Figure 17-1.

That point on the grid defined by the coordinates (9, 9) represents the highest level of managerial concern for both people and production. The related managerial behavior results in all members having a strong identification with the organization's goals and a shared commitment to their achievement. Such a work climate provides the surest path to organizational excellence. Though difficult to achieve, the development of a (9, 9) work climate is worthy of the best efforts of all managers. A recent study indicates that fully 85 percent of both the managerial and nonmanagerial work groups within our country are dissatisfied with their work situation. That means that most people spend 30 to 40 years working at something from which they receive little personal satisfaction. What a waste, not only in terms of human needs unfulfilled but also in terms of the unrealized productivity potential which is bound to result.

Table 17-1 pinpoints how a (9, 9) oriented managerial value system results in managerial actions which differ from those related to other value systems.

The managerial grid is based upon several widely accepted theories of behavioral science, such as McGregor's Theory X and Theory Y. Theory X is purely (9, 1), while Theory Y consists of a mixture of (1, 9), (5, 5), and (9, 9). Studying the grid as a framework for better understanding of individual manager and corporate concerns enables the organization's members to learn more about behavioral science concepts while providing a foundation for improving productivity.

As the Japanese are generally viewed as the "model" for improving productivity, it is interesting to note the result of an experiment conducted by Blake and Mouton involving both American and Japanese managers. After having studied grid theory for one week, managers participated in an experiment designed to answer the question: "What is the best way to operate an organization?" Twenty questions related to effective organizational performance were discussed. Each question had five alternative answers which the participating managers were asked to rank from "most sound" to "least sound" as the basis for operating an organization. Managerial judgments related to what the participating managers personally thought was sound, not necessarily to what actually happens in organizations. If any grid alternative was chosen as "most sound" in answer to all twenty questions, the score for that particular approach would be 100. If, on the other hand, any grid alternative was chosen as "least sound" in answer to all twenty questions, the score for that particular approach would be 20. The results summarized by Figure 17-2 illustrate that among both Japanese and American managers, there is equal agreement that (9, 9) is viewed as the best, or "soundest," way to manage; (9, 1) and (5, 5) were selected as second best, (1, 9) selected next, and (1, 1) selected as the least sound approach to managing an organization.

When this same experiment was conducted after the grid had been in use within an organization over a period of from two to three years, (9, 9) retains its strong first choice position, but (9, 1) is selected over (5, 5) as the choice for the second-best managerial approach.

**TABLE 17·1.** Characteristic Managerial Actions Resulting from Various Degrees of Managerial Concern for Production and People

| Element of Managerial Beahvior | Managerial Concern | | Characteristic Managerial Action |
|---|---|---|---|
| | Production | People | |
| | 9 | 9 | Attempts to pinpoint reason(s) for conflict and tries to resolve it |
| Response to conflict | 9 | 1 | Emphasizes winning position while curtailing conflict |
| | 5 | 5 | Tries to be "firm but fair"; seeks an "equitable solution" |
| | 1 | 9 | Avoids generating conflict, but when it does arise, tries to soothe feelings and keep people together |
| | 1 | 1 | Either remains neutral or doesn't get involved |
| | 9 | 9 | Expresses ideas and convictions candidly; willing to put forth an effort to resolve differences |
| Interface with others | 9 | 1 | Discussions on basis of look out for yourself; unwilling to compromise |
| | 5 | 5 | A willingness to compromise; to give and take |
| | 1 | 9 | Nonoffensive in approach; maintaining a friendly relationship is of primary concern |
| | 1 | 1 | Expresses ideas and opinions with little conviction |
| | 9 | 9 | Generates an ongoing examination of progress (measuring and evaluating operating results) for the purpose of learning and making improvement |
| Approach to evaluating results and improving effectiveness via teamwork | 9 | 1 | Finds fault with everything and everybody; unconstructive criticism |
| | 5 | 5 | Offers suggestions of what to do differently and how to do better |
| | 1 | 9 | Gives compliments while ignores faults |
| | 1 | 1 | Gives little or no attention to results or team action |

SOURCE: Based on R. Blake and J. Mouton, *Corporate Excellence through Grid Organization Development*, Gulf, Houston, 1968.

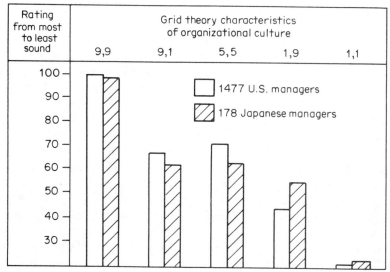

**Figure 17-2.** A survey of American and Japanese managers. (Based on Robert Blake and Jane Mouton, *Corporate Excellence through Grid Organization Development*, Gulf, Houston 1968, pp. 37–43.)

While grid training, in all probability, increases managers' awareness of the impact of their behavior and underlying concerns or values upon organizational results, I would guess that most experienced managers would express the same choice of (9, 9) managerial and organizational orientation as preferable in improving productivity without having the benefit of such training. While many, if not most, American managers intellectually acknowledge the desirability of high managerial concern for both people and "outputs," we have generally fallen short of modifying our value systems and our behavior so that we fail to do, on a consistent basis, what we know to be best. An awareness that improved productivity is dependent upon changing conditions within the organization, including generating an increased managerial concern for both people and "outputs," is encouraging. To utilize that awareness as the springboard to altering managerial behavior, so that actions coincide consistently with the (9, 9) value system and concerns orientation, is dependent upon recognizing and overcoming the barriers that create the variance between actual managerial concerns, as manifested in their on-the-job behavior, and the values or concerns they consider to be best related to improving productivity.

## Barriers to Managers Consistently Demonstrating a (9, 9) Concerns Orientation

If managers generally recognize the (9, 9) concerns orientation as generating a work climate most conducive to improving productivity, why then do so few of those same managers consistently demonstrate, via their actions, such an orientation? Blake and Mouton report that at the beginning of their organization development programs based upon the managerial grid, most participating managers evaluate "communications" followed by "planning" as the major barriers or obstacles to the achievement of organizational excellence. Poor examination of operating results in the form of measurements designed to evaluate progress and failure to properly provide direction in the form of organizational goals are further down the list. When participating managers reexamine organizational barriers in the context of teamwork development, measurements and goals shift upward in significance to first place. Examining progress via goal setting and measurements provides critical insight into problems and their causes and is the basis for improving organizational performance. The fact that the importance of goals and measurements is generally not appreciated among managers is an indicator that managers fail to do what they realize they should be doing simply because they don't know how to go about doing it. For a manager to exhibit a high level of concern for both production and people is dependent upon the implementation of goals and measurements. While goals and measurements obviously contribute to exhibiting a high level of managerial concern for production or the organization's outputs, they less obviously, but equally, contribute to exhibiting a high level of managerial concern for people. The process of setting goals contributes to quantifying what is expected from the organization's members, as well as providing the framework for communicating the significance of the individual member's role in achieving the organization's primary purpose. By increasing the objectivity of the basis for performance appraisal, goals and related measurements demonstrate a high degree of concern for people. The increased objectivity of managerial appraisal of subordinate performance usually results in an enhanced feeling of "fairness" among employees.

Goals and measurements, when properly communicated and implemented within a reward-centered work environment, are the foundation for managerial expression of a high concern for both production and people. With regard to production, they quantify expectations and provide a continuous means for managers and employees alike to gauge progress. With regard to people, they can readily be used in a manner which communicates the importance of the efforts of people, individually and in combination, to the fulfillment of the organization's purpose. The barrier to managers consistently demonstrating, via their on-the-job actions, a (9, 9) concerns orientation can be significantly reduced by showing them how to successfully implement and maintain organizational goals and measurements. In addition to such training, it is further required that managers gain some insight into how to deal more effectively with overt on-the-job behavior and its consequences. This knowledge can be a practical supplement to an awareness of traditional, but difficult to decipher, cause-and-effect relationships.

## Organizational Behavior Modification

Organizational behavior modification is based on the assumption that the behaviors exhibited by persons within organizations are dependent on the perceived consequences. The concepts describe how the work environment actually *controls* learned behavior. Note the key word here is *controls*, not *causes*. Behavior traced to its beginning must have some specific cause or causes. Although it would be valuable to isolate such causes of behavior, it is most often difficult, if not virtually impossible, to do so. Human resources can be managed more practically by recognizing the impact that "consequences" within the organization's environment have upon behavior. Figure 17-3 illustrates this contingency.

While the causes of behavior, as we know them today, are primarily hypothetical, the controlling mechanisms within the organization, and the behavior itself, is readily observable. Cues set up organizational behavior which, when demonstrated as a specific action by a member, is followed by various consequences. The nature of the consequences either increases, decreases, or maintains the probability that the behavior, or specific action, will be repeated.

*Cues* represent environmental conditions or specific stimuli. Cues take many forms within the organization: the behavior of supervisors and employees, as well as rules, formal and informal communications, instructions, schedules, physical objects, and available time. Singularly or in combination, these "things" within the organization serve to cue organizational behavior. Cued behavior, in turn, may have several consequences. Whereas money in the form of earnings is a common consequence within organizations, social approval, attention, status, privileges, and feedback related to performance are at least equal, and most often more important, consequences as perceived by members. Adverse consequences in the form of reprimands, discharge, demotions, social sanctions, and the docking of one's pay are also common in organizations today. While "general" or contractual pay increases and other rewards are commonly granted in modern organizations without regard to performance, other positive and negative consequences either already are, or if not can become, a direct result of a member's performance. On-the-job behavior is best-controlled if the cue-behavior-consequence contingency is understood by all the organization's

**Figure 17-3.** Basic behavioral contingency.

members and if each one is systematically and consistently identified and managed. Employees can then learn to associate certain cues with certain consequences which come only as a direct result of desired performance. Organizational behavior modification has been developed to help the manager learn how to improve performance by systematically and consistently managing the cue-behavior-consequence contingency.

Contrary to popular opinion, behavior modification is not some mystical psychological manipulation of people. Instead, it is a straightforward technology of learned behavior which has underlying principles and a procedured methodology. Behavior modification is based on three fundamental principles:

**1. The necessity for dealing exclusively with observable behavioral events.** Observable behavior within the organizational setting is a dependent variable. It is dependent upon stimulus control, stimuli, and reinforcement. The basic building blocks for the manager intent on modifying behavior within the organization are behavioral events, sometimes referred to as *responses*. Behavioral events differ from overall behavior in that they are only one instance (or "critical incident") of a larger class of behavior. While overall behavior is of some importance, the analysis of the cue-behavior-consequence contingency requires that you focus on the more specific behavioral event. In order to change behavior, the specific behavioral event must be identified. Table 17-2 illustrates how such events are identified.

**2. The use of frequency of behavioral events as the basic measurement.** What happens, or the specific behavioral event, is of secondary importance to the frequency with which it happens. Responses which occur fre-

**TABLE 17-2.** Identifying Behavioral Events

| Behavior | General Effect on the Environment | Example of a Specific Response on Behavioral Event |
|---|---|---|
| Approving behavior (verbal) | Increases the strength of the approved behavior | A manager comments to an employee, "I appreciate your help in getting that job out on time yesterday." |
| Disapproving behavior (nonverbal) | Decreases the strength of the disapproved behavior | A department store manager shakes her head and frowns in response to how a clerk treats a customer. |
| Disruptive behavior | Interrupts the productive efforts of others | A manager knocks on the closed door of his boss and interrupts a meeting that is in process for the purpose of communicating routine information. |
| Productive behavior | Contributes to the achievement of organizational goals | An employee meets the production standard without generating any defects. |
| Nonproductive behavior | Detracts from the achievement of organizational goals | An office worker reads the newspaper during working hours. |

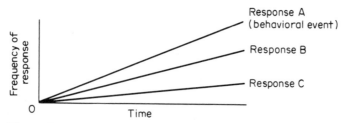

Figure 17-4. Recording an identified behavioral response.

quently are considered to be relatively strong, whereas responses which occur infrequently are considered to be relatively weak. The important thing is neither the size nor intensity of the event but how often it occurs. There are two important dimensions to response frequency, both of which relate to time.

**The past dimension.** As previously mentioned, a record of the frequency with which a certain response has occurred within a certain time period indicates its strength. Some response records are written and maintained in the form of filed reports; others exist only in memory. Response strength is a function of observed response frequency, and response frequency is the basic means of measuring behavioral events.

**The future dimension.** The other dimension of response frequency deals with the future and the predictability of behavior. The stronger a response, as indicated by its frequency of occurrence, the greater the probability for its reoccurrence. Likewise, the weaker a response, as indicated by its frequency of occurrence, the lower the probability for its reoccurrence.

With regard to the future, the manager intent on modifying behavior within the organization attempts to alter the probability of response by systematically and consistently managing the consequences of observable behavioral events. The success or failure of those efforts is revealed in the record of the response frequency (the past). In this manner, both dimensions of response frequency contribute to altering behavior.

Once a behavioral event has been identified and is under observation, the recording of its frequency of occurrence is easily accomplished through the use of a two-dimensional chart as is shown in Figure 17-4.

Inspection of the frequency chart shows the relative strength of the charted responses. When response frequency is measured prior to attempts to change a behavior, that period is called the *baseline*. The baseline plays an important role in any systematic approach to changing behavior as it is the reference point against which progress is measured. Measurements and subsequent charting of response frequency made after the initiation of efforts to change a behavior are said to occur in the *intervention* period.

**3. The importance of viewing behavior within the context of a cue-behavior-consequence contingency.** Behavior is either strengthened, weakened, or maintained by its consequences. This third principle ties together

**TABLE 17-3.** Organizational Behavior Contingencies

| Cues (Antecedents) | Behavior | Consequences |
|---|---|---|
| A manager approaches an employee at his or her work station. | The employee communicates that the work is progressing well. | The employee receives a compliment from the manager. |
| An exceptionally hectic day. | The manager berates the secretary. | The secretary's performance drops. |
| A computer program fails to run. | The program is rewritten. | The program runs. |
| A messy work area. | The manager asks all employees to clean up around their work station. | A clean work area. |
| A letter in the in-basket. | Answering the letter. | An empty in-basket. |
| A position description is posted on the bulletin board. | Applying for the position. | Getting the position. |

the cue-behavior-consequence contingency. Cues, or antecedents, represent events preceding behavior, while consequences are the result of that behavior. Table 17-3 provides an example of this relationship.

The basic procedures and techniques of behavior modification are derived from these three principles. Behavioral events are the common denominator, frequency of response permits the quantifying and measurement of behavior, and the cue-behavior-consequence contingency reveals the employee-environment interaction. The following places those principles into a "whole" context for a discussion of the "how to" of behavior modification.

## Intervention Strategies

Controlling behavior basically involves the management of cue-behavior-consequence contingencies. To manage those relationships, it is essential that you gain an understanding of how consequences affect the frequency of response. Over a period of many years, precise information has been developed for the control of response frequency with contingent consequences. Four general behavior modification strategies have emerged: positive reinforcement, negative reinforcement, punishment, and extinction. These strategies may be employed either singularly or in combination. Each strategy defines a class of consequences which has a particular effect on response frequency. It must be remembered, however, that the consequences must be contingent upon a specific behavioral event. The successful use of intervention strategies depends on the ability of the behavior modifier to efficiently present and withdraw environmental conditions in a contingent manner. These environmental conditions

**TABLE 17-4.** Behavior Modification Strategies

| Strategy | Cue (Antecedent) | Behavioral Events | Consequence | Behavioral Outcome |
|---|---|---|---|---|
| Positive reinforcement | A given environmental setting | B | Contingent presentation of an environmental condition | Increase in the frequency of response B |
| Negative reinforcement | A given environmental setting | B | Contingent termination or withdrawal of an environmental condition | Increase in the frequency of response B |
| Punishment | A given environmental setting | B | Contingent presentation of an environmental condition | Decrease in the frequency of response B |
| Extinction | A given environmental setting | B | None | Decrease in the frequency of response B |
| Combination strategies: Extinction–positive reinforcement or Punishment–positive reinforcement or Punishment–negative reinforcement | A given environmental setting | Incompatible responses B and C | Combination of consequences as listed above | Decrease in the frequency of response B; increase in the frequency of response C |

may include almost any changes in the environment, some of which may be subtle and not recognizable to the casual observer. Some examples include, but are not limited to, the withdrawal or termination of affection, a criticism, a layoff, a threat, a promotion, an invitation to lunch, an offer to buy a cup of coffee, extra work, and permission to take vacation when requested. Table 17-4 summarizes behavior modification strategies.

**Positive reinforcement.** Positive reinforcement strengthens behavior. A positively reinforced response has a greater probability of recurrence simply because it pays off. For example, you may repeatedly dine at a certain restaurant because the food is consistently good. The more frequently customers are positively reinforced by being served a good meal, the more successful the restaurant will be.

**Negative reinforcement.** Negative reinforcement is similar to positive reinforcement, the only difference being that negative reinforcement withdraws or terminates an undesirable consequence, whereas positive reinforcement provides a desirable consequence. An example of negative reinforcement is the employee who works harder to stop a boss from nagging all day. Negative reinforcement is sometimes confused with punishment. They differ in that negative reinforcement increases the frequency of a certain response, while punishment reduces the frequency of response.

**Punishment.** A response is punished when the contingent presentation of an environmental condition decreases its frequency of occurrence. A motorist is careful to drive within the speed limit because of being fined in the past for speeding. The fine is a punishment and is designed to decrease the frequency of the "speeding" response.

**Extinction.** Extinction is an unusual strategy in that it is based on doing nothing. Because learned responses must be reinforced to reoccur, extinction is a potent strategy of behavior modification intervention. Responses which are not reinforced decrease in frequency and eventually disappear. If a door-to-door salesperson rings the doorbell of a certain house on several occasions but can never find anyone at home, the response is extinguished and the salesperson stops calling.

**Extinction–positive reinforcement.** Combination responses are built around two incompatible responses, one desirable and one undesirable. Productive effort, for example, is incompatible with loafing. The two responses cannot be emitted simultaneously. They represent an either-or situation. A combination strategy of behavior modification such as extinction–positive reinforcement, can weaken the undesirable response, while strengthening the desirable response. An example might be a long-term subordinate who is overly dependent upon a supervisor. In the past, the response of contacting the supervisor for the purpose of resolving problems that the employee should be fully capable of handling has been positively reinforced. The supervisor has solved all the employee's problems in a speedy fashion. The dependent behavior, having been positively reinforced, increases in frequency. The practical solution to this problem would be for the supervisor to stop such positive reinforcement of the dependent behavior by the use of the extinction strategy while positively reinforcing independent problem-solving behavior on the part of the employee.

**Punishment–positive reinforcement.** This strategy is similar to the extinction–positive reinforcement strategy. The only difference is that undesirable responses are punished rather than ignored. Punishment may be chosen over extinction because the impact of the undesirable response is so disruptive or unsafe that the time lost in implementing the extinction strategy places the organization in a vulnerable position. For example, an employee who refuses to respond to the direction of a supervisor may require immediate disciplinary action. Positive reinforcement of the incompatible response of the employee responding to supervisory direction in a prompt and positive manner would constitute the other half of the punishment–positive reinforcement strategy in this case.

**Punishment–negative reinforcement.** The punishment–negative reinforcement strategy focuses on punishing undesirable responses until such time that the person being punished replaces the undesirable response with an incompatible desirable response. At that time the negative reinforcement is applied in the form of terminating the punishment. The supervisor who repetitively reprimands an employee for generating too much scrap and does not stop reprimanding until the employee is generating little, if any, scrap is using a punishment–negative reinforcement. The difference between the punishment and the punishment–negative reinforcement strategies as applied to this example is that the punishment strategy would be limited in the number of reprimands, the termination of which would not be contingent upon the emitting of a desirable response.

### Schedules of Reinforcement

In analyzing a specific behavioral contingency, a manager intent on modifying behavior must know "when" or "how often" the consequence follows the response in question, as well as "what" a contingent consequence is. The success or failure of a particular behavior modification strategy frequently depends on the scheduling and timing of contingent consequences. For example, whether a consequence is made contingent upon every instance of a particular response or every tenth instance will influence the strength of the response. Similarly, the elapsed time between contingent consequences has a distinct effect on response strength.

Studies have found, for example, that the schedule of reinforcement often has a greater effect on frequency of responding than does the size or magnitude of the reinforcer. One particular study consisted of two groups of employees that were paid the same hourly base wage for performing identical tasks. The first group was provided an automatic incentive of 25 cents for each piece produced. The second group was given a fifty-fifty chance to earn the same incentive of 25 cents for each piece produced, to be determined by the flip of a coin upon the completion of each individual piece. The second group outperformed the first group. Such results not only point out the significance of how reinforcers are scheduled but also emphasize the importance of properly administering wage-incentive systems.[1]

Surprisingly, an intermittent reinforcement schedule which does not rein-

[1]G. Yuke, K. N. Wexley, and V. D. Seymore, "Effectiveness of Pay Incentives under Variable Ration and Continuous Reinforcement Schedules," *Journal of Applied Psychology*, Feb. 1972, pp. 19–23.

force every response, such as a slot machine, tends to promote stronger behavior than does a continuous reinforcement schedule which reinforces every response. Continuous reinforcement highlights accidental oversights; for example, if you thank someone for a desirable response each and every time it is provided over an extended period of time, it is provided over an extended period of time; if you then fail to provide a thank-you for 2 or 3 times in a row, that desirable response is more subject to being terminated than were you to provide thank-yous on an intermittent schedule.

## Application of Organizational Behavior Modification Principles and Techniques

The following example is provided for the purpose of illustrating the application of principles and techniques of organizational behavior modification.

**Incident.** A manager summons a subordinate for an annual meeting concerning performance appraisal and warns the subordinate that unless an improvement in general attitude is demonstrated within the following six weeks, the subordinate will be discharged. Six weeks later the subordinate is terminated and complains of not knowing why.

Termination is the most severe economic sanction an organization can apply to its members. In this particular case, specifics were not provided the subordinate during the performance appraisal meeting. Not only was the performance appraisal subjective in nature, but no specific performance-related goals were set for the six-week period. The key question arising from the incident is, Did the subordinate deserve to be fired? Was the subordinate at fault, or was it the environment which was not conducive to performing properly?

The manager's strategy is apparent: the application of negative reinforcement in the form of a threat that the subordinate would be terminated unless there was an improvement in attitude. This action is a good example of the unwitting use of behavior modification. Even if the manager had been familiar with behavior modification principles and skilled in their application, negative reinforcement would have been difficult to apply effectively. While concerned with attitude, the manager should have been focusing attention on the subordinate's performance-related behavior. Was the subordinate wasting time, failing to produce the required quantity or quality of outputs, or failing to respond to the direction of the manager? These observable and measurable on-the-job behavioral events should have been addressed, not vague internal habits of thought commonly referred to as "attitude."

The manager skilled in principles and techniques of organizational behavior modification would have identified the subordinate's desirable and undesirable behaviors, collected data to serve as a baseline, and made an analysis to determine what consequences were supporting the behaviors in question, all before conducting the performance appraisal meeting with the subordinate. The format presented in Figure 17-5 provides the basis for such an approach.

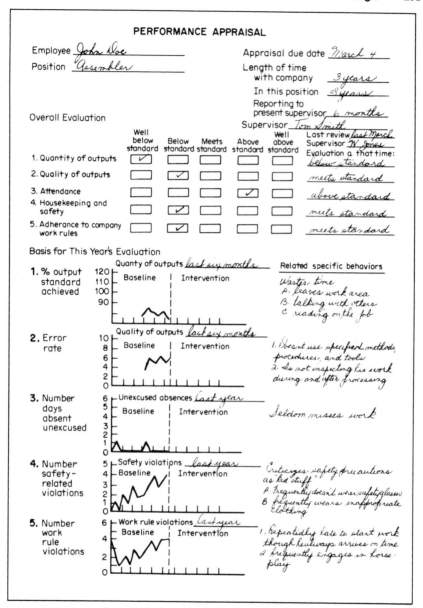

**Figure 17-5.** Sample of a performance appraisal.

As opposed to obtaining predictably poor results with a subjective evaluation lacking in specifics, this approach ensures objectivity and not only is backed up by specific results but also pinpoints the specific behavioral events behind those results.

On the basis of the information compiled in this performance appraisal format, the manager would meet with the subordinate to identify the problem behaviors, mutually determine some realistic behavior improvement goals, and outline the contingencies for the next six weeks. By extending the graphs provided as part of the appraisal format beyond the baseline period and into the intervention (and in this case probationary) period, response-frequency charts for the subordinate's behavior can be maintained. Unlike the baseline period, wherein response frequencies were charted on a monthly basis, the seriousness of the situation warrants recording those frequencies each week, if not each day. The subordinate's behavior should be monitored frequently by both the manager and the subordinate. The subordinate might even be instructed to personally update the graphs so as to ensure continuous awareness. Weekly meetings should be scheduled between the manager and subordinate for the purpose of reviewing the subordinate's progress. At the end of the six-week probationary period, the manager would have sufficient data on which to base objectively a retention or termination decision.

This example communicates the difference between the common subjective approach, which is usually based on fear and punishment, and the more constructive approach of a contingent manager who views the subordinate's behavior as learned and a function of the consequences provided by the organization. Not being able to identify the causes of behavior, the contingent manager focuses on the environment and the consequences it provides so as to control that behavior. The contingent manager strives to increase employees' willingness to contribute to the achievement of organizational goals by finding positive reinforcers which will strengthen the behavior associated with that willingness to serve.

## Identifying Positive Reinforcers

There exists no universal positive reinforcer that can be used to control effectively either all behavior of a single person or a single behavior in all people. The identification of reinforcers must be a case-by-case proposition. For example, while one employee may perform at a high level for occasional positive verbal recognition from a manager, another employee may respond better to money than to praise or recognition. Accordingly, it is essential that a concerted effort be made to identify those positive reinforcers that appeal to a particular employee. The following methods may be used to identify positive reinforcers for any employee in any specific situation.

**Analyzing histories of reinforcement.** This preferred method of identifying on-the-job positive reinforcers is to review and analyze their histories. If, with the presentation of some environmental condition, the frequency of response increases, that environmental condition (or consequence) is a positive reinforcer.

This method forces the manager to think in terms of antecedent (cue), behavior, and consequence (A → B → C) and thus use an organizational behavior modification approach to human resource management.

**Surveying reinforcers.** This method of identifying on-the-job positive reinforcers is based upon surveys which are designed to pinpoint and communicate what an employee perceives as desirable.

**An ipsative test.** An ipsative test is designed to determine the relative importance of each individual factor within a group of factors. M. R. Blood developed and tested a survey which gives the priorities of the importance of several potential rewards to the individual. Using the following ten reward categories, the individual is asked to rank each in order of preference.

Achievement or sense of accomplishment
Responsibility or control
Opportunity for personal growth
Recognition from family, friends, and the community
Job or company status
Interpersonal relationships or friendships
Pay or monetary reward
Job security
Provision for family
Support for hobbies and interests

Though the list is limited, the experimentally derived results seem to indicate the validity and application potential of this approach.

**Contingency questionnaires.** As a means of providing the practicing manager a reasonably good idea of what types of consequences are important to individual subordinates, the contingency questionnaire developed by H. J. Reitz is of value. He listed the following fourteen items, asking the respondent to select one of the six possible responses for each: "100% certain, very probable, fairly probable, uncertain, fairly improbable, and very improbable."[2]

1. Your supervisor would personally pay you a compliment if you did outstanding work.
2. Your supervisor would lend a sympathetic ear if you had a complaint.
3. You will eventually go as far as you would like in this organization, providing your work is consistently above average.
4. You would be promoted if your work was better than others who were otherwise equally qualified.

[2]H. J. Reitz, "Managerial Attitudes and Perceived Contingencies between Performance and Organizational Response," *Academy of Management Proceedings*, 1971, pp. 227–238.

5. Your supervisor would help you get a transfer if you asked for one.
6. Your supervisor's boss or others in higher management would know about it if your work was outstanding.
7. Your supervisor's recommendation for a pay increase for you would be consistent with his or her evaluation of your performance.
8. Your supervisor would show a great deal of interest if you suggested a new and better way of doing things.
9. You would receive special recognition if your work performance was especially good.
10. Your supervisor would do everything to help you if you were having problems in your work.
11. Your supervisor's evaluation of your performance would be in agreement with your own evaluation of your performance.
12. Your next pay increase will be consistent with the amount recommended by your supervisor.
13. Your supervisor would encourage you to do better if your performance was unacceptable and well below what you are capable of doing.
14. You would be promoted within the next two years if your work was consistently better than the work of others within your department.

While the data generated from this self-report instrument is not as precise as that obtained from analyzing histories of reinforcement, it can potentially identify behavior that requires reinforcement as well as already effective reinforcers. The responses of "low probability" to the statements represent an area that probably needs attention by the manager. Appropriate contingent consequences would have to be identified and applied.

A close look at Reitz's contingency questionnaire reveals that the rewards include a compliment, sympathy, promotion, transfer, recognition from higher management, a pay increase, attention, special recognition, help with problems, recognition from the supervisor, and support. Some or all of these rewards may be positive reinforcers that are currently maintaining goal-directed performance.

The book *Organizational Behavior Modification* by Fred Luthans and Robert Kreitner should be referred to for more information on this technique.

## Summary

The managerial grid is a concept for assessing any given manager's job-related behavior by quantifying concern for two key factors in the work place: coworkers and production, or the generation of outputs. The grid provides the means by which any manager can analyze her or his actions and the motivation behind those actions. It focuses on intangibles in the form of concerns as causes for specific behaviors demonstrated by subordinates within the organization.

In contrast, organizational behavior modification is based upon the more tangible, observable events occurring in the work place. The premise is that behavior is learned and is contingent upon prevailing consequences which are perceived by the organization's members individually as either desirable (rewarding) or undesirable. By identifying the contingent relationship between what triggers behavior (the cue, or antecedent), what results from certain types of behavior (the consequences), and how each individual reacts to specific consequences (the desirability factor), the manager can focus on identifying and applying positive reinforcers which will strengthen individual commitment to the achievement of organizational goals.

While employing approaches which focus on different factors, both the managerial grid and organizational behavior modification theory incorporate measurements, goals, and the interdependence of fulfilling individual and organizational needs as keys to improving productivity.

# 18 Epilogue

As managers, the realization of our organization's potential is dependent, in large part, upon our ability to improve productivity. As consumers, the maintenance of our present standard of living, not to mention improvements in that standard, are also dependent, to a great extent, upon improving productivity. As citizens of the greatest country in the world, maintaining our present position of leadership depends greatly upon improving productivity. While many factors impact productivity, common sense dictates that we focus our energies on those related factors which are most controllable by us, the resources for which we are responsible. By increasing the effectiveness, or quantity, of our work groups' outputs without a corresponding increase in the resources consumed in the process of generating those outputs, we are improving productivity.

Although productivity improvement is generally associated with changing things, such as acquiring new and better equipment, in reality, it is generally more dependent upon people or, more specifically, the managerial ability to relate employee needs to the needs of the organization. When viewed from the proper perspective, there exists an obvious potential for compatibility between the needs of the employee and the needs of the organization. As the organization works to satisfy its higher-order needs of effectiveness and efficiency, which just happen to be the components of productivity, the individuals' higher-order needs of self-esteem and fulfillment can be satisfied. In fact, as long as you are dependent upon people to realize your organization's goals, you will have to basically satisfy their higher-order needs to realize long-term productivity improvement.

A job and a paycheck make a significant contribution to the satisfaction of employee physiological and safety needs. The employees' need to belong and the company's need for direction can both be satisfied by the implementation of the process of goal setting and achieving. This process incorporates the phi-

**296**

losophy that employees at all levels of the organization have a right to know (1) the organization's purpose, (2) developments which relate to them and their jobs, (3) management's specific expectations of them in the work place, and (4) feedback on their performance. Beyond that knowledge, employee participation in the planning and problem-solving processes provides the potential for increasing employee contribution to the achievement of organizational goals.

The organization's goals must focus on end results rather than on activities. Some end results are more important than others in the sense they offer a greater opportunity for improving productivity and fulfilling the organization's purpose. Initial goal-setting efforts should be focused on these key end results. The achievement of improved end results in key areas of activity increases the organization's effectiveness, which is the next higher organizational need, while providing the opportunity to recognize employee contribution and thereby satisfy the employee need for self-esteem.

Productivity measurements provide the basis for gauging actual performance as compared to goal. Whereas, ideally, such measurements would include both total outputs and the total resources required to generate those outputs, such information is usually available only on a monthly basis and then only in the form of the organization's income statement. Should all elements of expense not be fully allocated to each component of activity within the organization as it appears on the income statement and backup reports, the concept of total factor productivity cannot be applied to component activities. Less complete productivity measurements will have to suffice as interim (between monthly income statements) indicators in most cases. While simple measures, such as output per hour, can provide false impressions related to the impact of productivity improvement efforts upon the organization's primary purpose, such as profitability, they do serve a useful purpose as interim indicators of progress.

In addition to the requirement that productivity indicators include as many of the outputs and related inputs as is possible, they must also be comparable between time periods, they must accurately reflect changes in productivity, they must be cost-effective, they should be applied to all activities within the organization, and they must be reported on a timely basis to the person(s) responsible. Calculating productivity measures in dollars, whenever possible, benefits all organizations. Dollars are specific and easily related to as a unit of measure. They relate directly to the primary purpose of profit-oriented organizations—profit—and by gauging costs, they relate to the amount of service a nonprofit organization can deliver at any level of available resources.

The "effectiveness" component of the productivity ratio, productivity equals effectiveness divided by efficiency, includes the quality of outputs, timeliness with which they are made available, and their quantity. Accordingly, quality measures and timeliness measurements are equally as important in the work place as quantity measures. Only by implementing and monitoring all three measures can you gauge your organization's productivity.

Standards, or goals, as communicated to employees should be based on methods and procedures that correct obvious problems, if not incorporate the "best method." In time, and with the support of a good working environment, it is conceivable that some employees can participate in setting goals related to their job responsibilities. Managers, including first-line supervisors, should always participate in the goal-setting process as it relates to their area of responsibility. Goals should be achievable. They should not represent ideals but rather what is realistically possible, though difficult. The positive reinforcement of progress made, if not goals achieved, is critical to maintaining positive employee motivation aimed at the achievement of organizational goals. Employees cannot feel good about themselves, the company, and their jobs if either they are unable to make progress toward achieving goals or those goals are so easy to achieve that their value system tells them they have not been required to work hard enough.

Obstacles exist and hinder the achievement of all worthwhile goals. Such obstacles must first be recognized, and a plan to overcome them must be developed and implemented. Participation of employees involved, in the development and implementation of a plan of action, serves two useful purposes: employee involvement tends to generate a commitment related to making the plan work and employee involvement provides management with the benefit of inputs from those who generally best understand either what action is required or what the result of a proposed action will be; that is, the person who does the job in question.

As a manager, your job is to influence what happens. You are a role model for your subordinates and for your peers. The manner in which you approach and carry out your assigned responsibilities is the most important factor determining the productivity of your work group. To improve productivity, you do not, generally, need additional resources. You do need a basic understanding of how to multiply your personal efforts through the efforts of your employees. You do not need an elaborate plan. The more basic and easily understood your approach, the greater your chances for success. Nothing worthwhile is ever achieved without effort. If you are willing to put forth that effort and to persist in spite of unforeseen problems that are likely to occur and frustrate you and your employees; if you are capable of accentuating the positive and viewing problems as opportunities; and if you are willing to apply the ideas presented in this book, then you can and you will improve productivity.

# Bibliography

Albrecht, Karl: *Successful Management by Objectives*, Prentice-Hall, Englewood Cliffs, N.J., 1978.

Besterfield, Dale H.: *Quality Control*, Prentice-Hall, Englewood Cliffs, N.J., 1979.

Blake, Robert, and Jane Mouton: *The Managerial Grid*, Gulf, Houston, 1964.

—— and ——: *Corporate Excellence through Grid Organization Development*, Gulf, Houston, 1968.

Blood, M. R.: "Intergroup Comparisons of Interperson Differences: Rewards from the Job," *Personnel Psychology*, 1973.

*Chicago Tribune:* "U.S. Productivity Falls for 6th Quarter in a Row," July 29, 1980.

Davis, Keith: *The Dynamics of Organizational Behavior*, McGraw-Hill, New York, 1957.

Dickey, H. Ford: "Hard Nosed Inventory Management," in Donald G. Hall (ed.), *The Manufacturing Man and His Job*, American Management Association, New York, 1966.

*Economic Report of the President:* Government Printing Office, Washington, D.C., 1979.

Feigenbaum, A. V.: *Total Quality Control*, McGraw-Hill, New York, 1961.

Filer, Robert: "Foreign Productivity Centers," *Management Review*, January 1976.

Gardner, John W.: *Excellence*, Harper & Row, New York, 1961.

——: *Self-Renewal*, Harper & Row, New York, 1963.

Greenberg, Leon: *A Practical Guide to Productivity Measurement*, The Bureau of National Affairs, Washington, D.C., 1973.

Hannan, Timothy: "The Productivity Perplex," *Business Review of the Federal Reserve Bank of Philadelphia*, 1980.

Heaton, Herbert: *Productivity in Service Organizations*, McGraw-Hill, New York, 1977.

Hornbruch, Frederick, Jr.: *Raising Productivity*, McGraw-Hill, New York, 1977.

Horngren, Charles T.: *Accounting for Management Control*, Prentice-Hall, Englewood Cliffs, N.J., 1965.

Juran, J. M., and Frank M. Gyrna, Jr.: *Quality Planning and Analysis*, McGraw-Hill, New York, 1970.

Krick, Edward V.: *Methods Engineering*, Wiley, New York, 1962.

Laurence, Paul, and Jay Lorsch: *Organizations and Environment*, The Harvard Press, Boston, Mass., 1967.

Lazzaro, Victor: *Systems and Procedures*, Prentice-Hall, Englewood Cliffs, N.J., 1968.

Luthans, Fred, and Robert Kreitner, *Organizational Behavior Modification*, Scott, Foresman, Glenview, Ill., 1975.

McClelland, David C.: *The Achieving Society*, Van Nostrand, Princeton, N.J., 1961.

McCord, A. Ray: "Total Involvement in Productivity," *Manufacturing Productivity Solutions Conference*, Washington, D.C., October 2, 1979.

Mager, Robert F.: *Goal Analysis*, Fearon, Belmont, Calif., 1972.

Mali, Paul: *Improving Total Productivity*, Wiley, New York, 1978.

**299**

Maslow, Abraham: "A Theory Of Human Motivation," *Psychological Review*, vol. 50, 1943, pp. 370–96.

————: *Motivation and Personality*, Harper & Row, New York, 1954.

Meyer, Paul J.: *Executive Motivation*, SMI International, Inc., Waco, Tex., 1968.

Morrisey, George: *Management by Objectives and Results*, Addison-Wesley, Reading, Mass., 1970.

Reitz, H. J.: "Managerial Attitudes and Perceived Contingencies between Performance and Organizational Response," *Academy of Management Proceedings*, 1971.

Simmons, David A.: *Practical Quality Control*, Addison-Wesley, Reading, Mass., 1970.

Sisk, Henry L.: *Management and Organizations*, Southwestern Publishing Co., Dallas, Tex., 1973.

Sloma, Richard S.: *No-Nonsense Management*, Macmillan, New York, 1977.

*Time*, "An Industrial Nirvana," Sept. 8, 1980.

Uris, Leon: *The Executive Deskbook*, Van Nostrand, New York, 1970.

*U.S. News and World Report*, "How to Stop Sag in Productivity," July 28, 1980.

Wareham, John: *Secrets of a Corporate Headhunter*, Atheneum, New York, 1980.

Williams, J. Clifton: *The Dynamics of Motivational Management*, SMI International, Inc., Waco, Tex., 1969.

Wilson, J. Watson: "The Growth of a Company," *Advanced Management Journal*, January 1966.

Winski, Joseph: "Turning Quasar around Proves Difficult—Even for Japanese," *Chicago Tribune*, September 17, 1980.

Yuke, G., K. N. Wexley, and V. D. Seymore: "Effectiveness of Pay Incentives under Variable Ratio and Continuous Reinforcement Schedules," *Journal of Applied Psychology*, February 1972.

# Index